STOURPORT-ON SEVERN

A history of the town and local villages

by

Anne Bradford

STOURPORT-ON-SEVERN

A history of the town and local villages

by

Anne Bradford
Edited by Michael R Kettle
Book design by John Bradford
Present-day photographs by John Bradford

Hunt End Books

Hunt End Books
66 Enfield Road
Hunt End, Redditch
Worcestershire B97 5NH, England
Telephone 01527 542516

Compiled in the year 2000
Published in 2002
ISBN 0 9519481 6 4

*The engraving on the cover is of the first bridge
and the canal basin in 1776.*

*The inside front cover is the first page of an
petition from the inhabitants of Bewdley to
Daniel Zachary, dated 1774, asking him not
to build a bridge at Stouport-on-Severn. Aaron
York is among the signataries.
Courtesy Worcestershire County Archives.*

*The inside back cover shows an advertisement
for the sale of the Tannery in 1873.
Courtesy Worcestershire County Archives and
Morton Fisher, Solicitors.*

ACKNOWLEDGMENTS

The following have given information or assistance
which has not been acknowledged in the text:

Kidderminster Shuttle
Worcester Evening News
Robin Whittaker, Senior Assistant, Worcestershire County Archives
Anita Blythe, Hartlebury Library
Miss L K Hart, Kidderminster Library
Mrs Lythall, Cultural Services, Stourport-on-Severn Library
A J Conder, The Waterways Trust
Roy Jamieson, National Waterways Museum
Rev Owain Bell, St Mary's Chantry, Kidderminster
Rev Paul Booth, Minister of Stourport-on-Severn Methodist Church
Rt Hon the Lord Sandys
A T H Baylis
Philip Calder, retired MD for British Wire Products
Linda Cook, Stourport-on-Severn Town Council
Michael Timmis & Sue Pattison of Forest Fencing plc
Tony Hyde, MD of Thomas Vale Construction Ltd
Carol Fullelove
Norman Gulliver
David Lukeman
Norman May, for information on Hartlebury School
Doug McLean of Forest Books Services
The Pheysey family, especially Josephine Bagby
John Roberts, publisher of the QuercuS series
Mike Stephenson
Four retired ladies who wish to remain anonymous

THE AUTHORS

Anne Bradford

Anne was one of Stourport-on-Severn's holiday makers. Her father built a wooden hut in a field near Bewdley where the family went camping at weekends, and twice a year she came to a school camp providing holidays for Black Country children in the Ribbesford woods. Anne is married to a retired graphic designer and has three children, all of whom have now flown the nest. Her varied career has covered the teaching of all ages from three to eighty. Since retiring, Anne has written and/or published two local history books and five collections of Worcestershire ghosts and legends.

Michael R Kettle

Although Mike was born in Redditch he has lived in Stourport for sixteen years. He knows Stourport like the back of his hand, not only has he worked at Brintons, Vales, Blunts and Foley Vehicle Hire, he was in the Special Constabulary from 1967 to 1972. Since retiring he has written three very popular books on canal walking.

It is hoped that this book will show how Stourport evolved through the centuries to become the town of today. The interviews for the oral history took place between August 2000 and May 2001.

Although every effort has been made to ensure the accuracy of the information, a great deal of this book is based on old records and oral history. Contributors have asked me to emphasise that all this happened a long time ago and memory sometimes plays tricks.

To quote the Victorian author of *Free Schools of Worcestershire and their Fulfilment*, 'If I am wrong, somebody no doubt will set me right'.

ISAAC WEDLEY

Very occasionally, perhaps only once or twice a century, there lives in a town an accomplished writer and artist who succeeds in capturing the essence of the town for posterity. Such a person was Isaac Wedley. Born in 1865, he lived in a large house 'The Laurels' on the Lickhill Road. He worked as the Registrar of Births and Deaths in Stourport-on-Severn but during his leisure hours he was a journalist, musician and photographer. For most of his life he was the organist and chormaster of the Methodist church and he taught the piano, cello and violin.

We have used many quotations and references from his books. He wrote 'Old Stourport' 1912, 'The Passing of Mitton' 1921, 'Twixt Severn and Teme' 1928 and various articles for the Kidderminster Shuttle. Some of these articles are not out of copyright and we are grateful to the Kidderminster Shuttle for allowing us to quote from them.

Isaac Wedley died in 1941.

(Photograph courtesy Kidderminster library)

CONTENTS

1. **Brindley's Memorial**   1

2. **Canal Mania**   7
    Trows, Narrow Boats and Barges   8
    Tugs   8
    Passenger Boats   8
    Improvements (or otherwise) to the Waterways   12
    Holt Abbott   16
    Summary   18

3. **Boat People**   19
    Lock Keepers and Toll Keepers   19
    Water Gypsies   20
    Tanker Men   28
    Steam Skippers   30

4. **The Dark Satanic Mills**   31
    Industries founded before the canal arrived   31
    Mitton Mill   31
    Boat-building   32
    The Tannery   33
    The Iron Works   35
    The Anglo American   36
    Enoch Baldwin and the Gas Supply   37
    The Carpet Industry   38
    Industries arriving after the canal   43
    The Vinegar Works (Holbrooks Limited)   43
    Thomas Vale   44
    Steatite and Porcelain Limited (Morgan Matroc)   47
    The Power Petroleum Company   50
    The Power Station   51
    Parsons Chain   53
    Larch Lap   56

5. **The Grand Tour**   62
    Area One - Bridge Street and to the West   63
    Bridge Street   63
    Maps   66
    Charles Hastings   69
    Riverside Lighting   69
    Raven Street (Off Bridge Street)   70
    New Street   70
    William Bullock Close   71
    Moor Hall Lane   72
    Galahad Way, Hafren Way, Gheluvelt Court   73
    Area Two - High Street, to the East and the Severn   74
    The High Street   74
    The Coffee Tavern   74
    The Post Office   78

Within Living Memory   79
The Bickertons   80
W H Grinnall's   81
Blunt's Shoes   83
Parkes Passage   84
York Street   84
Lion Hill   86
Mart Lane   87
Lichfield Street and Severn Lane, later Severn Road   87
Cheapside   88
Area 3 - Mitton St, Gilgal and to the north   89
Mitton Street   89
The Bridge over the River Stour   89
Gilgal   90
Baldwin Road   91
Mill Road   91
Worcester Road   91
Area 4 - Vale Road and to the west   92
Vale Road   92
Lombard Street   92
Co-operative Site   92
Tan lane   94
Foundry Street   95

6.   **Pubs and Publicans**   96
The Tontine Hotel   96
The Swan Hotel   98
The White Lion   101
The Red Lion or Steps House   102
The Round o' Beef   102
The Ring o' Bells   102
The Brindley Arms   103
The Old Rising Sun   103
The Bridge Inn   103

7.   **O Come All Ye Faithful!**   106
St Michael and All Angels   106
Methodists   112
Primitive Methodism   115
Congregationalists   115
Baptists   116
Roman Catholics   117
William Heywood   118

8.   **The Happiest Days of Your Life**   120
Tan Lane School   126
The National Girls School   127
The National Boys School   128
The First County High School   128
Stourport-on-Severn High School-Language College   129

9. **The Pace Quickens**   132
    Trains   133
    Trams   139

10. **Fun & Games**   141
    Annual Events   141
    Travelling Entertainments   141
    Mitton Wake   142
    The Carnival   142
    Fairs and Markets   143
    Clubs and Societies   143
    The Literary Institute   143
    The Horticultural Society   145
    Musical Entertainment   147
    The Music Society   147
    Glee Club   149
    The Instrumental Society   149
    Musical Evenings   149
    Sporting Activities   150
    The Boat Club   150
    Swimming   152
    Cricket   154
    Football   155
    Bowls   156
    Scouts and Guides   156
    Cinemas   157

11. **A Holiday Town**   158
    Caravan Parks   161
    Riverside Development   164

12. **Emergency!**   166
    The Floods   166
    The Freeze-Ups   170
    The Fires   172

13. **Poverty, Sickness and Death**   174
    Poverty and the Poor House   174
    Sickness   175
    Funerals   176

14. **Stourport-on-Severn Goes to War**   178
    The First World War   182
    The Second World War   185
    The American Camp   192

15. **Parish, Council, and Parliament**   199
    Boundaries   199
    Elections   200
    Councillors   200

VILLAGE LIFE 205

16. **Hartlebury** 206
Hartlebury Common 206
The Gypsies 207
Hartlebury Castle 209
The Civil War 213
Hartlebury School 215
Hartlebury Village 217
Waresley House 217

17. **Wilden** 218
The Baldwin Family and the Macdonalds 222
Wilden Church 224
Wilden School 226
Wilden Parish Hall 228

18. **Lickhill** 229
Newtown 230

19. **The Christian Shores** 231
Saint Bartholomew's 231
Church House 235
The Rectory 236
Areley Manor, later Areley Hall 237
Areley Court 239
The Walshes 239
Areley Common School 241
The Windmill 241
Areley Common 243
Murder on the Christian Shores 243
Redstone 244
Lincomb Lock and Weir 246
Lincomb Hall 248

20 **Astley** 249
Glasshampton 251
Andrew Yarranton 252
Frances Ridley Havergal 252
Stanley Baldwin 253

21 **Shrawley** 254
The Ford 254
Shrawley Wood 254
The Castle 256
The Hermitage 256
The Church 257
The Well of Saint Keyne 258
Fetes 258
Within Living Memory 258

People criticise things that were done in years gone by without any real knowledge of the conditions of those days. They try to put past events against today's backdrop. There is usually a practical reason for anything that happened in the past. History gets twisted round - what suits the present generation didn't necessarily suit people in the past. To truly understand history you have to go back and get the flavour of the time, not re-write it.

Bob Blunt

James Brindley (1716-1772), the founder of Stourport-on-Severn. He died before the town was completed.

1. Brindley's Memorial

About 1766, where the river Stour empties itself into the Severn below Mitton, stood a little alehouse called Stourmouth: near this place Brindley has caused a town to be erected, made a port and dockyards, built a new and elegant bridge, established markets, and made it the wonder not only of this county but of the nation at large. ... Thus was the sandy barren common at Stourport converted, in the space of thirty years, into a flourishing, healthy and very populous village.

Nash's History of Worcestershire

Stourport is the only town in England to have been built as the result of canals and the trade brought by those canals.

Even the name of the town came with the canals. The area had previously been known as Mitton, or Mytton, which could be an abbreviation of 'a mill town'. Another suggestion is that the name came from an old English word meaning a junction of streams, for it is here that the mighty River Severn joins the River Stour. Despite it being the junction of two important rivers there was no town here, only a barren, sandy heath. The Domesday Book of 1086 describes the whole area around Kidderminster as waste. By 1550, in the whole of Lickhill and Mitton there were only about 23 families. A few were farming the land, others were working the water mills running along the river Stour. At the junction of the rivers there was a mere alehouse, not even a hostelry, where the Severn bargemen met in the evening for a mug of ale and a whiff from their short clay pipes.

Then, in 1765, James Brindley arrived with the idea of building a canal which would run halfway up England from Bristol to the Mersey. At first the bargemen in the alehouse watched the teams of navvies digging the Lower Mitton basins with amusement. The ground was considered too spongy for building and the banks of any canal would need to be very high to prevent the River Stour running into it. However, as the project grew they became apprehensive as they realised that, from then onwards, their lives would be changed.

James Brindley was in his early forties when he became rich and famous beyond his wildest dreams. Brindley's family came from Staffordshire and moved to the Peak District when Brindley was ten. While his young friends were climbing trees and exploring the woods, Brindley was making little models of water mills. It was inevitable that he should become a millwright.

Brindley was a careful, solid man, always dressed in a gentleman's smart snuff-coloured coat and white cravat. Some folks said that he was argumentative, others have reported that he was 'kindly'. It has been said that he found intelligent conversations difficult, but he was often called before committees and was eloquent enough to persuade many of them to support his work. He was described as a plain-looking man but he was attractive enough to marry Anne Henshall, the daughter of a colleague, when she was 19 and Brindley was 49. The novelist, Arnold Bennet (1867-1931) was a descendent. It has also been said that he made the briefest of plans and that he wrote very little down. However, he left behind many notebooks and sketches. At that time it was customary to pass on instructions by word of mouth, as a high percentage of the population was illiterate. In any case, it was impossible to draw detailed plans because there were no reliable maps until 1844.

For the last fourteen years of his life Brindley was consulting engineer to the young Duke of Bridgewater. The Duke had a vision of combining the four great rivers of England, the Severn, Mersey, Trent and Thames. To help finance his dream, he gave up his life as a lord living frugally and in privacy. The only time he ate a lavish meal was when he was entertaining someone from whom he needed help. The first step was to build a canal from his coal mines at Worsley to the ready markets at Manchester. He needed a brilliant and innovative engineer to build the first canal with aqueducts, long tunnels, canal lifts and a series of locks. It was arranged that Brindley and the Duke should meet and it was not surprising considering their mutual passion for engineering and canals that they took an immediate liking to each other. This despite their age differences, the Duke was in his 23rd year and Brindley was 43 years old. It was decided that Brindley should build the canal under the supervision of the Duke's agent. It was opened in 1761 and was considered to be the eighth wonder of the world. The Duke was persuaded to extend his canal to Runcorn.

At that time England was largely undeveloped, covered by dense forests and undrained marshlands. There were only two ways of transporting goods, the one was by carts and packhorses over deeply rutted, unmade roads, the second was by rivers which were notoriously erratic. The fast-flowing River Severn was not neatly channelled, as it is today, but meandered here and there, creating bogs and swamps. For several months of the years, it was unusable, either in flood or too shallow from drought. In spite of this, it was usually easier to take goods along the waterways than the unmade roads and the Severn was the second busiest river in Europe. Bristol was the first seaport of the kingdom and traffic was passing constantly along the Severn between Bristol and Gloucester, Worcester, Bewdley, Bridgnorth and Shrewsbury, even as far as Welshpool.

Francis Egerton, third Duke of Bridgewater, threw himself into canal-building after an unhappy love affair. He had a vision of linking the four great rivers of England. James Brindley was his consulting engineer.

Brindley was then asked to survey for two canals, the Trent and Mersey and the Staffordshire and Worcestershire. This would mean that goods could go north and south halfway up and down England by canal and the great ports of Gloucester and Bristol could be reached be river and canal. Various alternative routes were proposed but in the end it was decided that the two canals should meet at Great Haywood, east of Stafford.

The problem was, where should the Staffordshire and Worcestershire canal join the Severn? Six towns made an official request for the canal port: Bewdley, Wolverhampton, Walsall, Willenhall, Stourbridge, Kidderminster and Dudley. The most obvious choice was the flat Stour valley and so the wasteland then known as Lower Mitton was chosen.

Bewdley officials were annoyed that they had not been selected and said that they hadn't wanted the 'stinking ditch' anyway. Before Stourport was created, most of the River Severn goods arrived at Bewdley either by packhorses to be transferred to boats or by boats to be transferred to packhorses. There were often as many as 400 packhorses tethered there. When the Staffordshire and Worcestershire canal opened, Bewdley was by-passed and the rows of stables for pack-horses were empty. The town had seven hundred poor inhabitants and the wealthy were paying 10/6d (52p) in the £ to support them.

The enthusiastic James Perry was the promoter of the Staffordshire and Worcestershire, raising funds and nursing the Act through Parliament. The surveying and costing were done by Brindley's two brothers-in-law, Hugh Henshall, who was his wife's brother, and Samuel Simcock, who was probably married to Brindley's sister.

An Act was passed on the 14th of May, 1766 authorising the Trent and Mersey on the same day as the Staffordshire and Worcestershire. It was

The Basins at their Height

1. *Clock Basin, also known as Main or Lichfield Basin, opened 1771.*
2. *Lower Basin, opened 1771.*
3. *Town Basin, built by 1810.*
4. *Second Lower Basin, built by 1810.*
5. *Engine Basin, pumped water into higher basin, built by 1810.*
6. *Furthermost Basin, built by 1812, filling-in commenced about 1955.*
7. *Cheapside Basin, built by 1812, filled in about 1866.*
a. *Boat Locks*
b. *Barge Locks*

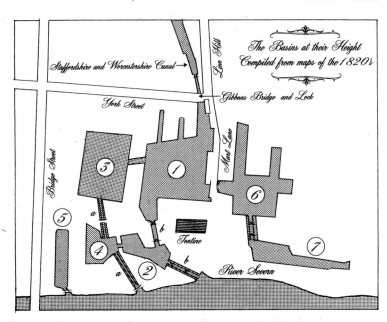

3

customary for the Principal Engineer to work on several canals at the same time, consequently Brindley was asked to oversee three canals, the Duke's extension to Runcorn, the Trent and Mersey, and the Staffordshire and Worcestershire. His role was to decide what route the canal should take, then he would be responsible for its construction. Brindley spent his time riding from one end of the site to the other, living mostly in inns, sorting out any problems such as unexpected geological difficulties or unresolved disputes. By law the canal builders had to give the land-owners a fair price for their land. Sometimes, land owners refused to sell until the canal had been partly built so that they would get a good price. When a problem arose, Brindley was in the habit of going to bed for three days and emerging with the problem solved.

The twenty-three families of Mitton no doubt wondered what had descended upon them. A huge piece of land was purchased by the Canal Company in 1769, stretching from (what is now) Stourport bridge almost to the mouth of the Stour and extending townwards to what is now known as York Street and Lichfield Street.

Hundreds of men arrived. A local brickworks was set up and stone and timber brought in. Stone masons chiselled away. Gangs of men arrived with picks, shovels and barrows. Some of these were men who had lost their homes through the Enclosures Act. The navvies, or navigators, were the skilled men, the labourers were often vagrants sent to do some useful work. On the whole, the builders were a rough, tough lot, prone to fighting, swearing and stealing.

Along the line of the canal an enormous ditch was dug with sloping sides, with the earth from the ditch piled up on each side. The ditch was lined with rocks, stones and pebbles, known as puddling. In porous ground the canal bed was given 18 inches (45 cms) of puddle below and 3 feet (90 cms) at the sides. In retentive soil, puddle was only needed at each side to prevent leakage through the sides which would have weakened the banks. The floor line or bottom of the canal was made twice the width of the largest boat likely to enter, plus 6 to 8 inches (15 to 20 cms) each side and 12 to 18 inches (30 to 45 cms) more than the draught (the depth to which a boat sinks) of the boat.

The size of the narrow boats most often seen on today's canals were set by Brindley. He asked that the craft for his first canals should measure 70 feet by 6 feet (21 metres by 1.8 metres), draw 2 feet 6 inches (75 cms) and carry 15-20 tons (tonnes). Later, this was lengthened to between 70 and 72 feet (21 metres to 21.3 metres), widened to 6 feet 10 inches (2.04 metres) with a lower draught to carry 25-30 tons. These are the dimensions generally in use today.

Brindley avoided complex engineering projects as much as possible, consequently he tried to keep level and to follow the contours of the land. His early canals were narrow and winding. When a Birmingham man complained, Brindley said that if the canal had not curved, less people would have been serviced by it.

Not only was Brindley working on the Duke's canal and the Trent and Mersey, he was also surveying for other canals such as the Lichfield to Coventry, the Oxford to Coventry, the Birmingham to Oxford and the Birmingham to Wolverhampton. The actual construction of the canal at Stourport was left chiefly to Samuel Simcock and Thomas Dadford, Sen-

Constructing a canal.
Courtesy National Waterways
Museum, Gloucester.

ior. Samuel Simcock was also absent for a great deal of the time, as he was working on the Birmingham to Oxford canal.

Josiah Wedgwood of pottery fame, said of Brindley in 1767:

"I am afraid he will do too much, & leave us before his vast designs are executed; he is so incessantly harassed on every side, that he hath no rest, either for his mind, or Body, & will not be prevailed upon to have proper care for his health ... I think Mr. Brindley - the Great, the fortunate, money-geting Brindley, an object of Pity! ... He may get a few thousands, but what does he give in exchange? His Health, & I fear his Life too.'"

The first basin was officially opened on 1st April 1771 and was simply a dock basin, in which vessels waited before they were transferred to their docks. Two locks connected the basin with the river, made to accommodate barges. When the canal first opened it only reached the River Trent at Tettenhall or Compton (on the western outskirts of Wolverhampton). It passed, and still passes, beneath Kidderminster, past Wolverley and runs to the west of Wombourne to Tettenhall, a distance of 24 miles. It required 22 bridges and two acqueducts. The difference in water level between Tettenhall and Stourport was as much as 294 feet consequently 31 narrow locks had been built. When it was completed in 1772 it joined the Trent and Mersey East of Stafford, a distance of just over 48 miles.

As well as surveying the canal, Brindley also supervised the development of the early town. Round the first basin, warehouses were built, together with sheds, cranes, weight houses, offices and public houses. The

Long Warehouse and the Iron Warehouse were the first to be built. There was a house for the engineer, a canal office with a superintendent, a house and office for the chief toll-collector and one for a resident clerk, together with his staff.

Other buildings were added as the need arose, such as stables, a boat repair yard and a dry dock, where the water could be drained out for the repairing of boats. Workmen's cottages were required, and a splendid house for the Wharfinger. He was in charge of the public wharf, where vessels were unloaded on a bank of timber or stone.

Stourport was not built to any overall design, but simply extended according to demand. Fortunately, it was built at a time when architecture was particularly attractive so that it has several roads full of elegant Regency houses. Builders tended to use pattern books, so that many of the houses are similar, which gives an overall unity.

Brindley never saw Stourport completed. The project was still unfinished when, in 1772, Brindley was put into a damp bed wearing damp clothes at Ipstones in Staffordshire. He was discovered to have diabetes and this, together with a kidney infection, proved fatal. He lies in the churchyard of Newchapel in Staffordshire.

Hugh Henshall took his place as Principal Engineer. Only a few days after Brindley's death the canal system reached as far as Stoke-on-Trent, where a temporary wharf was opened.

As for the Duke of Bridgewater, he saw his dream realised in 1790 when the Birmingham/Fazeley/Fradley/Coventry/Oxford line was finished. His canals became very profitable and when he died in 1803, his enormous fortune went to a cousin.

Brindley built other canals and developed other villages but Stourport was the only town he created out of nothing. There is no statue to Brindley in Stourport but there is no need for one, for the whole town is his memorial.

The Clock House from Mart Lane

2. Canal Mania

This place (Stourport-on-Severn) is becoming the resort of people of fashion. The Beauty of the Country around about it, the fine navigable Canal now compleatly finished, the spacious Bason for the Vessels, the River Severn, and the New Bridge over it, form altogether a pleasing Picture. Scarce a day passes by but several Parties of Ladies and Gentlemen come there in their Carriages. Regattas (the fashionable Term for Water Parties) are not unusual.

Berrows Worcester Journal, 1784

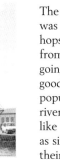

This photograph of a trow at the National Waterways Museum, Gloucester docks, gives an impression of its size and height.

The barren, sandy heath became a flourishing town. Stourport-on-Severn was the great market place for the West Midlands. Coal, iron, grain, flour, hops, apples, salt, chinaware and other products arrived along the canal from Birmingham and the Black Country and were transferred to river-going vessels and sea-going ships while sugar, tea, spices and other foreign goods were transhipped by donkey or horse and cart inland. By 1796 the population of Mitton and Lickhill had grown to 1,300 inhabitants. The river was covered with trows and barges, the masts of the vessels looking like a forest of trees shorn of their leaves. Sometimes there were as many as sixty or seventy canal boats waiting their turn to pass into the canal for their journey up to the Black Country.

More basins were added until, by 1810, they were as large as they are today. In about 1812, two more basins were added which have now been filled in, making seven basins in all.

By 1783 a £100 share on the Staffordshire and Worcestershire canal was worth £400. When people saw that handsome profits could be made, new canals began springing up all over the country and everyone wanted to invest in them. The success of Stourport, together with that of the Staffordshire and Worcestershire and the Trent and Mersey canals, brought about the Great Canal Mania.

Between 1790 and 1797, 56 canals were constructed and many others had been proposed and turned down by Parliament. By the 1830's over 4000 miles of canal and navigable rivers were in use. So many Acts for canals were going through Parliament that it was difficult to find time for any other business.

Before the canals arrived, each town or village was self-contained. People ate what they could grow locally and worked at cottage industries that sold their goods to the immediate area. They had local customs, dialects and beliefs. With the coming of the canals, all that changed. The whole of the centre of England was opened up by this new method of transport. Canals also helped to increase England's general prosperity by making it possible to move the coal, iron and finished products of the Industrial Revolution cheaply and easily round Britain.

TROWS, NARROW BOATS AND BARGES

Both the River Severn and the canal were very shallow and, at times, difficult to negotiate. Consequently, only three types of boat were seen at Stourport. The first was the magnificent trow, used only on the river, the second was the narrow boat, built for use on the canals, and the third was the barge, strictly speaking twice the width of a narrow boat and too large for most canals. The trows could be as long as 100 feet (approx 30 metres) with a main mast and a top mast as high as 80 feet (24.38 metres). They were flat-bottomed to cope with the shallow water and could carry between 40 and 80 tons (tonnes). In 1797 28 trows were sailing weekly between Bristol and Stourport. The last trow was built in 1851 and named 'The Times'.

TUGS

In the middle of the 1800s the Severn Steam Tug Company brought 'The Enterprise' from London. It could tow a line of ten or twelve barges from Stourport to Gloucester in fifteen or eighteen hours and was such a success that they ordered two more. The steam driven tug began to replace the horses, despite their huge boilers and the large area needed to store a supply of coke. The first motor driven tug arrived in 1930 with a little 14 hp engine.

Taking a tug through Lincomb lock (about two miles south of Stourport) was so difficult and took such a long time that it was decided that the tugs should not go through the lock. Instead, there was just one tug, the Margo Newman, running to and fro between the lock and Stourport. The lock-keeper at Lincombe would ring through to Stourport to tell them when the tug was required.

PASSENGER BOATS

By the year 1800 boats from Stourport could reach London by canal and in 1802 a regular service was in place for passengers as well as cargo. It was a most comfortable and pleasant ride, smooth and noiseless, with

The Tug, Athlete, in about 1890 at Lincomb cutting. On board is Captain Hodges, his engineer, Mr Weaver, and three passengers. Courtesy National Waterways Museum, Gloucester

Four horse boats, the Lydney, Aston, Berkeley and Holt moored at Stourport in 1900. They belonged to the Severn & Canal Carrying Company which began in 1851. By the end of World War I they had a fleet of barges collecting cargo from ports around the Bristol Channel and taking them on to Stourport for transhipment.
Courtesy National Waterways Museum.

The Beatrice, in about 1953. The pathway under Stourport bridge is known as Beatrice Walk.
Courtesy Ray Franks

one's own cabin. The only problem was that the trip took 20 to 25 days. Three years later posters were appearing advertising fly boats which could carry both goods and passengers and went via Wolverhampton and the Grand Junction to Paddington. These only required one overnight stay.

Len Holder is writing a book about steam-powered passenger boats and provides the following information:

"Steam powered passenger boats were being built and used in Stourport-on-Severn as early as 1821. The Severn Steam Yacht Company constructed two boats and launched them in the summer of 1821. The first was Sovereign, a paddle steamer described in adverts of the time as a Steam Packet intended to carry up to 500 passengers and light parcels between Stourport and Gloucester each day. A large number of people gathered amidst a 'carnival' atmosphere to watch the launch. A 21-gun salute was begun using a small cannon to celebrate. However, the gunner was killed when the cannon exploded. The boat only ran occasionally for about a year. The second boat that was launched by the same company was called The Twins. It was of a catamaran-type design having two hulls joined together side by side. The boat also only ran occasionally for about a year.

'About thirty years later, Mr John Tyler from the Tontine Hotel purchased the steamboat *Severn* at auction for £305 and operated the boat only for a short time. Following the completion of the locks along the river, several passenger steamers called regularly at Stourport. One of them was Perseverance, originally built as a paddle steamer in Worcester in 1868, and later converted to a propeller driven vessel. This particular boat had the Town Crier announce its arrival and departure times.

'A few steamboat proprietors were based in Stourport. One of them was Mr Harry Hatton. He lived at the Angel Hotel and had various steamers from about 1904 including Lady Foley, Lady Honor, Lady May and Bonavista.

'Another owner-operator was Mr Samuel Palmer who had steamers such as Windsor Castle, Berkeley Castle and Amo. When he first moved to Stourport he lived aboard a houseboat moored near the bridge. By 1911 he had founded the Severn Steamboat Company and later moved from his houseboat to 11 Bridge Street.

'Captain Hatton and Captain Palmer were bitter rivals and would stop at nothing to gain an advantage over each other. Their feud was so great, according to hearsay, that it became a violent and dangerous rivalry with both men as bad as each other. There were collisions between their boats, and employees of both companies became involved with the arguments. Lawsuits were issued by each against the other and it is said on numerous occasions actual fistfights occurred. They would argue over the custom of one passenger, or over rights of way (river rage probably) and over the placing of advertising posters. They both had problems with authorities too. Both had Court appearances for misdemeanours relating to navigation regulations.

'Mr Thomas Bailey had two passenger steamers based at Stourport from 1905. They were Empress and Beatrice. His fare for the return trip from Stourport to Holt Fleet before the First World War was one shilling. After selling his boats he operated five buses from about 1925 to 1933, when he sold his bus services to the Midland Red Company.

The old Clock Warehouse in 1951, before it was renovated and occupied by the Stourport Yacht Club. At that time it was used by Larch Lap.
The warehouse was probably built in the early 1800s, storing grain and general goods. The clock itself was installed in about 1813 and was a gift to the warehouse by the people of the town. The Staffordshire and Worcestershire Canal Company, who owned all the buildings, donated £25. Built by craftsman clock-maker Sam Thorp of Abberley, it had the reputation of showing four different times on its four faces, nevertheless it kept going until 1978. It was renovated in 1980.
Courtesy Florence Phillips, formerly Mrs Abbott.

Two columns of narrow boats passing on the River Severn in 1831.
Courtesy National Waterways Museum, Gloucester

'At the end of World War Two, Mr George Head and his family moved from Bristol to Stourport and acquired the Severn Steamboat Company. He purchased Kingstonian from the Thames and had it delivered by road transport to the Severn. The company also operated Beatrice and Amo. Gradually these wooden steamers were all converted to diesel power, but not until after the 'Suez' Crisis' was over, because there were fears of fuel oil shortages, and there was still plenty of coal available. Probably Mr Head was the last proprietor to operate a steam powered passenger boat on the Severn during the mid 1950s. During the 1960s the Severn Steamboat Company modernised again and replaced the old boats with steel-hulled diesel-powered passenger 'steamers', River King, Miss Jason and Carbolate. The type of trade had changed and the design of boat needed to change. Early steamers had carried passengers almost as a 'bus' service, then for leisure excursions, perhaps with a 'banjo man' playing and singing during the 1920s and 1930s. The passengers of the later 1960s wanted room for 'rock bands' and discos."

IMPROVEMENTS (OR OTHERWISE) TO THE WATERWAYS

The Staffordshire and Worcestershire canal and the basins at Stourport were one of the first to be designed by Brindley, consequently they were not perfect. The canal was so shallow that sometimes boats were stuck on the bottom, and it curved to and fro, making it difficult to negotiate. Some of the locks in the basins were a tight squeeze for the larger boats. Despite being so profitable, no-one ever spent any money improving it. One reason was that nobody bothered, but a second reason was that from 1793 to 1815, the Napoleonic wars were taking place. There were blockades and counter-blockades, European markets would be open, closed then open again. Investing in anything, including canals, was an uncertain business.

The River Severn also caused problems, with its outcrops of hard rock and shoals of gravel. In winter it was often in flood and in summer it dried up and was too shallow. For a month or two each year the river was impassable.

It was decided, in 1790, to build a canal to Birmingham which would join the Severn below Worcester. Consequently, the Canal Company tried to deepen the river by building timber and stone jetties to increase the speed of the current in order to scour the river bottom. The boatmen didn't

The Clock House today, now the home of the Stourport Yacht Club.

like them and found that they were difficult to negotiate. The company was taken to Court and ordered to remove them. The following year an Act made it possible for them to collect £10,000 to remove shoals of gravel but the watermen said that this spoiled the river and they destroyed the works during the night.

William IV came to the throne in 1830, and in the same year, the prosperity of the canal at Stourport began to decline. Other canals were built which took trade away from Stourport, particularly the 1835 branch from the Staffordshire and Worcestershire canal to Shrewsbury. The conditions of the roads began to improve. And, worst of all, was the coming of the railways. Seventy years of canal mania ended with railway mania. In 1850 the Worcester to Birmingham railway was completed which took much of Stourport's trade away, and in 1862 the Severn Valley Railway arrived.

The Canal Company and other interested parties began to panic. They decided at last that the River Severn and the canal between Stourport and Worcester should be improved to take larger vessels. A tremendous battle broke out which continued for years through petitions, meetings, and pamphlets. The merchants, land owners, canal companies and iron masters of Worcestershire, the Midlands, Shropshire, Gloucester, Here-fordshire and Staffordshire were all involved, some for and some against the improvements. The two main reasons for objecting were that tolls would be increased to pay for them and that it would mean loss of trade for some other river and canal ports.

The Transhipment Warehouse

The Canal Company closed and in 1835 the Severn Navigation Company took over the reins of management. They wanted to improve the waterways to take barges of up to 100 tons (tonnes), providing 12 feet (3.6 metres) of water to Worcestershire and 6 feet (1.8 metres) from there to Stourport.

The controversy and arguments reached a climax when the Bill proposing the work was presented to Parliament. Isaac Wedley writes, 'there was a terrific battle unprecedented in the annals of private Bills in Parliament'. At first the Bill was thrown out, mainly because it would mean imposing a tax on a free river. Then, in 1842, it was passed in a modified form. The Severn was to be dredged between Diglis and Gloucester, and the canal was to be increased to a depth of 6 feet 6 inches (1.95 metres) to Worcester and 6 feet (1.8 metres) to Stourport. Locks were to be constructed at Holt, Lincombe, Beaver and Diglis. The Severn Navigation Company was dissolved and the Severn Commission, made up of landowners and local dignitaries from Gloucestershire and Worcestershire, was appointed. The Staffordshire and Worcestershire Canal Company agreed to guarantee the Commission's bonds up to £180,000 which provided the money for the locks to be built and for the river to be dredged lower down.

Towards the end of the nineteenth century, the merchants of Tewkesbury and Gloucester were forced to accept improvements. The Chamber of Commerce and the Corporation of Cardiff wanted to encourage trade with Worcester and so recommended to the Severn Commission that a depth of seven feet should be obtained from Stourport to Worcester and ten feet from there to Gloucester, and that all the locks along the route should be deepened. Work began in 1891 and was completed three years later. The improvements were a failure with no increase in trade, and Cardiff merchants admitted that they were despatching timber by rail. The Severn

Commission had borrowed heavily to pay for the improvements, now its debt increased by £3,000 a year.

The basin at Cheapside began to silt up, and when the gas works on Cheapside were built in 1865, they filled in and built on part of the basin. A few years later the entire basin was filled in.

George Cadbury is famous for his chocolate, less well-known is the fact that he saved the Staffordshire and Worcestershire canal by making it profitable. During the First World War the Severn and Canal Carrying Company Ltd was subsidised but even with a hand-out from the Canal Control Committee of the Board of Trade they were unable to make a profit. After the war, the subsidy ceased and there was disagreement among the interested parties as to how the canals could be made profitable. Most thought it was impossible. The docks at Stourport had fallen into disrepair and the warehouses stood empty and derelict. George Cadbury heard about the difficulties in the 1920's and took over as Chairman. He modernised the longboats and facilities at the docks. He persuaded the Dock Company Ltd, who hired boats, levied tolls and rented out warehouses, to reduce their charges. He ran a publicity campaign promoting the waterways. The result was that by 1938, not only was the canal profitable but also the outstanding debt had been cleared.

In 1927, an oil depot was established at Stourport. New riverside wharves were built to serve large craft which were carrying petrol and oil. Within a few years the oil and petrol traffic began to transform the river's finances, helped by a substantial revenue from the sale of condensing water to power stations.

The canals gained a new lease of life during the second world war. The hustle and bustle of war and petrol rationing meant that any method of transport was useful and so the waterways were in demand. They were taken over by the Ministry of War (who pocketed any profits), consequently the management of the canal and river from Stourport was combined with the Gloucester and Sharpness canal. It was recommended that the Severn should be upgraded to take vessels carrying petrol and oil coming from the estuary at Avonmouth. In 1942 an extensive warehouse and distributing service equipped with cranes and mobile trucks was opened at Nelson Wharf, to the south of Stourport. A basin was constructed for loading onto petrol tankers which is now Stourport Marina. In 1944 a new wharf with a quay 320 feet (nearly 100 metres) long and an engine shed were opened at Diglis near Worcester. Vessels could come straight from the Severn estuary at Bristol to depots at Stourport and Worcester for distribution by road. Ten years later new oil wharves were added at Diglis.

However, by the early 1950's, the waterways were in serious difficulties again. Even one or two founder members of the Inland Waterways Association thought that many of the canals were redundant and should be filled in. Jo Corbett's timber yard on the edge of the Furthermost basin desperately needed more room. The General Works Manager, Bill Hughes, explains:

"The basin on the western side of Mart Lane had not been filled in except for one small part which were our premises. The yard was so small that the tails of the trees used to hang over the cut, as we called the basin. The mill was surrounded with mud, it was like a quagmire, you had to work in wellingtons. Alf Pratley used to have loads of stones delivered but

Holt Abbott, who worked to save the canals, with his wife, Florence, and daughter.
Courtesy Florence Phillips (formerly Mrs Abbott).

The narrow lock leading on to the River Severn in the early 1950s. This is a 'staircase lock' ie one central gate between two chambers which is less common than 'flight locks'.
Courtesy Florence Phillips.

you only had to have a shower of rain and the stones would disappear and you would back to mud again. There was an elderly chap by the name of Ernie Spragg - he worked a big old saw they put in years ago. He had a young chap working with him, his mate. One day Ernie went to Alf Pratley and said, 'Can I send my mate home? - he fell in the cut'. Alf asked, 'How far did he fall in?'. Ernie told him only up to his ankles. Alf said, 'I aint sending him home just because he got his boots wet'. Ernie answered, 'He fell in head first'.

'When the carriages (huge lorries) came into this tiny yard with the timber, they couldn't turn the carriage round to drive it out because the canal was on three sides. They had to run these trailers out backwards into Lichfield Street and turn as they came out, but where it had to turn houses were right opposite. One day, we were moving one of the lorries when the big wheel slid on a stone in the yard. The yard was on a slope and the big bar sticking out at the back went straight through Mrs Weaver's front room, just missing her big window. She certainly wasn't very happy.

'When the coal for the power station ceased there was no use for the basin any more . We badly needed more ground, then Paul Timmis and one of the directors came up to me and they just said, 'We need the basin filled in, Bill, we leave it in your hands'. Some of the infill we got from Steatite, that filled in quite a lot. I went to contractors building all the ring roads in Kidderminster and said, 'Do you want a quick dumping area?'. I had all the bricks and rubble from them dumped in the basin. Ted Edwards, the carpenter, had the job of concreting over it all."

HOLT ABBOTT

Fortunately, at that point Holt Abbott arrived on the scene. There is a tribute to him in the Gloucestershire Waterways Museum, and a plaque to his memory in Stourport on the wall of the canal near Lion Hill which reads:

A DEDICATION TO
HOLT ABBOTT RTN
CANAL BOAT BUILDER 1951-1978
A FOUNDER MEMBER OF THE IWA
IN RECOGNITION OF HIS CONTRIBUTION TO THE
PRESERVATION OF THE CANAL BASINS OF
STOURPORT-ON-SEVERN AND THE PROMOTION OF THE
INLAND WATERWAYS AS A LEISURE FACILITY FOR ALL

Holt's widow, Florence, gives a brief outline of his life and work:

"When I first met Holt he was on the managerial staff of the GEC, Witton, having done an engineering apprenticeship there. We were married in 1942. Holt was always very fair, very just and he treated people well. He was pretty calm in any emergency but he could get het up about an injustice. He was not bad-tempered but quite determined, he would persevere and not let something drop.

'In those days property was difficult to come by and so, just after the war, we had a little boat near Wolverhampton. We both loved boats. We put the boat together, the hull came all the way from London, up on the canal through Gloucester. I did a lot of painting and quite a bit of carpentry. It was a lovely boat, the 'Rothesay', 43 feet long with a teak wheel house. We had a bathroom and central heating from an Ideal boiler. Then we moored down at Kempsey, near Worcester, and Holt travelled into Birmingham each day to work.

'In 1947 Holt was found to have a collapsed lung, and advised to give up industrial work. While he was convalescing he read 'Narrow Boat' by Tom Rolt, that's what sparked his enthusiasm for canals. One summer afternoon in 1947 we were moored for a few days in Diglis basin in Worcester and who should come into the basin but Tom Rolt himself and his wife, Angela. Their boat, Cressy, happened to draw up alongside. We got talking and became very friendly with them, Tom was a lovely person. Tom said to my husband, 'Why don't you put more boats on the canal? You've done a good job with your own boat, and it's an up and coming thing'. When Holt was better we went to Gloucester and took over a Scout Hut at Saul, on the Gloucester and Sharpness Canal. That's where we built the first two small boats of our fleet and hired them out, the Avonvale and the Severnvale. We moored there for a couple of years and while we were there I had Julia, our first daughter.

'Tom Rolt asked my husband if he would join the Inland Waterways Association which he had just got off the ground. We went to the very first Inland Waterways rally, cruising all the way to Market Harborough.

'Our business went well. The hiring business was in its infancy when we started, we were only the second people to go into it. We were one of the first to put a trap over the propeller, so that if the propeller of the boat became tangled with weed or something, you could just open the trap door above the propeller, disentangle the blades and close the trap door again.

The lock-keeper's cottage and office by York Street. The earlier maps refer to the lock as Gibbon's Lock but the old boatmen know it as Cotton's Lock, named after one of the first lock-keepers.. The white house in the distance used to be the stables.and is shown in the lower photograph.

Some of the old stables have survived, such as this one in Mart Lane. A stone slab floor sloped into a central gutter so that, when swilling down horses or scrubbing floors, the water could be thrown into a central gutter and carried away by a culvert.

Our first boat, a shallow draft craft designed and built for inland waterway use, won an award for the best-designed canal craft other than a narrow boat. We needed larger premises and in 1955 we found them at Stourport. We had three boats to bring all the way from Saul to Stourport, our own and the two that we had built. We brought the 'Rothesay' under power, then one of the small boats had an engine so a friend brought that and towed the other boat. It was Whitsun and when we reached Stourport there were all these crowds of holiday-makers. I thought, 'What have we come to?!'. But when the holiday was over, the little town was so peaceful and the shopkeepers were so friendly.

'Our premises were by the basins in the building by the lock with the rounded wall. We continued our boat-building and hiring business, naming it Canal Pleasurecraft Ltd. Holt built a slipway into the basin, which is no longer there.

'Then we exchanged premises with British Waterways who owned the listed buildings running alongside the canal from York Street. We had the toll house next to the Lock Shop and all the buildings up to the one standing at right angles to the canal. There are old stables at the back, at right angles to the rest, those were our offices and stores. We rented them, we tried to buy them but British Waterways refused to sell. My sister-in-law used the toll house as an art shop where she sold her canalware paintings. The Lock Shop was a general grocers supplying hirers with provisions. The hirers would send us a list of groceries that they needed and the Lock Shop would make them up, ready for when they arrived. By this time we had bought a house between Bewdley and Stourport - I had had my second daughter and it is not advisable to live on a boat with two little girls.

'We built small cruisers, not only for hire but also for everyday ownership, about 35 in all. They had to conform to a certain size, otherwise they wouldn't get through the locks. An Australian engineer, Ashley Moulden, came to help and we had another assistant and an apprentice. We used to hire extra people when there was a big painting job, although I did some of the painting of decks and hulls. We had cleaners, too, to clean the boats after the holiday-makers.

There was once a bridge under Mart Lane leading to the Furthermost basin. The photograph shows a working boat about to pass under the bridge in the early 1950's.
Courtesy Florence Phillips (formerly Mrs Abbott).

'By 1954 canals were choked with weed, the main basin at Stourport had a pile of mud in the centre and nearby residents were beginning to complain about the smell. The waterways at Stourport were no longer used commercially, the power station was receiving coal by road and petrol was arriving by pipe to the petrol storage facility.

'Then Holt read in the papers that the council had decided to fill in the main basin and turn it into a charabanc park. He was devastated. This would mean that the canal would be cut off from the basin and therefore from the river Severn. There are 2000 miles of waterways in England and to cut off the branch of one of them would be disastrous.

'Holt went to see the local councillors and he wrote to everyone he could think of, the national and local newspapers, county councillors and eminent personalities. He was able to rally most of the members of the Inland Waterways Association round him. He also wrote to the Rt Hon Gerald Nabarro, our MP. Gerald Nabarro was a member of a special parliamentary committee set up to encourage inland waterways use for both commercial and recreational purposes. He took the matter up in the House in June 1955. After asking questions, the government allocated some half million pounds to help stop the decline of the canals and enable emergency remedial works to be carried out. The following year, in 1956, parliament voted a further five and a half million pounds to the renovation and regeneration of the canal systems. This saved the inland waterways.

'Eventually most of the councillors came round to his point of view and they dredged the main basin."

SUMMARY

For two hundred years the fortunes of the canal repeatedly rose and fell. Fortunately, Stourport did not depend entirely upon the canal for its prosperity. Brindley's thriving canal complex had attracted a whole range of industries, not only those which you would expect to be built by the waterside such as boat building and carriers, but also a variety of factories attracted by the plentiful water supply and the cheap, convenient transport. Raw materials could be delivered easily and cheaply and the finished products could be despatched by a canal network across England as far as Bristol or the Humber, from where they could be shipped abroad.

The travel-writer, J Randall, wrote in the early 1800s:

"Houses, warehouses and inns ... sprang up as if by magic, the magic which wealth-creating industry usually gives; and iron foundries, vinegar works, tan-yards, spinning mills, carpet manufactories, and boat-building establishments were added."

As we shall see in the fourth chapter, these flourished largely irrespective of the fortunes of the canal.

3. Boat People

The boat people were a strange lot. They kept themselves to themselves. They would argue and rant but if one of them was in trouble, they would do anything to help.
Everybody used to dress up for May Day and they would dress the horses up as well. Different horse brasses came from different areas so you could tell where a horse was from by looking at his brasses.

Jo Clarke

A horse brass commemorating Queen Victoria's Jubilee in 1887

Hundreds of people earned their living in this busy port. The first census, in 1841, shows that in Bridge Street about a dozen of the inhabitants were watermen, while the next popular occupations were those of lawyer, tailor and carpenter, with about four members of each trade. This short street also contained shoemakers, labourers, drapers and foundry-workers, plus one accountant, chandler (candle-maker), ironmonger, grocer, plasterer, shopkeeper, servant, shoebinder, cleaner, painter, baker, schoolmaster, office executive, porter, sailor, gutterman, clerk, weaver, gardener and boat-builder.

LOCK-KEEPERS AND TOLL-KEEPERS

Lock-keepers and toll-keepers were given a house, a coal allowance (to keep them from temptation) and wages. In 1832 a lock-keeper at Stourport received 14s (70p) a week and 4s (20p) in night wages. Toll houses now seem extremely small but these were days when large families were raised in cottages of one room up and one room down.

The first tolls were set by an Act of Parliament but in 1845 Canal Companies were given the power to vary them. From that point onwards tolls became more and more complicated as certain goods were given a low toll if competition was keen. For example, iron was given a huge discount at Stourport if it travelled via Stourbridge and Dudley to Selly Oak to discourage it from travelling on the rival Worcester and Birmingham canal. One discount led to another and carriers were lost in the maze. Short-distance carriers protested that they often had to pay more than goods going a long way. Also, no-one ever knew what the rate was, it was always being altered by some company or other. After the Second World War, in 1958, the toll system was replaced by licensing.

At first, traffic was allowed through the locks only between the hours of 6 o'clock in the morning and 8 at night. Then, in 1816, express or 'fly' boats came into being, they travelled all round the clock and by paying a licence fee, could use the locks at any time. By 1830, competition from other canals had increased and so it was decided that any boat could use a lock at any time. These 24-hour locks meant that the poor lock-keeper could never be absent, nor could he get a good night's sleep.

BOW-HAULIERS

When the basins were first opened there were few towpaths along the River Severn, most paths in the Worcester and Stourport areas were not built until 1804. Boats had sails, but if the current was against them and there was no wind and no towpath for a horse, how did the boat manage to move? The answer is - by manpower.

A team of men, anything from eight to twenty, would pull a boat along the river by a rope tied to the mast head. They had to wade through marshland, scramble over rocks and up steep banks and struggle through overgrown thickets. The fifteen miles from Bewdley to Bridgnorth along the River Severn was considered to be a day's work. Only the roughest, toughest and most aggressive men could cope with the life. They were always quarrelling and fighting among themselves.

A tow path was made in the 1790s along the Severn from Stourport to Gloucester so that horses could be used instead of men. The bow-hauliers objected strongly and mobs of hauliers used violence to stop the horses working, but despite their protests horses were increasingly used. One man pulling three tons cost three shillings per mile, whereas one horse cost one shilling per mile and could pull eighteen tons. The bow-hauliers are said to have died out at least 150 years ago but one Stourport senior citizen re-members seeing them at work.

WATER GYPSIES

From the 1830's onwards, as the prosperity of the canal waned, wages were lowered and the families of watermen began to make their homes aboard narrow boats as it became more and more difficult to pay the rent on the family house. People were born, lived and died on the boats. Be-cause they were a mobile community the Factory Acts and the Education Acts did not apply to them. The whole family, including the children, often worked eighteen hours a day for seven days a week as unpaid helpers.

Bill and Bert Hughes are the grandchildren of Joby Clarke who worked as a boat carrier for the LMS Scottish Railway:

"His boat was the Idriss and it's now in the museum at Ellesmere Port. It was not an ordinary, run-of-the-mill slack boat but it was a fly boat. It just kept going, if anybody got in the way, they ended up in the canal. He worked the boat with his son, Charlie, they went from Wolverhampton to Stourport - the trip took two days if they didn't spend too long in the pubs.

'Stourport was the end of the line, the barges couldn't go any further. They were usually in pairs, a barge and a butty. The barge would be pulled by horse, or later, fitted with an engine, and it towed the butty.

'He carried general goods - bicycles, parcels, shoes - anything. One of his sons, Tim, worked for the railway on a three wheel lorry and trailer. He would take the goods from the boat (or any other boat) and he had a deliv-ery round.

'All Grandad could write was his name. There was a big tin tray hanging on the wall of his boat with a surface rather like a mirror and he would write his name on it in big letters with soap. He wore white corduroy trousers with leather straps just below the knees. The straps were to stop the rats running up his trousers. The warehouses and every-where were full of them, there was no method of controlling them as there is today.

Tokens of the Severn and Canal Carrying Company. At one time, men would be paid with these tokens. They had to spend them in shops and pubs owned by the company.
Courtesy National Waterways Museum Gloucester.

Joby Clarke with the LMS flyboat, the Idris. Tim Clarke is leading the horse.
Courtesy Jo Clarke.

Jessie Hughes with Mick. They worked for Staffordshire and Worcestershire Canal Company Ltd.
Courtesy Bill Hughes (his son).

'Our grandmother was a proper boat lady. She had thirteen children and they all lived on the boat. There was a cabin at the front for the children and one at the back for their parents. Bill asked her once why she had had so many children. She said, 'Well, it's a bit naughty of you to ask, but if you really want to know, I couldn't get away from your grandad. There was nowhere to run on a boat'. Her children would get their schooling wherever the boat stopped to unload for a couple of days.

'The women did the same work as the men, they helped load and unload as well as keeping the boat clean and looking after the family. On the whole, the women were very rough, they were left to their fate. If a wife hit the side of the lock with the barge or made some clumsy manoeuvre her husband would smack her ear'ole. He would be quite violent, it was a hard, tough life.

'Grandmother wore a black apron and boots with hooks and laces. She tied her hair back in a bun and put a scarf over it. She used to take snuff and smoke a clay pipe. On one towpath there was a series of steps, grandmother fell down them and split her head open. Grandad gathered her up, pushed her head together and she lived to be 93.

'We can remember her taking my grandfather's best suit to the pawn shop every Monday. She would get five shillings (25p) on the suit. Every Friday she had to go back and fetch it and pay 5/2d (nearly 26p) so that grandad would have his suit to wear at the weekend

'One day, grandfather and his two sons, Charlie and Jo, took the youngest member of the family, Tom, on a trip with them. Tom was then eleven years old. When they arrived at Stourport the lock was empty and they opened the paddles. While doing this, one of my uncles went to the front of the boat. The boat tipped, and Ben fell into the lock. There are paddles at the side of each lock, the paddle hole is only about a foot (30 centimetres) square but the water rushes in. He was sucked into the paddle hole, they couldn't get him out and he was drowned.

'Most of their sons continued working on the canals when they were older. Our father worked for the Staffordshire and Worcestershire Canal Carrying Company at their yard at Stourport, in a building between Parkes Passage and the canal, where the canalside houses have recently been built. These used to be repair sheds, he stoked the boiler and worked the machinery doing canal maintenance. Occasionally he would have the canal shut down for a fortnight. Sometimes he used to have to ride on his pushbike as far as Wolverhampton, carrying some old coats for bedding. He slept on the boat while he was doing the repairs, usually he was only away for a night or two but sometimes he was away for a fortnight. He was only paid once a fortnight and in 1939 he was earning £2 a week. He had to pay rent every fortnight of about four shillings (20p) - that was for a house in the slums.

'In about 1935 we used to visit dad at work in the repair sheds and we watched him build the last icebreaker. At one time father used to drive the ice-breaker in the canal so that the boats could get through with slack to the power station, it was a terribly cold job.

'During the war father worked on a dredging boat. The canal used to get silted up so that the boats would stick on the bottom. If a boat was carrying slack and if the boatman thought this was likely to happen he would throw some of the slack off to make the boat lighter. This would silt the canal up further for the people behind but they didn't care as long as they themselves got through. The dredger had a winch at the front and a big spoon-type device with two handles. Dad would lower it over the side of the boat and winch the spoon into the mud, then the mud would be tipped into the boat. When the boat was full he had to go up Stourport by the churchyard near Gilgal, then he had to jump into the boat on a board and shovel the silt out in a wheelbarrow and tip it out. There was a lot of coal mixed up in the mud and Stourport people used to come and dig in the mud for coal. Later he had a steam dredger. Dad was exempt from the army because his job was vital to keep the canalways open. Most nights they would put stop planks in certain places on the canal in case it got bombed.

'People who worked in the basins were given nicknames. There was Blackberry, Tingalacre, Peter Black, Chocolate Charlie and so on. Sometimes the name was given to them according to the job that they did, Chocolate Charlie worked on the Cadbury run. Father also went up the Severn and carried petrol, tobacco, margarine, teak, dried fruits in crates - anything. Then it was craned off at Nelson wharf for Birmingham. All the local farmers brought their wheat to Nelson wharf, they emptied it into a pile and vacuum cleaners blew it into barges for Gloucester to be made into flour.

'The tollkeeper measured the height of the boat above the water and he would write this down, together with the number of the boat and the log. Teddy Ward was the lock-keeper at Stourport during the war. It was a busy waterway, there were a lot of foodstuffs - tea and margarine and raw chocolate for Cadbury's called crumbs. Dad used to get bags of the stuff for us.

Tim Clarke with his lovely shire horse at a show. He originally worked on the canal, later for the LMS.
Courtesy Jo Clarke

During the war there were so many boats going up and down with slack and so on, they were never-ending. They would be through a lock in a couple of minutes.

'Everyone used to fight over who was going through the lock first. The first boat through a lock would have a full lock but it would be empty for the second boat going through. You used to do anything to get into the lock first. You used to race the horse, or the Captain used to race ahead on his bike. Occasionally, in the scuffle, a butty would get cracked and then there would be an argument as to whose fault it was.

'Another trick was to put the feeding bag over the horse's nose when a motor boat was coming so that they would think that the horse had stopped for a feed, and not be in any hurry to get ahead of us, then as soon as the boat had gone round a bend the nosebag would be off and we would chase after the boat to get in first. When the first motor boats came we used to drop barbed wire and bits of string into the canal to get round the propeller. We used to come back later in the day and see them repairing the boat and we would be so sympathetic, saying something like, 'Good Lord Jack, how did that happen?'.

'There used to be a saying that you could insult a man's wife but not his horse. On the whole, the horses were treated better than the women. Some of the horses were wonderful, Jo had a horse, Tommy, for 21 years, and he was almost human. When he was in the middle of a feed you could say to him, 'Don't eat that' and he would stop eating. Jo used to bring him back to Stourport along the road and take him into a pub for a pint, and Tommy would drink it out of a glass. Not all horses were like that. When Bert was about ten or eleven father took him up the canal in the boat. Bert was steering the boat and had been told to keep it to the side but he liked to go up the middle. The mate was leading the horse, but when it was breakfast time, the mate left the horse, jumped on the boat and started cooking the bacon. Suddenly, the horse started to run back, taking the line with him. The boat was stuck in the middle of the canal with no power.

'We had a cousin who worked for T & S Element. Their boats used to go down from Cannock to Stourport with slack for the power station. At that time there were no motors, the boats were all horse-drawn. He was behind the horse when suddenly this horse kicked him full in the face. It smashed his face up. He was taken to Barnsley Hall Hospital which was then a hospital for soldiers and it was twelve months before his face was back to normal. We went to see him in hospital, his face was black and he had all tubes stuck out of his mouth. They did a wonderful job. You can't tell now that he had had a bad accident when he was young.

'Sometimes you would see a chap steering a boat and the horse would be on its own but it would keep going, and its head would be nodding. This was because the chap would put a pebble in its ear and the horse would keep shaking his head to try and get rid of it.

'Jo Corbett had an old barge, Hearts of Oak, which was used to take tree trunks under Mart Lane bridge and across the basin to the wood yard under the clock. You had to be quick to get to the clock before the barge sank and you had to 'pole' the boat, pushing it along with the pole. Bert, who worked at Corbetts, was taking Hearts of Oak under Mart Lane bridge, when he saw another barge being poled out of York Street lock, about to bump into him. The other boatman saw him, and went to go back, but as

Boat lock leading to a lower basin, the dry dock and the River Severn.

Joby Clarke with the horse, Tommy, at a show. Tommy pulled the fly boat Saturn. Courtesy Jo Clarke.

he swung the pole round it hit his mate on the front of the boat, knocking him in the water.

'Some boatmen took a real pride in their boats and they were spotless. The rope was wound into a shape called a 'Turk's Head' and they used to scrub the rope until it was white. If you threw a line near them they would shout, 'Don't drop that dirty line on my boat!'. Uncle Tim used to be able to do castles and roses on the furniture and all the utensils. It was a proper skill but he just picked it up.

'Mother had four children and we lived in a little rented cottage on the canalside at Kidderminster. In about 1935 we moved to a canalside cottage (by the Bird-in-Hand) at Stourport. How did we move the furniture? Well, my uncle Fred worked on the boats taking steel from the railway sidings to the steel works at Stourvale and on the return journey, when his boat was empty, our furniture was piled on the boat.

'We were in a communal area, with two washhouses, each containing a cold tap, and you were allotted one day a week as your washday. Then you had to get up at six o'clock in the morning and light a fire. Sometimes, if you were a bit late getting up, somebody else would nip in and take your place and there would be a fight with the line props. Mother was very good at this, nobody dared to take her place.

'We had paraffin lamps and a tin bath hanging on the wall. The toilet was a wooden seat down the garden, you had to go down with a bucket, put the bucket under the seat and remove it afterwards and bury the contents. The house fronted right on to the canal. Bill was only two years old and out playing when he fell into the canal. He was wearing a coat with a little half belt. The children called to my mother, 'Bill's thrown his coat in the canal'. Stan James, who lived nearby and later came to be mayor, thought he would rescue the coat for my mother so he reached in, grabbed the coat and pulled it out and there was Bill, inside. We lived there for about 12 months. Although it was a slum house all our neighbours were lovely, real family people. Then we moved to a Council house, 21 Bullus Road. For the first time we had modern conveniences. We could just flick a switch and the light would come on. We turned a tap and water came out and even better,

24

we turned another tap and hot water came out. We even had a bath. The rent was 5/2d (nearly 26p) a week - 2d (nearly 1p) for the shed."

An Act of 1877 limited the number of people who could live on board a boat. A further Act of 1884, making schooling compulsory for canal boat children, was usually ignored. Tom Mayo, who was working on boats by the time he was nine years old, taught himself to read and write:

"I was what was known as a water gypsy. I come from a boating family - my grandad was 84 in 1939 and he was nearly born on the boats. My dad worked a cargo boat for the Severn and Canal Carrying Company Limited, the only carrying company going all the way to Stourport. My mum used to help him on the boat, even when she had two children, but then she had another lad so she had to stay at our house in Gloucester. My two sisters went with him for some time to help. My mother had seventeen children but there were only ten alive at any one time. In those days you had no help at all from the government, dad was the only breadwinner so we all had to help to bring in some money to keep us alive. I remember going up to Stourport just after 1928 with my dad when I was about nine or ten. I only went to school when I was back home in Gloucester.

'I used to drive the horse and generally look after it. Sometimes I would steer the boat, it was quite normal for young children to do that, I have seen children as young as five steering. It's quite easy. My dad used to do all the loading. He carried any sack work - sacks usually weighed 2.1/4 cwt (127 kilos) each, but things like barrels of oil weighing 4 cwt (203.20 kilos) were craned in.

'Ours was a live-in boat, we used to sleep on board. It was very comfortable. We had a coal fire and a pot-bellied open stove. Inside was what we called a 'mother' with hooks on for the meat. The fat ran into the drip pan and we would use a spoon to baste the meat - chickens, rabbits, ducks, anything. We often used to buy from the shops in Stourport, the Lock Shop was a general grocers and we got food from there. Then there used to be farmers on the side of the canal. You could buy ducks from them or fresh eggs, always thirteen - a baker's dozen - for a shilling (5p). Later, when the motor boats came in, we had a range to cook on. The bed was let down from the wall and was the full width of the boat so we had plenty of room. It was on steel lathes with a flock mattress and a feather mattress on top. During the day we would roll the mattresses up and put them in a cupboard. If we were in Stourport for the evening we used to go to the films at the Electric cinema. These were the silent films.

'Even though dad did all the loading, it was still hard work on the locks, winding the ratchets and opening and closing the lock gates. People would be walking round muffled up in coats and we would be in our shirt sleeves. We had to work with our arms, we couldn't work a windlass or carry a whip if we had something on our arms. If it was cold and we had nothing to do we would put on a balaclava and an overcoat but this wasn't very often.

'I loved the work. The only thing I didn't like was getting up in the morning. Sometimes I had to get up at three o'clock, but that was only when we had to load up at Gloucester. We usually left Gloucester at eight, then we would get to Worcester at night when we would have to wait for the tug to take us to Stourport. It went up once a day and down once a day and didn't run at all on Sundays. You had to make sure you didn't arrive after Saturday lunch time because then you couldn't get away until Mon-

Below top: Traditional narrow boats, mostly converted for leisure use, moored in the Clock House basin.

Below bottom: The old and the new side by side along York Street overlooking the Town Basin.

25

Boat people from the River Severn in the 1920's.
Courtesy National Waterways Museum, Gloucester.

day morning. If the tug had a big tow (a lot of boats), we would start at six o'clock in the morning and get to Stourport at eleven or twelve. Some days I would work from 6am to 9pm then another day I would only have to work for two or three hours. It just depended on what you were carrying and where you had to get to.

'After each cargo you had to scrub down and wash all the decks - everything, even the sides of the boat. Each boat had a false bottom of planks, the boat could take three inches of water without the cargo getting wet. You had to get the bottom up and clean all the muck out. I'd sooner have coal than sand. The sand silted down between the cracks.

'Sometimes there would be a horse waiting for you at Stourport, at other times it would be allocated to you at Worcester and you had to go and fetch it. The horses could be quite troublesome, usually because they wanted to go back to their stable. I collected a horse at six o'clock one morning at Worcester and he wouldn't let me ride him out of the stable. I had to pull him all through the town. A constable saw me and said, 'How far have you got to go with him?' I told him, 'Stourport', and he said, 'Lord help you'. I must have pulled the horse for at least three miles and I got to where you turn off for Birmingham and road goes straight on to Stourport (Holt Heath?) before I could get on his back. I was only ten or eleven at the time and I had taken four horses up the day before.

'You had to be very careful with the horse when you were taking a boat through the lock. You had to unfasten the line from the horse to the mast, take the boat through and fasten it on again afterwards. If the horse started before you were ready it could take the mast off. The locks between Worcester and Stourport were very deep which made them awkward. We also had problems with the horses pulling the boats along the Staffordshire and Worcestershire canal because it was so shallow. We had to unload some of our cargo at Stourport basin so that we could get along the canal. We ran aground once at Cookley and so I jumped out and waded to the bank to pull us free. To get some extra leverage I sat on the bank - straight in a wasp's nest. I got stung right between the eyes - I had two beautiful black eyes!

'My sister nearly had her head cut off not far from Cotton's Lock early in 1924 or 1926 when she was about twelve. She was leading the horse under the bridge by the Black Star, when the horse realised that if he bolted down Lion Hill and Mart Lane he would be back in his stables by the Tontine. He turned round and away he went but the line got twisted round her neck. She was taken to hospital and she carried the scars for the rest of her life. My dad was careful on that approach ever after. Nine times out of ten he would drive through the bridge himself and he wouldn't let us handle the horse - not until we got a good way from Stourport.

'On another trip the rope nearly took the end off my finger. We were just below Kidderminster locks, there were side branches and you had to go over the top. The irons on the bridge had been cut away by the lines and I didn't know and the rope got twisted round my finger. The flesh was hanging off and the bone was sticking out. I put the top of my finger back on, wound a bandage round it and that was that. I never went to hospital or anything. My finger healed completely except for a white scar all the way round my finger top.

'In about 1930 engines were put in the barges and they became motor boats. This was a great improvement, we didn't have to cope with the horses and we didn't have to wait for a horse or a tug. However, they couldn't carry as much, they could only take 27 tons instead of 33.

'Petrol barges didn't come in until the late 1930's. The first to arrive were Russian Oil Products. They had grey boats, very plain, their names were the Sincerity and the Loyalty. They were the first to take petrol to Stourport, before Cleveland and Shell and before the Severn & Canal Carrying Co."

Tom left the Severn and Canal Carrying Company in 1939 to work at the Stoke Prior Salt Works near Droitwich.

TANKER MEN

Fifty years ago, the River Severn was much busier, with all kinds of commercial activity and huge tankers going to Stourport and Worcester. There was the Regent King, the Regent Queen, the Regent Jack, the Regent Jill, the Trader and two tugs, the Progress and the Enterprise. One of these tanker men was Mr B A Lane, author of *Severn Tanking* (published in 1991 by Douglas McLean). He started work for the Regent Oil Company, which was attached to the Petroleum Board, in 1946. His life was full of adventure and incident. On many occasions his scalp 'crawled with fright'. During the war years it was essential that supplies got through and the Masters had to sail whatever the weather. He negotiated floods, frozen rivers, gales and fogs, and once he was nearly hit by a bomb. There was often only a few inches below the flat bottom of the boat and the river bed. In thick fog the Master once asked the look-out if he could see anything. He said, 'Aye Cap'n, some sheep under our bow'. This was one of the many occasions that the tanker had run aground.

One small cabin was shared by three men. The cold was horrific in winter but during the summer they often slept under the stars - until they were visited by a sudden shower. He writes:

"You can imagine the scene. A sudden storm, two or three men sleeping on deck, and only one small hatchway. Bedclothes and mattresses were thrown down the companion way closely followed by the crew. Then came the business of sorting out whose bedding was whose before retiring ...

'Our life was hard; the living accommodation sparse. The wheelhouse had no doors, only a canvas dodger each side to keep out bad weather. Doors were eventually fitted but this was many years later.

'By other standards on shore, our wages were very good, but the hours were abnormal. For instance, we would leave Sharpness on the tide at three o'clock in the morning for Avonmouth, load there, and when we returned to Sharpness that following night, it was around five or six o'clock in the evening before we had finished. In that one day we would have worked fourteen to fifteen hours. The following morning we would be away from Sharpness about five o'clock to go to Stourport and discharge our cargo and then head back to Worcester to moor up. By then it was about eight or nine o'clock at night which made a fifteen or sixteen hour working day. Next morning we were away at five o'clock again, to arrive at Sharpness at around two p.m., a nine hour day, making a long three-day trip. We could then have a few hours off to go home. ... We had to keep going, day in, day out.

'When we arrived at Stourport in those days it was nothing to find several craft waiting to discharge. We had to wait our turn which could be at any time during the day or night. Someone had to stand by the craft until it was empty then he returned to his bunk until sailing time, which again could be from 5.30 a.m. onwards.

'To get away from the depot, you had to swing round and face down river. The width of the river was barely a length and a half of our craft, so we had to swing on the jetty posts by putting a rope around it and back around the stern of our vessel. Then we could let the bow lines go and swing out on the rope. When the motor was halfway round, she could slip the line and keep the prop turning ahead to let her continue on round. The

The Severn Merchant traded from Stourport to Cardiff.
Courtesy National Waterways Museum, Gloucester.

28

dumb (towed) barge would have started swinging just before, it would be three quarters of the way round when the motor would drop alongside, pick up the tow rope, fast forward and away we would go to Lincombe Lock."

It was always a rush to catch the tide, 'sometimes barges were loaded so quickly that it was a wonder they didn't blow themselves up and save the Germans the trouble'. He adds:

"Men that work the river now in bad or foggy weather, don't know they are born. They have radar, sound equipment, radio and all the mech-anical aids to navigate that river. All we had was compass, a clock and a hell of a lot of river knowledge, but most of all a lot of luck."

Mr Lane stayed until the last vessel was sold in the mid 1960's. When he finished he described it as a 'sad, sad day' and his final comment is:

"I married a Stourport girl and we still visit there where I sometimes walk on the Red Cliff overlooking the old depots and I can look up and down the river and remember the old days."

STEAM SKIPPERS

Terry Crewe was the last Steam Skipper on the river:

"I worked mainly on the Amo which carried 240 passengers but there was also the SS Beatrice (190 passengers) and the Kingstonian, named after the place where she was made, Kingston-upon-Thames. The Kingstonian was 80 feet (nearly 24 metres) long, she arrived on three Pickwick trailers. She had an old petrol paraffin engine put in her which went back to 1918. You would start her up on petrol then when she was warmed up you would change to paraffin. The Amo would go at 15 knots if you pushed her.

'I started with the company round about 1955, and I soon found out that it was hard work. You had to be down there at 5.30 in the morning to load up three tons of coal before setting off. That would carry you through for the day. You had to keep the engine at just the right temperature and you were very crammed, there was no room between the engine and the boiler. The shovel had to be very small to fit in and the engine wasn't encased as engines are now. By the time you got to lunch time you were like a piece of wet rag. If you had a good engineer who lasted the day you were lucky.

'The company I was working with eventually converted the Amo from steam to diesel."

The lane under Stourport bridge has been named *Beatrice Walk*.

4. The Dark, Satanic Mills

Stourport is not only important for its traffic, but it is equally so for its productions; few places can boast of such an extensive household ironmongery and kitchen range manufactory, and here is one of the largest tanneries in this part of England; many barges and boats are built in the numerous yards; considerable quantities of sail-cloth, carpets, and vinegar are manufactured; the coal, corn and timber trades are very important, and employ much shipping; in the season for hops and fruit, vast quantities change hands here every market day; and from the central situation of the town, from the almost unparalleled facilities for business, Stourport bids fair for progressively increasing in population, intelligence, and wealth.

Bentley's History Directory of Worcestershire, 1841

INDUSTRIES FOUNDED BEFORE THE CANAL ARRIVED

Mitton Mill

Until Brindley arrived, the only buildings of any importance on the northern bank of the Severn were the small mills along the river Stour. Tucked away along Mill Lane is the oldest industrial site, so ancient that it is mentioned in the Domesday Book of 1086 as being a corn grinding mill held by the 'King's Bailiff' and having a value of seven or eight shillings. A century later we find it in the hands of the monks of Maiden Bradley who, in their turn, relet it to the local landowner at a rental of one mark of silver, on the understanding that he should keep it in repair at his own expense, but might claim the assistance of the monks if he needed them. By the nineteenth century it possessed two separate water wheels and five massive pairs of millstones.

The mill was put to various uses according to general demand. During the thirteenth century, when nearby Kidderminster was famous for its cloth, it was used in cloth-making as a fulling mill. When, in the eighteenth century, English iron and steel was called for, the Knight family bought up most of the mills on the Stour from Halesowen to Lower Mitton and converted them into iron forges. They owned Mitton Mill for 150 years. In 1816 flour made from home-grown corn was in short supply and so the mill was used for corn-grinding under the Blundells. It was a flour mill during the shortages of the 1914-18 war. The Elf Manufacturing Company took over in 1947, producing wooden bobbins used in the making of Kidderminster carpets, and other wood products. Unfortunately, a fire and flood in 1955 partly destroyed the mill.

The Ward family purchased the remains of the mill and the dilapidated Mitton Mill house, together with a few other old buildings, but were undecided as to what they should do with them. The next development came when their daughter married Richard Hoare in 1972. Richard was both a musician, having played in the Birmingham Philharmonic for three years, and a qualified, experienced engineer. Eventually, he began to upgrade the site:

The River Stour at Wilden. Like rivers and streams throughout the country in medieval times, the River Stour was used as a source of power to drive many mills along its banks. In the 19th century, there were about 30 water-powered iron works along this river.

31

DANKS, VENN & CO.

Having taken up the Business lately carried on by

BELSHAM & Co.

RESPECTFULLY INFORM THEIR FRIENDS THAT THEIR

LOCK-UP TROWS,

REGULARLY SAIL TWICE A WEEK,

TO AND FROM

Bristol, Glo'ster, Worcester, Stourport & Bewdley;

And by their own Boats to Stourbridge, &c.

By which every description of GOODS, particularly Wines and Spirits, are safely and expeditiously conveyed for the undermentioned Places;

LUDLOW	WOLVERHAMPTON	BIRMINGHAM	MANCHESTER	AND ALL PARTS
SHREWSBURY	THE STAFFORDSHIRE	COVENTRY	AND ALL PARTS	OF THE WEST
KIDDERMINSTER	IRON WORKS AND	LEICESTER	OF THE NORTH	SWANSEA
STOURBRIDGE	POTTERIES	DERBY	BATH	AND
DUDLEY	WALSALL	LIVERPOOL	EXETER	SOUTH WALES

FOR PARTICULARS OF FREIGHT, &C., APPLY TO

Wm. Bird, Wharfinger, } *Stourport;* ANTWIS & STURLAND, Castle Fields,
Danks, Venn & Co. } *Manchester*, or Duke's Dock, *Liverpool;*
John Danks, Wharf, *Birmingham;* W. Kendall, Wharfinger, *Gloucester;*
Crowley & Co. *Wolverhampton;* T. Y. Venn, Wharfinger, 6, Tontine
Hood & Wall, Diglis, *Worcester;* Warehouse, Quay Head, *Bristol.*

D. V. & Co. request the favor of their Friends to be particular in directing Goods UPON THE PACKAGES to be forwarded by their Trows.

[MARY NICHOLSON, PRINTER, BRIDGE-STREET, STOURPORT.]

An advertisement showing a trow, probably printed at the beginning of the 1800s. The Danks family were well-known carriers in Stourport. Courtesy National Waterways Museum, Gloucester

"We had to choose whether it should become residential or commercial. This is such a lovely spot that we couldn't bear the thought of turning it into roads and houses so we decided on a commercial site. Mitton Mill House was demolished and replaced by the first industrial unit in 1983. The site was prone to floods from the river Stour, in fact part was a marshy swamp, so one of our first jobs was to raise the whole area. We gradually developed it and we now have eight industrial units. Two of these are occupied by my company, Richard Hoare (Plant & Machinery) Ltd, the remainder are let to other companies.

'When we reconstructed the old mill, the council stated that we had to preserve a square where the old mill wheel had been. If you look at the wall by the side of the bridge, you can see the outline in the brickwork."

Richard buys, renovates and sells plant and machinery. His expertise has earned him the title of Honorary Doctor of the prestigious Saint-Petersburg State Marine Technical University.

Boat Building

Boats were being built at Stourport even before the canal arrived. Thomas Monk was born in 1765 into a family who had been boat-builders at Lower Mitton for generations. Although he was only a few years old when the canal arrived he was fascinated by it all. Thomas was an ambitious young man and, with a view to expanding the family business, he moved to Tipton. However, he still maintained an interest in the family concern at Stourport. He specialised in long-distance craft on narrow canals which are still known as Monkey boats. Eventually he owned a fleet of 130 boats sailing the length and width of England. He was one of the first to build boats with a shelter for the driver and a small living cabin to house the crew and, sometimes, the mule, donkey or horse. In 1820 he launched 'packet' boats, built for carrying passengers and parcels, which were a great success.

Monk had eight sons and a daughter. Two of his sons died young, the others were trained in boat-building then each one was given a boat-building yard along the Severn. As for the daughter, she married a boat-builder!

32

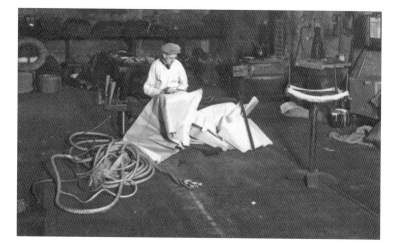

Samuel Danby at work in the Tarpauling Workshop, Long Warehouse. He worked until he was over 80 and died in 1946 when he was in his nineties.
Courtesy National Waterways Museum.

Left: A narrow maintenance boat passing through the staircase lock in the 1950s. The dry dock is the building on the left-hand side of the photograph.
Courtesy Florence Phillips (formerly Mrs Abbott).

Below: The dry dock building today. The two narrow boats are probably being repaired.

The family continued working at Stourport where they built many trows, using oaks from the Wyre Forest.

Most of the trows built by the Monk family came into the hands of the Dock Company at Stourport early in the twentieth century. Here, these wonderful and unique craft were converted into anonymous dumb barges in the Dock Company dockyard and workshop. They also overhauled their own vessels at Stourport. The Dock Company were a huge concern with offices at Bristol, Worcester and Birmingham as well as Stourport.

Another boat-builder in Stourport was William Bird who owned a dock off Cheapside and the house opposite. He and his wife are shown on the 1841 census as wharfinger, barge and boat builder, block and mast maker. He built two of the finest vessels on the Severn, the Water Witch and the Prince Albert. When the Prince Albert was being built it was discovered that the upper part was too wide to get it out of the dock, so the boat was taken half-built to the engine basin and finished there.

Boat-building continued after the World War II. Some of the first pleasure boats to be built after the Second World War were built at Stourport by Holt Abbott of Canal Pleasurecraft Ltd.

The Tannery

In medieval times, every village had its tannery, supplying leather for anything from horse harnesses to belts for water-powered machines. The Stourport tannery was built in 1702, probably by the Nash family. No doubt they were delighted when the canal arrived and they were able to expand to such an extent that they became the largest tannery outside London.

The works stretched across both sides of Lombard Street, backing onto the canal where the company had a wharf, for it received raw materials by barge. From the canal side you would have seen the men patiently pushing the hides down into the pits with their long poles. Worcester Street was built by the Rogers family for Tannery workers.

Wagons used to arrive bringing in great loads of bark from Ribbesford woods. Stripping bark was considered to be a woman's job. The bark was piled into huge ricks, like gigantic hayricks. An elderly lady by the name of

Betty Birch brewed ale at the back of the Tannery and the tables were loaded with bread and cheese, so that carters and dealers were never sent away empty-handed.

There were several ricks in the tannery grounds, one in Tan Lane and another in Lion Hill. These were, of course, highly inflammable and one of them was once set on fire by small boys playing with matches.

The Tannery chimney was built in 1831by Thomas Ward and remained a local landmark for years. It was 203 feet tall and 25 workmen could sit round the top, an impressive piece of work. One of the workers once climbed to the top 'and waved a flag to his missus'. Thomas Ward is remembered for the carvings he donated to the Methodist Church.

Sometime later, in about 1860, the tannery was almost completely burned down. No-one knows how the fire started, perhaps small boys were playing with matches again. It began on the Saturday and burned until the following Tuesday week. At that time it was owned by two brothers, John Crane Rogers and Joseph Rogers who had come from Martley. Joseph Rogers was fetched from Areley House by one of his workmen and when he saw the raging flames from the top of the street 'he was speechless'.

HENRY

THE TANNE

TELEPHONE 17.

Oak and
Chrome
Leather Belting,
Laces, ...
Combing Leathers
Pickers and Bands.   Chrome Tann

A splendid new factory was built, even the great chimney stack had a crack down it and had to be rebuilt. The new factory had an ornate Gothic tower complete with clock, a useful addition for the many people who, in those days, could not afford a watch. Not everyone was delighted by the clock. There was only a clock face on the works side so that the time could not be seen by the town folk. Twenty years later it seemed to have acquired a mind of its own, for when the little finger was at nine and the big one at two, the clock would strike ten and the workers would know that it was half-past four.

After the rebuilding of the tannery Mr Rogers seems to have lost interest. Isaac Wedley says that the tannery 'suffered from his predilection for horses and hunting', and hints at a lawsuit. The tannery went into liquidation and was sold for a quarter of its value, then it changed hands again at twice the figure and was bought by a Mr Henry Hall Beakbane in 1880 for £5,000. The name is Celtic and means a worker in bone and skin so perhaps his family had been tanners for hundreds of years. He came from Cheshire where his business had flourished, despite the fact that he and his family were Quakers.

At first he must have regretted his move to Stourport. Local materials were disappearing, and the cutting back of the Wyre forest greatly affected the supply of oak bark. With the railways replacing horse-drawn transport the need for harness leather decreased and even the craftsman cobbler was put out of business by factory-made shoes. The tannery ran at a loss for a while until it closed in 1901.

Then in 1908 Mr Beakbane's son, also named Henry, returned from America having learned new methods of tanning. The old tannery was reopened and modernised and the great chimney stack demolished. The yard turned out leather for driving-belts, pimp cups, washers and other engineering requirements. There was a recession during the First World War but when peace returned new lines were started.

The tannery began to supply fine sheepskin leather to the Worcester glove trade in 1927. They changed over to a light leather for shoe uppers, gloves, coats and handbags using both sheep and goat skins from India. The

AKBANE
URPORT.

TELEGRAPHIC ADDRESS:
"BEAKBANE.
STOURPORT."

Chrome
Cup and
Ram Leathers,
Hydraulic Butts,
P   and Valve
a Speciality.   . . . . . Leather.

An idealised illustration of the Tannery. Tanneries have always been notorious for their terrible smell. Courtesy Ray Franks.

great demand for this high quality material encouraged skilled men to come to live and work in Stourport. The Beakbane family was still running the business until the early 1960s, when there was another terrible fire. An eye-witness says:

"The tannery had slatted windows and you could see the silhouettes of rows of skins hanging up and you could hear them popping in the heat. On the other side of the road was a petrol station and the owners of the garage were very worried!"

It was never rebuilt and the business was transferred to Kidderminster. For many years, Thomas Vale & Co Ltd used the site but it is now the home of the Co-operative Society.

The Iron Works

If the Baldwin family had not settled in Stourport it would now only be about half its present size. Their iron factory in Foundry Street expanded until it filled the site now occupied by the public library, police station, fire station and medical centre. They founded the giant Anglo American Tin Stamping Company. They built houses, schools, churches and a hospital. At one time or another the Baldwins owned almost every industry in Stourport except for the Tannery and the Vinegar Works. They created the village of Wilden. One member of this illustrious family, Stanley Baldwin, even became prime minister of England three times!

The first member of the Baldwin family to arrive in Stourport was a Shropshire ironmaster, Thomas Baldwin. He arrived in about 1791 to work at Joshua Parker's works in Foundry Street. English iron was in great demand, Dud Dudley in Worcestershire and Abraham Darby in Shropshire had experimented with the use of coal or coke instead of charcoal, which resulted in the superiority of English iron. There were not many foundries about and these works were the only ones of their kind for miles around. Customers came from Hereford and Ludlow and even further afield. Thomas was a hard-working, enterprising young man and must have had the most senior position as he lived in the house next to the Foundry. He began to specialise in the manufacture of cast iron hinges, Baldwin's Best Butts became known all over the country for their excellence. One of Baldwin's best known works is the bridge that crosses the main road from Worcester to Tenbury.

Thomas acquired the works in about 1814 and they became so prosperous that he began buying up local mills. There were about thirty waterpowered iron works along the River Stour including slitting (cutting) mills, forges and wire mills. In about 1860 his sons bought Lewty's factory at Wilden, which became the Baldwin family's major iron works.

Thomas was a dedicated Methodist, putting his heart and soul into the hymns with his fine singing voice. Although he lived in a time when there was a great divide between the managers and the workers, he never hesitated to get down with the workers whenever there was a problem.

The Foundry became one of the main sources of employment in Stourport for five generations. The fires of the forges glowed all night. Fred Rimmel's uncle worked there:

"Baldwin's factory was in Foundry Street and Worcester Street. My uncle said that it was a terrible place to work with all those furnaces. When he got home each day he was black, he looked as if he had just walked out of a mine. Baldwin was very supportive and did his best to make life bearable for them. Interestingly, they didn't have a hooter or a siren but a bell to summon the workers. You could tell the time by the bell. Worths and the other factories had hooters or sirens right to the end."

The Foundry closed in 1956.

The Anglo American

The Anglo-American Tin Stamping Company Limited was one of the triumphs of Stourport. At the end of the nineteenth century enamelled steel hollowware was only made in America, then in about 1879 Baldwin and Son secured the patents for cast mottled enamelware. A Mr Quinby came over from America to supervise its manufacture and the enamelware was first named 'Baldwin and Quinby's Patent Mottled Enamel' but it was later known as 'stone iron ware'. It was only the fourth factory in the world to manufacture this enamelware. The promoters were Alfred Baldwin, Enoch Baldwin, and two others.

They took over a disused factory on the Worcester Road opposite Gilgal. The site had been originally used as a spinning shed for the manufacture of carpets, first by Samuel Broome and then by John Brinton of Moor Hall but it had been seriously damaged by fire five years previously. The new company was known as the Anglo-American Tin Stamping Company.

They made kettles, saucepans, water bottles, mugs, dishes, plates - anything where enamel could be used. If any local housewife discovers that she has in her kitchen cupboard an immaculate piece of enamelware which is a light bluish grey, splashed with dark blobs and patches and with frequent pinholes, it would be wise not to send it to the local charity shop as in a few years time, it may become a collector's item. These were made from a secret process which has died with the inventors. It had a major advantage in that it did not chip.

Some of the floors had acid swilling about on them, consequently the workers wore heavy wooden clogs.

An artist, J Darbyshire, was called in from the Worcester China Works to decorate the enamelware; he painted beautiful studies of fruit, flowers and rural scenes which were later japanned (varnished) to give them a finishing touch. However, this process proved to be too expensive and transfers were used instead.

In 1915, during the first World War, the Anglo American Tin Stamping Co combined with Archibald Kenrick's of West Bromwich and changed its name to Anglo-Enamelware Ltd. Kenricks also had a foundry near to the present police station. The company expanded into Baldwin Road (known in those days as 'Farm Bed') and took over the empty buildings of Harrison's screw works next door.

The company was selected by the war office to supply the army. They made hand grenades, bomb casings and domestic items. Margo Addison worked at the Anglo during the war:

"I was on the hand presses, making mugs, hot water bottles, plates, bowls, pans, colinders, anything enamel. I put the holes in the salt cellars and pepper pots with a little hand press, then they went to be enamelled. We supplied water bottles for carrying drinking water to the troops. They were flat and slightly curved to fit round a body. A

36

One of Baldwin's factories, the Anglo-American. It was only the fourth factory in the world to manufacture enamelled steel hollow-ware.

lady would cut out the pieces on a press and they were bent by hand on a shape on the bench. Although we were supplied with gloves they wore out in no time. We took it in turns to do that job because your hands got so sore. Then somebody else would weld them and put the tops on. Afterwards they would be finished off on another press and go to be enamelled."

The Anglo went into liquidation in 1956 but the site is still known locally as Anglo Corner.

All the Baldwin family were known for their benevolence towards their workers. They created an enthusiastic and committed workforce. One of the townsfolk remembers her father going in every Sunday morning, unpaid, to check on the furnaces. No strikes have been recorded and the only disagreement between a Baldwin and the townspeople occurred over the supply of gas.

Enoch Baldwin and the Gas Supply

According to the Thomas Memoirs which spanned the twentieth century, 'Lighting in Stourport-on-Severn was first candles, then oil lamps followed by gas which was a naked flame until mantles were introduced'.

Birmingham had a lead in the gas industry and in 1824, a gas works was built by Enoch's company, Baldwin & Son, in Foundry Street, to supply the town with gas. Earl Baldwin later mentioned in one of his speeches that the streets of Stourport were lit by gas before the streets of the city of London.

As this gas was expensive, at about 10 o'clock every night Enoch used to turn down the gas by his tap in the kitchen and the town had to do with half supply. Enoch was a member of the Methodist Church and ensured that they had a supply but this, too, was rationed. He installed a gas tap under his seat in the sanctuary, and when the sermon began he would stretch out his hand and gently turn down the lights until the building was 'dim and religious'. As soon as the preacher reached his conclusion, the light would become brighter. After his death the chapel keeper continued to do this, operating it from the meter, and on one occasion he turned it too far and the congregation was plunged into darkness.

A few years after the first gas works had been built, Baldwin, Son & Co decided that they would like to light the streets of the town with the 'new illuminant'. A 'town meeting' was called in the church, which anyone could attend, to consider the application to lay down new pipes. The residents said that they were not happy with their supply of gas. They said it was too expensive, of poor quality and insufficient in supply. The local factory owners and businessmen asked Enoch to enlarge his plant but he refused, he also refused to supply the gas for improved street lighting. They therefore formed the Stourport Gas, Coal and Coke Company in the mid 1860's and built a gas works in Cheapside. This provided larger quantities of cheaper and better gas. The gas company offered to compensate Enoch but he turned them down and his gas works fell into disuse.

Gas lamps were still around in the 1930's. Senior citizens remember the lamplighter going round in the evening with his long pole, hooking the end through the chains hanging from the lamps and pulling them to turn on the lamp.

The Baldwins lie in Mitton cemetery, beneath monuments made not from stone but in iron, wrought at their own workshops. The memorials are still there today.

The Carpet Industry

A few years ago a local resident went to the Adelaide Theatre in Australia. They had just had a new carpet laid and she was amazed when she found that it had come from her home town, Carpets of Worth in Stourport!

The history of the carpet industry is complicated. Over the years there have been more than three-hundred manufacturers in Kidderminster and Stourport alone. Many of them were registered before the mid 1800's when the hand looms were scattered in the houses of the town. Melvyn Thompson, who is currently writing 'Woven in Kidderminster' gives a brief outline of the industry and its association with the town of Stourport:

"Many towns in Worcestershire were involved in the cloth weaving industry. With sheep on the hillsides and a good river for the washing and dyeing of the yarns, Kidderminster was one of the most important in the county. The weavers were progressive and always looking for new products. They were known for a heavy weight cloth named 'Kidder Stuff' but in 1735 they introduced a flat weave carpet which was called after the name of the town. 'Kidderminster' sold well and in 1749 they added 'Brussels' which had a looped pile. The demand for patterned carpets grew rapidly and the industry responded with many new companies being formed to meet the orders.

'In the days of the pack horse, delivery was a major headache, rolls of carpet were not easy to transport! James Brindley solved the problem in 1772 when he built the Staffordshire & Worcestershire canal through Kidderminster following the River Stour to the point where it joined the River Severn near Lower Mitton. Kidderminster, at the heart of the country, soon became the 'Carpet Capital' as access to the canals and waterways opened up new markets.

One of two similar gravestones for the Baldwin family in Mitton churchyard.

38

'The company owners, the Carpet Masters, quickly became very rich but their weavers were forced to work long hours in appalling conditions to make a living. 'Fall day' was pay-day and the weavers immediately went to one of the many public houses of the town to drown their sorrows. They pooled their grievances about pay and working conditions and decided to form a Weaver's Committee. In the 1820's the relationship between the Masters and the Weavers became very strained and in 1828 the weavers went on strike for twenty-one weeks in a dispute about rates of pay. This total stoppage was a disaster for the town and the canal transport business.

'But the industry was still developing so the manufacturers decided to look outside the town boundary for other places to get weaving away from the influence of the Weavers' Committee. Around this time the carpet industry was established in Lower Mitton.

'Remembering that the factory dyehouses needed to be on the river, Lower Mitton was ideal since the River Stour actually split for a short distance creating an island just big enough for a factory. And so, with the industry still in the hand loom era, in this area of Stourport the first factories came to the town.

'Early records indicate that a Robert Shirley was in business around 1825. But it seems that the first carpet factory was established in the same year as the General Strike when Tyler and Humphries started business at Farm Bed. The factory was named 'The Farm Bed Carpet Works'. In later years the factory was owned by George Harris. He was quite a character, he lived alone in the High Street and was so fond of his horses that he frequently fed them port wine and biscuits. He seems to have had a good head for business and considerably enlarged the factory and the turnover.

'When George Harris retired in 1854 he was eventually succeeded by his factory manager, Charles Harrison. It appears the workers called the departing George Harris, Harris-off and the new owner, Harris-on. Mr Harrison was born in Liverpool in 1830. When he was a young man he came to Stourport to work for the wharfinger but he soon realised that the carpet industry offered better prospects. In later years he was MP for Bewdley and Stourport and lived at Areley Court.

'The 1850s was a period of change when the Industrial Revolution hit the carpet industry. Charles Harrison, with the backing of spinner Samuel Broome and old George Harris, further expanded the business and installed a steam engine to drive the line shafting for the first power carpet looms. In 1896 he transferred his business to Long Meadow Mills in Kidderminster and left the town.

'In earlier years, Samuel Broome was also responsible for building a spinning mill called 'The Mitton Works' near Lower Mitton Bridge, currently the site of Anglo House. A number of other companies made their mark in the area. Island Mills was the home of Fawcett & Watson and later Richard Smith & Sons. In 1894 Smith financed Anderson, Lawson & Co who specialised in Chenille Axminster rugs. In the 1930's they became part of The Carpet Manufacturing Company in Kidderminster and the factory was sold. Many other companies occupied the factories of Lower Mitton including John Brinton who was, for a while, affiliated with Samuel Broome. However, the best known name associated with the Stourport carpet industry is 'Bond-Worth'.

'In 1831, William Henry Worth was a partner in the Kidderminster company, Butcher, Worth & Holmes. Thirteen years later the partnership split up and William Henry decided to set up his own company with his two sons, William and Joseph. In 1850 he retired, the company was re-named Worth Brothers and a younger brother, Thomas Bond, entered the business. In 1853 Worth Brothers moved to Stourport setting up at Broome's old Mitton Works. They soon extended the factory and installed the latest Brussels-weave power looms.

'On the retirement of his two brothers, Thomas Bond, who was becom-ing a wealthy man, joined in partnership with John Head. By 1866 he had dissolved all partnerships and was putting all his energies into the building of Severn Valley Mills on the meadowland further downstream between Severn Road and the Stour.

'The Severn Valley Mills factory was completed by 1868. Initially, other carpet companies leased areas of the factory but eventually they left and Thomas Bond Worth was able to take over the whole site. He lived in Lichfield House, near the factory; more recently, the house was the offices of Carpets of Worth. In 1896 Bond-Worth became a limited company and about the same time bought a mill in Stroud. T. Bond Worth & Sons Ltd was, by now, world renowned for their extensive range of quality woven carpets.

'The company continued to grow and in the late 1920's they added a new large weaving shed which was so large that when 1,000 workers and their families sat down to a lavish meal to celebrate the opening they were only in one corner. By 1935 T Bond Worth was the main employer in Stourport with well over 1,000 employees. Another 400 were employed in the factories in Stroud.

'In the war years all carpet factories ceased production and became involved with the war effort. After the war, the 1950's and 1960's were the boom years as the country built houses on a grand scale. Rugs and carpet squares were superseded by wall-to-wall carpeting, the industry was extremely busy! Bond Worth were also expanding their operations and in 1963 they bought the established Kidderminster weaving company, Jelleyman & Sons.

'And so, the 60s were good years with full employment for Bond Worth and the carpet industry."

Traditional patterned carpets made by Bond Worth of Stourport. Carpet samples supplied by Carpets of Worth.

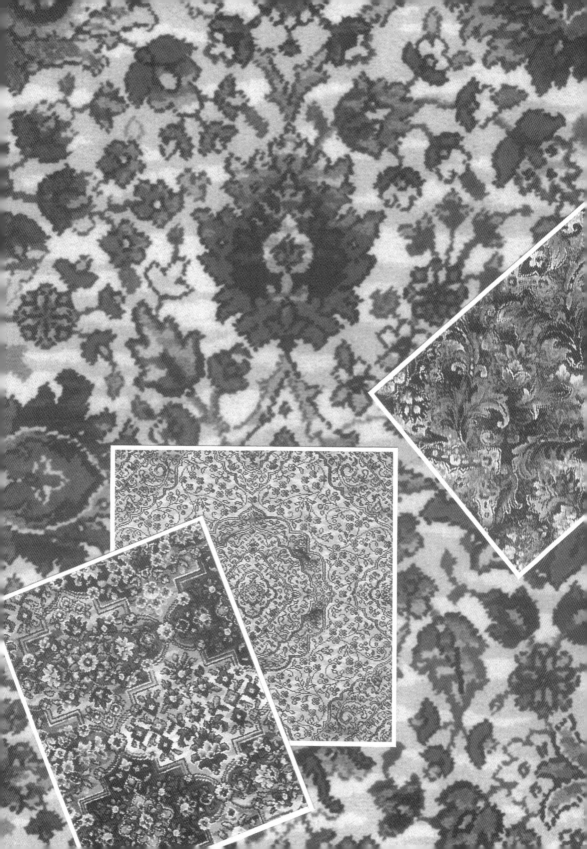

Two retired ladies, now living in Areley Kings, worked there before the war:

"We both went to Bond Worth, hundreds were working there and we were either weaving, setting or picking. In picking, you had to pick the mistakes out of the carpet. We started at about 7.30. From 8.00-8.30 was a half-hour break for breakfast, then we had an hour at 1.00 and we finished at 5.15. On Saturdays we worked from 7.30 until a quarter to 12. You had to clean down on a Saturday, that was a terrible job.

'The wages when you started were 7/6d (about 38p) a week with 4d (nearly 2p) stopped for insurance. After four weeks if you were OK you had a 1/6d (about 7p) rise. Our parents gave us 9d (about 4p) a week pocket money and we had to buy our own stockings

'You had to queue for your money on a Friday after you had left work. You had the cash in a little tin with a lid on and your number on the top. When you had taken your money out you threw it into a bucket ready for the next week. The wages were fairly standard so there was no use in changing from one job to another for more money. Most jobs were in the carpet factories so if you left Bond Worth's you would have to work in another carpet factory in Kidderminster, then you would have your tram or bus fare on top."

Betty Bickerton worked in the design department:

"I was a student at Stourbridge Art School for three years, after which, in 1953, I got a job at Bond Worth in the design department . It was very humble. I would empty the water jars and grind away with the pestle and mortar. They were all powder colours in those days mixed with Gum Arabic.

'You had all these designs in front of you and you had to transfer them on to squared paper. Each square represented a tuft of carpet. The designs were then sent down to the factory where they would follow the design and weave the carpet.

'The youngsters (like me) would be allowed to do some designs. We would have a flat wash on a piece of paper and we would doodle patterns on it. A Wilton carpet would just be based on five colours whereas an Axminster could have thirty or forty. Then the doodles would be submitted to the Directors and they would select those they thought were saleable. A few of my designs were chosen, among them one called Galleons Reach which had a black background and broken lines of blue and red - it was like a treasure chest with broken chains and jewels.

'Constance Spry came quite often. She would suggest things and send us various plants, leaves and flowers. The senior designers would work on those. One design was a medley of leaves like a jungle, another was of soft pastel roses. She sent a parcel from Scotland where she had been inspired by the colours of lichens and bracken but when we opened it in the studio it was just a muddy splodge. Mosses and lichens looked vibrant on the hillside but they dried up on their way to Stourport.

'I was there for ten years. Nowadays designers use computers."

Melvyn concludes:

"In the 1970's the whole industry was influenced by overcapacity and uncontrolled imports from abroad. Many companies failed to survive and in 1977 Bond Worth Holdings Ltd, as they were by then known, went into

Top photograph: The number 1 gate entrance to Bond Worth in about 1960.
Courtesy Worcestershire County Archives.

Above: A recent photograph of Bond Worth No 2 gate entrance.

receivership. But it was still a fine company and a group of Middle Eastern businessmen bought the business and renamed it Carpets of Worth.

Towards the Millennium Carpets of Worth made plans to reorganise. Sadly these plans involved the vacation of the Severn Valley Mills that had been their home for over 130 years. Ironically, the business was transferred to the old Jelleyman factory in Kidderminster - less than half a mile from where William Henry Worth started the business all those years ago! Today the carpet industry no longer relies on the river and the factories of Lower Mitton. It has moved to the Sandy Lane Trading Estate where new, smaller companies continue the industry that has had, in the past, such a major influence on the lives of the townsfolk of Stourport."

INDUSTRIES ARRIVING AFTER THE CANAL

The Vinegar Works (Holbrooks Limited)

In Mitton churchyard lies Hickin Bold, the founder of the world-famous sauce factory of Holbrooks. He had a little vinegar works in the centre of Stourport in 1781 but in 1798 Charles Swann from Tenbury offered to finance his expansion, and Swann & Company was born. They built a malt vinegar brewery in the wide angle between the River Severn and the River Stour at Cheapside. The site was chosen because of the quality of the local water, pumped from the Bunter Sandstone, and the fact that the canal nearby would provide convenient transport. The only problem was that it was subject to flooding from the River Stour. To prevent this, 2,000 tons of earth were imported from (what is now) Worcester race course. A wooden ramp was built which folded back on itself for loading and unloading from the River Severn.

At first they made only malt vinegar from barley, malt, water, yeast and invert sugar, but they were soon experimenting with other sauces. A report by Health Commissioners in 1852 said that, although most of the sauces they tested were highly dangerous and adulterated with oil of citriol, sauces from the Swann's factory were found to be pure.

Then came disaster. In 1879 the brewery was burned to the ground. Some of the large vats were made entirely of wood and the heat was so intense that the walls near the Severn bulged in the heat. In 1882 it was rebuilt and the name changed to the Birmingham Vinegar Brewery Company Incorporated. During those three years the company had not only been planning a new brewery but they had also been experimenting with new sauces. One of these was Holbrook's Worcestershire Sauce, made from a recipe provided by 'a nobleman of the county' who brought it back from India. It was originally made as a thin sauce. The name 'Holbrook' came from a salesman in Manchester who sold more than anyone else.

By 1894 the demand was so great that they needed to expand. They therefore decided to build the three largest vats in the world. The two names to remember of this magnificent enterprise are William Knott, who was the Foreman Cooper, and William Newbury, the engineer. The walls were of Siberian Red Deal and 3,000 yards of iron bands were required. Each vat held 140,000 gallons of vinegar, enough to fill a row of thirty five-roomed houses and large enough for 150 workmen to sit down side by side inside to eat their lunches. One of the workmen, John Hobley, was a champion cyclist and while the men were sitting at the bottom of an empty vat eating their lunches he would put in his practice by cycling round and round inside the vat above their heads. Fred Rimmel recalls that sometime in the 1940s one big vat burst. 'The surrounding houses had cellars, and the cellars all filled up with vinegar'.

By the year 1900 the sales of Holbrooks Worcestershire Sauce had become so great and the product so well known that the Birmingham Vinegar Brewery Company changed its name to Holbrooks Ltd. Eleven years later F D Ratcliff, of Stourbank House, became manager and his son, Tony, succeeded him.

In 1935 another disastrous fire destroyed much of the brewery. This may well have been a blessing in disguise for as the result of the rebuilding, Stourport possessed one of the most modern malt vinegar breweries in the country. They produced vinegar in three colours to meet regional demand, for natural golden vinegar is preferred in Manchester, distilled colourless vinegar in Scotland and Northern Ireland, and vinegar darkened by caramel finds favour in the South of England. Some of the vinegar was sent to their Birmingham factory for bottling or using in pickles and Worcester Sauce, and the rest was filled into casks for distribution throughout the country and world.

The factory was taken over by British Vinegars in 1954 who used the trade name of Sarsons. It was extended in 1978 and 1988 but was bought by Nestle who closed it down in April 2000

A friend of Bob Blunt's dismantled one of the vats and was allowed to have the timber. Bob says it was beautiful stuff, 100 years old and well-seasoned. He asks, 'Will Worcestershire sauce ever be the same again?'.

Thomas Vale

From humble beginnings, Thomas Vale created a huge civil engineering company of tremendous expertise. The reinforced concrete bridges at Evesham and Upton-on-Severn are just two of their constructions which are used by hundreds of people every day. They donated the land for Vale Road which is named after them. Vale Industrial Site is built on location of 'The Firs' which was owned by them. They also gave the land for the Memorial Gardens to the Council.

Thomas Vale came to Stourport in 1869, working for a Birmingham company who were building the brickwork portion of the present bridge. He liked Stourport so much that he decided to make it his home and founded Thomas Vale & Sons.

Fred Rimmel was working for Vales in the 1930's:

"When I started work I was in the office at Vales. I earned ten shillings (50p) a week, rising by half-a-crown (12.1/2p) per year. Some of their projects were the Dudley sewage works, the gas station at Weymouth and the bridge at Upton-on-Severn. At Upton they dug up quite a big churchyard and the carpenter at Vales spent several weeks making coffins in which to put the remains. They were reinterred in consecrated ground."

Reg Hughes was born in a bungalow on the riverside. He started working at Vales when he left school in 1941.

"They were a nice family. Three directors were the sons of Thomas Vale: Fred, Robert and Ernest. Fred lived at Ravenhurst which is now a nursing home. Robert lived at Sandbourne, Bewdley, now a housing development. He used to invite the staff there for tea. Ernest lived in

House on the corner of Cheapside and Severn Road, the only remaining house of a row on Cheapside. Was it built with a curved corner to facilitate the passage of wagons along this narrow road?

A recent photograph of the Vinegar Works.

Kidderminster by the golf club. Ernest had two sons and one of them, Guy, followed him into the business. Guy was known as the Black Prince because he was dark and well-liked. He knew all about the business and was respected. He left Vales in 1951 and went to George Law's Limited in Kidderminster.

'Another gentleman was Charles Vale. He was quite a character and did all the work for the farmers. Then there was Ted Vale, who owned the sand pit which is now a communal tip. It was a special type of sand, probably for retort work.

'They were one of the country's leading civil engineers . They changed many a sky-line across England and Wales. They built the Smethwick Drop Forgings factory in the Minster Road and John Foulkes Foundry which has recently closed. They worked at Garringtons in Bromsgrove, Worth's carpet factories and the British Sugar factory. They built the sewage disposal works at Tettenhall, Abergavenny, Oldbury and Lye and they installed mains at Pershore and round the Martley area. Stourport Drill Hall and Lickhill Middle School, which used to be the High School, was theirs. They constructed reservoirs at Burlish, Wolverhampton and in the Cotswolds. While they were building a new bridge at Bransford (just outside Worcester) the Teme flooded and the Contracts Manager, who was staying at a local pub, was marooned for several days. They also built Lickhill Road.

'Their first contract with a gas company was at Redditch in 1901, this was followed by work for several other gas companies. Harold Tyler was in charge of building the gas works at Llandudno, he was one of the main Contract Managers, another name to be remembered is Spencer Brown.

'They also built the embankment and railway line to Stourport. You can still see the bridge and abutments on the Hartlebury Road. The Vales put the main sewers through Stourport, they went under the river bridge and up to Areley Kings. There was a bit of a friendly rivalry between the different gangs. Fred Warner was the foreman at the Areley Kings side and Lawrence Bradley at the Stourport side. Bradley discovered that his compressor (which you use to break the road surfaces) wasn't working properly so early one morning he sent his driver over to the other side to pinch Warner's compressor before he got to work and left his faulty one.

'Bradley was doing some work in Foundry Street and so that he could do the work without interruption he closed each end of the road with barriers. He hadn't had permission to do this, and who should be coming from Kidderminster but Mr Ernest Vale himself. He had a slight stammer and he said to Bradley, 'W-w-what do you think you are doing?'. Bradley said, 'I've got to get on with the work, Mr Vale'. Mr Vale's reply was 'D-d-don't tell anyone I've been here, will you?' and he made a hasty retreat and made a detour down Worcester Street to get to his office another way.

'Apart from being one of the largest employers in the area, the Vales were very considerate towards their employees. They rarely sacked anyone. You were kept in gangs, and each gang had its own expertise. The Vales had purchased a lot of land in Stourport which they used for housing development and if there was a shortage of major construction work they would send their employees to work on the houses. I suppose you would call this 'spec housing'. They owned several gravel pits, I know that they had one in Lickhill Road at the back of Steatite because they kept various small gauge wagons, tracks and hoppers there and, when I was younger, I used to play in them with a gang.

'The company had an old diving suit kept in the stores, the type with the screw-on helmet. We used to hire a diver from Gloucester by the name of Joe Lane. He used to go down and examine the piles in the River Severn - I think they're still there. One day, the diver was down in the river when the Contract Manager said, 'He's been down there too long, we'll get him up' and he gave the rope a pull. The diver didn't come up so the foreman gave the handle of the air pump an extra crank or two and blew him out of the water! He came up a lot quicker than he intended.

'During the war the Civil Defence had a Rescue Gang formed from Vales' employees, who practised mock rescues from beneath tons of rubble. Their uniform was blue with a steel helmet. They were called over to Coventry the night that it was bombed. Vales worked at the Rocket Research establishment at Summerfield on the Worcester Road near Kidderminster, and at the testing ranges in the Wyre Forest. They also worked at Drakelow near Wolverley on the conversion of tunnels into units for secret government establishments. All the workforce had to have special security screening, this was possibly one of the reasons that they got the work at the Drakelow establishment."

Tony Hyde, the present managing director of Thomas Vale Construction Ltd, adds that in about 1906, the company constructed Dudley Road in the West Midlands, and were operating a number of steam driven items of plant. When the contract was completed the steam roller was donated to the Birmingham Museum of Science and Industry.

Their offices were the old tannery manager's house in Lombard Street which is now the Co-operative store. To their surprise, when the company were renovating their works in 1988 they pulled down a wall to discover

Jimmy Preece's old forge, standing exactly as it had been the day it was closed. Thomas Vale Construction Ltd now has a head office in Worcester Road.

Steatite & Porcelain Products Ltd (Morgan Matroc)

On 17 May 1930 Stourport woke up to find itself famous. A new factory had been appearing in the fields at Lickhill, overlooking the Severn Valley and this was its opening day when the press were invited. The factory was along the Bewdley Road and was a quarter of a mile long, occupied 70 acres, and was to employ 700 people on a recently invented process.

Steatite is a naturally occurring mineral, otherwise known as soapstone, which when processed makes a strong ceramic with very good electrical insulating properties. In 1907 in London it had been discovered that a patent process made it suitable for magnesia rings and nozzles for the in-candescent mantle trade. The process was developed in Germany, then America, and this was the first plant to be built in Great Britain. The plant made everything from the smallest components of television sets to the huge insulators, some of them higher than houses, seen outside power stations.

The site was chosen partly because the company needed a good water supply. Steatite used a lot of china clay brought up from Cornwall and had a rail running right across the Bewdley Road. At frequent intervals during the day they would stop the traffic and take the trucks across the road. In the early days the company was making its own gas.

It was opened by the Prime Minister, Stanley Baldwin. Among the dig-nitaries who were taken on a tour of the factory was Isaac Wedley, who describes the High Tension Laboratory as follows:

"The spectators stood there, the doors were closed and the lights turned out. All was darkness. Then sparks began to flicker and a tapping was heard as if 100 typewriters were at work. Flames leaped about the room, "400,000 volts" said a voice. Then blue lights had the intensity of street lighting. "800,000 volts" said the voice. Forked lighting played round the laboratory and there was a crackling and howling inferno culminating in a thunder clap. The building shook. "1,800,000 volts" said the voice."

Fred Rimmel reminisces:

"Steatite and Porcelain were a German firm, they came over and set up but they used mainly British labour. Although it was about eleven years after the end of the First World War, there was still a nervousness about the Germans. If the towns' people saw someone approaching them who was obviously German they walked on the other side of the road.

'Steatite took their social responsibilities seriously, bringing unemployed potters from the Potteries to do the craft work on the insulators, and un-employed miners from the Rhondda valley as labourers."

A housing estate was built for about sixty of these families along the Bewdley Road. During the war the company increased in size and were experimenting with the early development of radar and the whole field of telecommunications. In the 1950's it became a subsidiary company of Imperial Chemical Industries Ltd and ten years later it was employing over a thousand people. Keith Newnham was one of them:

"I began at Steatite and Porcelain as an apprentice toolmaker and I fin-ished as kiln superintendent. The ceramics were placed on a truck which

Bond Worth Staff Outing in 1922.
Courtesy Kidderminster Library.

was about 10 feet by 12 feet and mounted on rail tracks with a tunnel beneath for inspection purposes. They took about two days plus to go through the kiln. The industrial porcelain had to go through at 1200o centigrade. Eventually, the kilns got smaller as the ceramics got smaller and had to be fired at higher temperatures. A lot of the products were lumina-based. They had innumerable uses in computers, lights, radios and so on. They were in the national grid and were also used for body protection, for example, in the seats of helicopters."

During the 1960's they closed the High Tension Factory where they made the huge insulators and sold out to Morgan Matroc, now known as Morgan Advanced Ceramics. Half of the building has been sold off to Midland Industrial Plastics and a housing estate has been built on the recreation ground.

The Power Petroleum Company

A storage depot had been opened at Stourport in 1928 by the Power Petroleum Company. It was the furthermost up-river point at which oil barges could operate. At first, the oil was transported in dumb barges such as Shell Mex Seven, but by 1935 new motor barges had been built by John Harker Limited. These were diesel-engined tanker barges, the modern successor to the trow.

The tankers were built in pairs, the first with an engine, the second (the dumb boat) without and the first towed the second. They were given matching male and female names, such as Queen and King, and the engined boat was the female. The carrying capacity was usually about 150 tons (tonnes) for the first and 180 tons for the second but some craft could carry 250 to 300 tons. The Regent craft were powered by 140 hp marine diesel engines. Sometimes the dumb barges went alone and were pulled by powerful tugs.

The Severn tankers were nicknamed 'Severn Submarines' because they sat so low in the water when fully laden. From the mast to the wheelhouse only six to twelve inches were visible above the water. In bad weather, all the hatches were battened down so that the water quickly ran off again.

The usual run was Avonmouth/Sharpness/Gloucester/Stourport then back to Gloucester/Sharpness/Avonmouth by river and canal. The crew were paid per run which usually took three days. During the war there were four depots at Stourport, one at Worcester and five at Gloucester.

Terry Crewe ran Regent Oil Tankers from Bristol to Stourport:

"The tankers were 120 feet and made to fit the locks exactly so that when they went into the lock the gates would close behind them. I've been to every port and I used to run the river in all conditions - from summer, (when the river was low) to flooding. To get under the bridges when the water was quite high you had to take everything off the deck - the wheelhouse had to be flattened and anything on board, such as bicycles, had to be hung over the side. Then any crew on the deck would lie down flat and you had to take the bridge fast. At one time we were running when the river was in flood and we went smack into Haw Bridge near Tewkesbury. It twisted a pillar and all three arches collapsed. The bridge came crashing down - it killed the skipper who was in the wheelhouse."

Originally the depot received supplies by barge only but during the war it was essential to keep supply lines hidden from enemy aircraft, and so hundreds of miles of underground pipeline was installed.

An enormous Power Station, first known as the Electric Power House, opened on the south-eastern side of the town in 1927. Before it closed in 1985 it had been supplying electricity to three counties. A housing estate now stands on the site, one of its roads is named Power Station Road. Courtesy Ray Franks.

Regent finished with this trade in 1969. General freight barge traffic ceased altogether in the early 1970's forcing the closure of the depots at Worcester and Stourport. The remains of the huge wharfs installed for the oil tankers can still be seen on the river bank near to Stourport Marina and almost opposite Redstone caves.

The Power Station

One of the highlights of the town's life this century was the opening of the Power Station on 2nd June 1927. A thousand children lined the road and, in the days when few people had cars, 500 were parked in the town. The Power Station covered 32 acres between Severnside and the Worcester Road, with an addition of twenty acres to link with the Canal and Great Western Railway. The site was chosen for three main reasons, first it was at the centre of the area to be supplied with electricity, secondly, the River Severn was available to supply condensing water (240 million gallons each day) and thirdly, transport was easily available by the canal or the Severn Valley railway.

It was opened by the Prime Minister, Stanley Baldwin, but in his speech he described it, rather unfortunately, as a nightmare. These were the days before Spin Doctors. He said:

"To those of us who, like myself, have played cricket and football on the site of this Power Station, it seems like a nightmare to stand here in this crowd."

The foyer was immense, a local comment was that 'it was like entering a cathedral'. Towering over it all were four tall smoke stacks, painted in brown and green patches for camouflage during the war.

Arthur Mee, in his series 'The King's England', describes it as follows:

"From the bridge over the Severn is seen one of the two important buildings of the town. It is a station giving 100,000 horse-power to supply the needs of most of three counties. To it come the pylons marching from every quarter across the countryside, meeting and merging in a gigantic medley of wires, insulators, and girders."

The British Electric Authority, in their brochure, stated that it was not an ordinary station. 'Apart from its high pressure sets and a steam rising plant, it contains other up-to-date and unusual features, including hydrogen-cooling of the alternators and molton ash disposal'.

First of all, the Staffordshire, Worcestershire and Shropshire Electric Company Ltd supplied local power by means of two 18,000 kw turbo-alternators. Gradually more and more towns were supplied. A second power station was started in 1943 and extensions added in 1953. It finally had ten times the capacity of the first installation and supplied electricity for the whole of the three counties.

Richard Scarth says that he is a Brummie and he used to work in Birmingham:

"When my colleagues heard that I had got a job in Stourport they said, 'That's the place where people go for their holidays!'. It was a huge joke to them. Occasionally, I worked on bank holidays and when I went into the town it was full of holiday-makers.

'My boss was the efficiency engineer and at the end of each financial year he had to calculate how many thousands of tons of coal were left in the coal stocks. There were various scientific methods of calculating this, however he would say, 'I know there was more than that, we had a flood in so-and-so, the river must have washed some away'. You see, the less coal we used, the more efficient the power station was said to be.

'Sometimes I went with my boss to inspect the culverts under the power station. That was a really weird feeling. We were below the level of the river and the water was held back by huge steel gates, about 8 feet by 12 feet wide and 10 feet high, known as Penstock valves.

'When Stourport was supplied with electricity it could come either from the grid or from the power station. As long as there were

The view from Stourport barge locks, looking along the Severn, past Cheapside and across the Stour. The first factory on the left is the Gas Works (now Tube Plastics), the next is the Vinegar Works, and last is the huge Power Station, with its arched central section.
Courtesy Florence Phillips (formerly Mrs Abbott)

This drawing by Sam Keenan illustrates the way that coal was taken by road to Stourport Power Station between the 1940s and 50s, before a railway line was provided from the Stourport Railway yard to the Power Station. The trailer carried 20 tons at a time and seven loads were taken each weekday .The man standing between the tractor and the trailer was known as the 'Vanguard' and this was Sam's job in his mid-'teens.

enough transformers to take the electricity from the grid you didn't need to have the power station switched on for the local area. This one day one of the grid transformers broke down, which meant that the newer part of the 'A' station had to run to generate electricity. The problem was that the ash chain, a crude device which carried ash away from the boilers, had broken down and all the hot ash was dumped on the floor of the power station basement. Everybody who was available rallied round and shovelled all the hot ash off the floor. If we hadn't done that the ash would have built up, the station would have had to close and Stourport would have been without electricity. There was a very good community spirit at the station.

'We had an accident at the station when a flashover killed one of our best and much respected engineers. The electrical switch had three phases, one or two of them were not opening correctly and the engineer had to investigate why this was so. One or two of the phases had stuck in and that was his downfall. His colleague was standing close to him, he wasn't hurt but all the keys in his pocket welded together."

The power station closed in the mid 1980s. The National Grid went nuclear and the power station became too expensive to run. There is now a housing estate on the site and the only remaining evidence of an enormous power station is the name of the road - Power Station Road.

Parsons Chain

The Great Parsons Chain company, for more than 70 years the largest producer of chain assemblies in the British Isles, began in 1902 when Harry Parsons fell off his bicycle. He was an engineer and a cycling enthusiast based in London, and his bike slipped sideways on wet grass. He reasoned that if he threaded whipcord through the spokes of his wheels and round the tyres, this would prevent his bike slipping. The same idea could also be applied to the tyres of a recent invention - the motor car. Patents were filed and the next year, Parsons Non-skid Company Limited was formed, working from Harry Parson's cellar. The invention was a great success both at home and abroad, especially in the USA.

In the late 1920s the company decided to manufacture chains as well as assemble them and for this the London factory needed larger premises. Bill Harper takes up the story:

Jack Smith at Parson's Chain in about 1947.

"The managing director in 1927 was Mr Carrington and his chauffeur was a man named Stan Hay. One day, Stan took Mr Carrington to Stourport for a drive and as they were going along the Worcester road they saw this empty factory. The building was all concrete, even the roof, it had been built during the 1914/18 war for the Anglo Enamel Company. Mr Carrington asked Stan to stop and went to have a look at it. Then he made enquiries about it and bought it. That's how Parsons Chain came to Stourport.

'Parsons Chain was American-owned and had two sister companies, also American-owned, the National Standard making braided wire for tyres, and British Wire Products making dill valves and tubes for car tyres. The National Standard moved there first, followed by the other two companies. Mr Carrington owned 53% of the shares in Parsons Chain and his wife owned a percentage of shares in National Standard.

'I started as an engineer in 1933, eventually becoming works engineer. At that time Parsons Chain were making non-skids chains, side chains and cross chains. All the skid chains for cars were tumbled, polished and copper plated so that they wouldn't rust during storage. In 1938 another factory was built on the site.

'During the war Parsons made non-skid chains for the war effort especially the Orian pad tyre chains needed to get around in the desert. British Wire Products took over the manufacture of fire extinguishers for jet Rolls Royce engines from the Derby factory. When the war was nearly over, they started to make cables for aerelons (flaps for planes). After the war a specialist research laboratory was built at Parsons Chain. One of their developments was a chain made from alloy steels, so strong that one inch of crain could lift a weight of 80 tons.

'About 1947 Mr Carrington died. Because he owned 53% of the shares they had to be sold to the American Chain and Cable Company who had to get somebody to take his place. Two people rushed over to America, John Spence, manager of Parsons Chain, and Major Hopcraft. John Spence was also a director of National Standard. John Hopcraft got the job as Managing Director of Parsons Chain and British Wire. John Spence became managing director of National Standard and they moved to the Kidderminster Road. John Hopcraft was a very popular manager and he liked the people to have something for services rendered. For every five years served a worker was presented with a pewter tankard, for every 30 years a silver egg cup and for every 40 years a silver tray. When he finished as director all that stopped.

'In 1956 we started a programme for mining and another new building was put up. We did all the work from the cage to the donkey house. We also made the old pit props for mines. Today they are held up by hydraulic equipment. What used to happen was that we used to have to persuade some farmers to have their trees cut down then we would use the timber as pit props. To pull them out from the mine we made multiblocks, which were aluminium blocks on a chain with a ratchet. We made thousands of those because they used to get buried in the coal dust and the miners wouldn't go back and look for them, so they used to have a new one every day.

A 1903 10 hp Decauville showing Parsons 'Non Skidder' fitted to the rear wheels. All Parsons Chain photographs are courtesy Philip Calder.

The original workshop of Parsons Chain in about 1947.

'The programme started to get to the stage where bigger chains were required and so in about 1960 another building was built for the heavier chains. By 1964 the company was making a turnover of one million a month and needed to expand, so British Wire Products moved to Baldwin Road.

'About 40 years ago a lot of employees got together and we asked if we could have a club, so the directors built us a big club house. It's still there, along the Kidderminster/Stourport road. Since there are only a few Parsons Chain people left, it's now shared by Parsons and Brintons. There are facilities for bowling, football and cricket. Mind you, we had to pay for it, 1d or 2d per week.

'The American Chain and Cable Company sold out to Babcock International in the 1970s. The result was that we still had orders coming from America but all the staff changed. Unfortunately, our heavy involvement in mining meant that when the coal industry began to decline, orders dropped."

Larch Lap

Mrs Mann remembers the timber yards. She says: "I used to take the children to see the timber works. It was marvellous to see these huge cranes lifting all the timber out of the boats. There weren't just one boat, there were two or three fastened together. The wharfs are still there but they're now used for repairing boats."

The overlapping fencing panels which surround many English gardens were, it is said, invented and developed in Stourport. The success of the garden products turned a little timber yard into a modern factory stretching from Mart Lane to Severn Road and from Lichfield Street to the site of the old gas works, together with a piece of ground on the other side of Severn Road.

The company was begun by Jo Corbett, the son of Jo Corbett & Son. In 1930 or 31, Jo decidedthat, as well as using portable mills, he would build a permanent shed in Lichfield Street next to Stourport basin. In it was the biggest horizontal sawbench in the Midlands with the longest running bed, about 42 feet long. When the sawbench was being put in it broke the wall of the canal so that water poured out and flooded the cellars in

Lichfield Street. The timber-carrying barge, 'Hearts of Oak' was his, now sadly sunk among the debris in the in-filled basin.

Bill Hughes went to Jo Corbett's straight from school in 1949:

"As well as the Lichfield Street site, Jo also had a sawmill in the red brick building under the clock and that's where I started. You had to work hard. It was a hard life, not like it is now with earmuffs, gloves and unions. Jo Corbett used to make sure you knew he was the boss. He would come to the mill every Wednesday afternoon and walk round with the manager. He was very old, perhaps in his eighties. He would come up to me and say, 'Do you work for Mr Corbett young man?'. I had been told to call him 'Sir'. You would say, 'Yes sir,' and he would say, 'Then take your coat off, young man'.

'Old Jo Corbett died, I think it was when I was in the army, between 1952 and 1954. His daughter, Phyllis took the mill over."

In the early 1950's, Phyllis sold out to Paul Timmis. He was one of three sons of Jock Timmis, a farmer at Chaddesley Corbett. He had been in the RAF and with his demob packet at the end of the war, he had started an English timber felling company in a shed at Woodcote on the Kidderminster/Bromsgrove road. The shed is still there to this day. He had a couple of timber carriages (long lorries) and he used to go into Corbett's yard with the timber.

Bill Hughes continues:

"The person I knew most was Alf Pratley, the works manager. He was the main timber valuer for the whole of Worcestershire and very experienced. When I was a lad I used to think, 'When I grow up I want to be like him'. I thought he must be brainy to run and control all these blokes and know what timber was to be cut up into what. He was, I think, well into his sixties and became too old to continue as works manager so he moved into the gatehouse. That was an important job. When the factory got modernised there were enormous amounts of timber going in and going out and it all had to be checked. He worked almost until the day he died. The years rolled by and eventually I became works manager.

Roy Wilkes and Jock Hall in the early years of Larch Lap.

'Around 1960ish old Alf Pratley went on holiday. When he came back he called me into the office and he used to have a habit of drawing things in the dirt with a stick. He drew this rectangle on the floor, and then he drew some wavy lines over the rectangle. He said, 'What do you think that is, Bill?'. I told him that it looked like a rectangle with wavy lines. He said, 'No, its a fencing panel. I reckon we could make some of those'. Alf told me he had thought that up when he was on holiday.

'He got some six foot lengths and took them into the mill and, sawing on the old circular push bench saw, we cut some lap boards about a quarter of an inch thick, then we took them outside and nailed them together. Lo and behold, it made a panel which looked good. Then he said, 'What do you think about that Bill?' I said, 'It looks good but it needs something else doing to it.' 'Like what?' 'Like colouring to bring the wood out.' 'Do you mean put some creosote on it?' 'Not that black stuff, it needs something golden to bring the colour out of the wood.' So we mixed some creosote with paraffin and then we dipped various pieces of wood in that mixture until we got a golden brown and then we painted that with a brush on the panel. When Paul Timmis came we showed it to him and he was impressed.

56

A new crane at Larch Lap in the 1970's. The old crane has been replaced by one on concrete pillars. All photographs of Larch Lap supplied by Forest Garden plc.

That's how Larch Lap came about. I felt quite chuffed that I was involved with that first panel.

'Having worked in the old saw mill under the old methods I knew there was usually an easier way of doing something . I spoke to Alf one day and said, 'You know this one saw, if you fitted another one next to it that would be more efficient. I could feed in enough wood for the two machines'. It did work, and then I had the idea of putting five 36 inch band resaws lined up one after the other, so instead of having ten men employed on the five resaws we would only need to have two, one feeding in and one taking off. This idea was put to Paul Timmis and a few weeks later he told me that he had contacted a French firm called Gillette in France. We went to this site in France where they had set up five resaws of their own make in line on a temporary structure. We spent a quarter of a million on debarking equipment and five resaws, together with the systems required to make the resaws work. The mill was set up in England in Lichfield Street and turned out 40,000 boards a day. Business boomed. I worked seven days a week and I was paid for five. Every Sunday morning I sat at home working out the wages from the cards."

In 1955, John Hawker came out of the navy and was looking for work:
"My brother was right-hand man to Paul Timmis, so I was offered the job of timber mating and carriage (hauling). Eventually I became opera-

tions manager and a director of the company. One of Larch Lap's little jobs was the miles and miles of motorway fencing for the M50 in the mid 1960s.

One of the saw mills was under the Clock House, and when the workers were sky larking they would throw files at the face of the clock to see if they could hit and stop the clock. The clock is about 35 feet (10.66 metres) in height and the files would go 'ping' if they struck the face. The name of Sid Massey went down in history as the man who managed to stop the clock by wedging a file under the clock hands.

Twice in the 1960's I can remember the 60 foot crane collapsing into two. Each time, the crane driver got a rollicking. He had let the jib free fall then tried to put the dog in, (a piece of metal which locks the cog) but the footbrake hadn't held.

Sometime in the late 1950s my brother and I, together with two timber fallers, had a mishap at Binton churchyard. The vicar had asked us to cut down a huge tree in the churchyard, I think it was a Douglas fir, and it twisted as it fell. Shall we say that numerous headstones were dislodged? The vicar went bananas, that was an insurance job. I think the stump of the tree is still there.

On the southern end of the basin were dry docks where the barges used to go for repair. We built an incinerator in the deepest of the dry docks to burn timber waste. We called it Mr Martin's folly because after the first two burnings the cast iron rods at the bottom of the furnace collapsed and the 30/40 foot (9.14/12.19 metres) chimney got a list of about

Larch Lap's first gang: from the left, Ernie Spragg (half cut-off , in background), Graham Bennet, two unknown workers, then Bill Hughes, who tells most of the Larch Lap story. On the extreme right is David Childe.

15° from the upright position. The incinerator got so hot and buckled so much that when we once emptied a bucketful of creosote sawdust on it the smoke blacked out York Street. The chimney had to be taken down later because it was unsafe.

I had a phone call in the middle of the night in the early 1980's to tell me that the factory was on fire. The fire brigade were only round the corner, they had arrived promptly and forced open the gates so that by the time I arrived it was all over. The five-in-line machine was destroyed and the sawdust extractor. We didn't lose any orders as we had a large stock of components. We think it was caused by a cigarette end but this was never proved.

Before the incinerator was built we had a huge open fire in the docks. The fork lift truck used to go up to the edge of the dock and tip the rubbish in. We used a huge larch tree about forty feet long and twelve inches in diameter near to the edge of the incinerator so that the fork lift trucks would know that they had to stop when their wheels hit the tree. Once, the tree burned through on the underneath without my knowing it, the truck didn't stop and took me and the truck into the fire. Down it went, 30 or 40 feet, into the fire. Fortunately, I managed to jump out to the right a fraction of a second before it went down.

(Bill Hughes adds: We went to get a hosepipe but all that we could find was a garden hose. We fixed it on to the tap by the toilet and we turned on the water. There were so many leaks in the hosepipe the water was spurting out all over the yard and only a dribble was coming out the end of the hose. I can't repeat what we said. We did get the truck off, we managed to get a chain attached, got another truck and pulled it up).

'When I started, there were 45 employees at Stourport, plus eight men falling and fetching the trees, and ten at Bromsgrove. At its height the company was employing about 170 men in two shifts, one shift ran from 6am to 2pm, the other from 2pm to 10pm, plus overtime on a Saturday morning and Sunday morning. We had so much work we couldn't cope with it. I worked from 6 o'clock in the morning to 6.30 at night, and most Saturday and Sunday mornings."

Paul Timmis sold the business to a company called Banbury Buildings in the late 1960's and joined their Board, becoming responsible for their fencing division which included another fence panel manufacturer based in Bridgwater, Somerset. However, a period of ill-health caused Paul to take early retirement in 1974. By this time Banbury Buildings had become part of the London Brick Comany. Several changes of ownership followed which mostly resulted in neglect and lack of investment in the company. Meanwhile, Paul Timmis' health had recovered and he set up a rival business - Forest Fencing - based at Stanford Bridge in the Teme Valley.

In the early 1980's Bernard Atkins was an Independent Commercial Advisor in Redditch, and he was approached by a company of accountants and business consultants on behalf of the parent company, London Brick Limited, who were concerned that Larch Lap at Stourport, despite a million pound turnover, was losing money. He was asked to run a project looking at the business. Bernard says:

"Having read the consultancy report, inevitably the invitation came for me to implement it. I was therefore appointed to run the project, first as general manager, then as managing director.

'First of all, we increased the range and quantity of products offered. We built trellis, garden sheds, bird tables and feeders, pergolas, gazebos and other decorative products. Previously Larch Lap's goods had been supplied to small garden centres but now the DIY superstores such as B & Q were opening up across the country, and gardening centres such as Webbs were expanding rapidly. It was a case of channelling our products through different outlets. We also developed a range of DIY flat-packed goods to put in the car for assembly at home.

'The bark and the woodshavings used to be called waste products. I encouraged the workforce to call them co-products, I had to put into people's minds that everything had a value. The bark was sold in garden centres as mulch, and it was bought by local authorities for their gardens and play areas. We even sold huge quantities to race course gallops. Sawdust was used for chipboard and multi-density fibreboard. Nothing was wasted.

'The company became a huge commercial success. Everything turned to gold. We became a very profitable company, so much so that Forest Fencing ultimately bought the company back at a greatly increased price.

'We were so successful that in the 1990s we opened a new site on Hartlebury Industrial Site. It was a huge move to go to much bigger premises. The Stourport-on-Severn site was owned by British Waterways and the lease was due to expire in about 1998. They were thinking of renovating the basin on which we were situated and extending it as a leisure centre. We were therefore encouraged to vacate and we moved to the Hartlebury site which has now incorporated all the Larch Lap industries."

The new combined company (Larch Lap and Forest Fencing), has recently changed its name to Forest Garden plc, and has over 700 employees working at six sites.

When Larch-Lap move to Hartlebury, they were missed by Stourport folk as each Christmas they had provided the town centre with a thirty foot Christmas Tree. Happily, this tradition was recently revived by Forest Garden.

SUMMARY

The products of Stourport reached all corners of England. Holbrooks Vinegar made Stourport a household name. The arrival of Steatite & Porcelain Products Ltd put Stourport on the front page of the national newspapers. There is hardly a middle-aged or elderly housewife in the country who has not used bowls, dishes or colanders from the Anglo American Tin Stamping Company. The builders, Thomas Vale & Sons ensured that Stourport would be recorded in many a town or village archive. The names of Canal Pleasurecraft Limited and other Stourport boat-builders have sailed up and down the British waterways. Carpets from Worth's have been used as far away as Australia!

The prosperity of Stourport was saved by the development of ancient industries and the arrival of new. By a strange quirk, the enterprises attracted by the canal outlived the usefulness of the canal itself.

Motor boat, Severn Merchant,
carrying steel. Traded from Cardiff
to Stourport.
Courtesy National Waterways
Museum, Gloucester.

5. The Grand Tour

As a child I was born into a town which was a little faded, a little old. You could still see what it had once been. The canal business still operated, boats came up the Severn from Bristol with petrol and coal, canal barges were still carrying manufactured goods and coal but you could feel that it wasn't as busy as it had been in the last century. The warehouses were empty and some were derelict. The wrecks of some boats were there - old trows and the steamer 'Areley Castle'.

Robert Blunt describing Stourport-on-Severn before World War II

By 1834, the town was well-established. The population had risen from 1,603 at the turn of the century to the 3,000 mark. The town had its own power house, savings bank, public library, Sunday School library and a variety of clubs and societies. Apart from beer retailing, the most popular trades were boot and shoe businesses, of which there were sixteen, and grocers, of which there were six.

Despite its prosperity, the Medical Officer of Health, Dr Masterman, was not happy with the town and described it as being packed with small, badly-planned houses. There was no organised system for the removal of ashes and similar refuse which led to a 'pervading frowsy smell ... most evident in courts and alleys'. The town was without sewers and many wells were polluted. There was a careless discharge of smoke. The town was not nearly as healthy or clean as it ought to be, mainly because of dampness of air, overcrowding and personal uncleanliness. The lower and middle classes were in the habit of sleeping in flannels they had worn by day. Rheumatism was aided by the damp atmosphere and by 'excessive use of hard cider'. A public baths and a washhouse was urgently needed. In addition, the roads were in a very bad state, and were impassable in wet weather. A paved causeway from the top of High Street to Lombard Street was 'much needed'.

Dr Masterman's advice was evidently followed, for 50 years later, Kelly's *Directory of Worcestershire* states: 'The town is neat and clean and contains some well-built houses, and the streets are paved and lighted with gas'.

In those days, commuting was unheard of and it was the custom for all those who worked at a factory to live nearby. This included the factory owner as well as the workers. The Baldwins lived in Foundry Street and Lombard Street, the Rogers lived in Lombard Street with a large garden next to the Tannery, and Hickin Bold & Swanns had Stour Bank House adjoining the brewery. Stourport streets were therefore a mix of factories, large houses, rows of worker's cottages and a generous sprink-ling of public houses.

For the purposes of the tour, we have divided the town into four areas: area 1 is Bridge Street and to the west, area 2 is the High Street, going east and down to the River Severn, area 3 is Mitton Street, Gilgal and the roads to the north, and area 4 is Vale Road and to the west.

AREA ONE - BRIDGE STREET AND TO THE WEST

Bridge Street

Until 1775 there were no bridges at all across the Severn between Bewdley and Worcester. Those who wanted to get across had to go more than half a mile (about one kilometre) to use the ferry at Redstone.

Then, in 1773, it was proposed that a bridge should be built across the river Severn. Although it was known as 'Brindley's Bridge', Brindley had died the previous year, perhaps it was built to his design. This first bridge was a tremendous enterprise, with 52 arches, three of them over the river. The central arch was 50 feet (15 metres) high to allow tall masts to pass beneath. It cost £5,000 and took two years to build but unfortunately, one of the worst floods on record arrived in 1794 which demolished not only Brindley's bridge but also several other bridges along the Severn. There was a sudden thaw and a flood brought down a quantity of ice, smashing against the bridge and wrecking it. Stourport was then without a bridge for twelve years, until a second bridge was built in about 1806. It was a single iron arch spanning 150 feet (46 metres), a great engineering feat. The second bridge lasted for 60 years and was replaced in about 1870 by the present bridge. The building of the second bridge was a relatively simple matter because it was not used by many people, but by the time the third bridge was built 200,000 pedestrians were crossing the bridge each year. Consequently, a temporary bridge had to be erected which was a fragile wooden structure and passengers, particularly horses and carts, wondered if it would hold until they reached the other side.

A view of old Stourport with the first bridge in the left-hand bottom corner. The bridge was carried away by floods in 1794.
The engraving is from the Victoria County History, where it is said to be by Peter Mazell after James Sheriff. Other sources state that the original sketch was by Samuel Ireland, who was a Spitalfield weaver but became a connoisseur of books and pictures. Both agree on a date of 1776.

The first bridge, opened in the mid 1770s and destroyed by floods in 1794. The town was then without a bridge for twelve years.
From Samuel Ireland's engraving in 'Picturesque Views on the Severn, Volume 11 page 4.
Courtesy National Waterways Museum, Gloucester.

Left centre: The second bridge, built in 1806. It was quite an engineering feat, having a single span of 70 feet, and was said to be constructed at local forges.

The present bridge, an attractive Victorian construction of 1870. The building of the bridge brought ThomasVale to the town to found his nationally well-known company.

Anyone going across Stourport bridge had to pay a toll, pedestrians being charged 1d (approximately 1/2p). The tollhouse was on the Areley side of the bridge and is still there. Benjamin Bradburn began collecting tolls on the bridge in 1850. Most of the tolls came from riders of horses at 1d with the occasional gig or carriage at 3d (approximately 1p). The house was on one side of the road and the kitchen on the other, consequently, when Mrs Bradburn was cooking she had to run backwards and forwards across the road. She was given a new house a year before the 1870 bridge opened.

Occasionally, there was trouble at the toll house. One day, a stranger on horseback refused to pay the toll, so when he attempted to leave, Peter Snider, the last tollkeeper, hung on to the bridle. The man whipped the horse which made it jump and Peter was thrown to the ground. Evidently a struggle followed, because his wife, Betty, tried to separate them and was struck in the eye and knocked against a porch so that a hairpin stuck in her head. She was 'blind with blood'. After that the stranger offered to pay his toll but Peter refused it and took his name and address instead. Then he made the stranger go back and come through the toll again, this time to 'pay proper'. Betty soon recovered but Peter was in bed for some weeks. The case went to court and the stranger was fined three shillings (15p) for not paying his toll, six shillings (30p) for assaulting Peter and sixpence (2.5p) for assaulting Betty. The magistrate also told him to pay each of the two solicitors a guinea (£1.05p). One of the solicitors said that he would not lower himself to take it, so the magistrate raised it to two guineas which the solicitor promptly pocketed.

The tolls fell hard on those who had to use the bridge frequently, such as workers who lived in Areley Kings but were employed in Stourport. Many children had to cross the bridge to and fro on their way to school. A meeting was held to discuss the possibility of dispensing with the tolls. A town crier went round announcing the meeting but Isaac Wedley says that he used such dreadful language that the organisers denied responsibility for him.

Mr Danks, a local businessman, presided at the meeting and he explained that the bridge had cost £10,000 to build and only half of this had been paid off. Furthermore, the working man living in Areley Kings had a newer and better house with a larger garden and lower rents and rates than if he had stayed in Stourport. Another member said that the people of Areley Kings may not want all the black sheep of Stourport on their side of the river, inferring that the law-abiding citizens lived on the Areley Kings side. This is how the old saying arose that the inhabitants of Areley Kings 'live on Christian shores'.

Four years later a petition was presented with 3,084 signatures asking for the tolls to be abolished. By this time, two-thirds of the tolls had been paid off and so, in 1893, the bridge was made free. People knew how to celebrate in those days! Wedley reckons that 15,000 people descended on Stourport to join in the festivities. There were organised sports, a roasted sheep, a carnival procession and, in the evening, a torch-light procession.

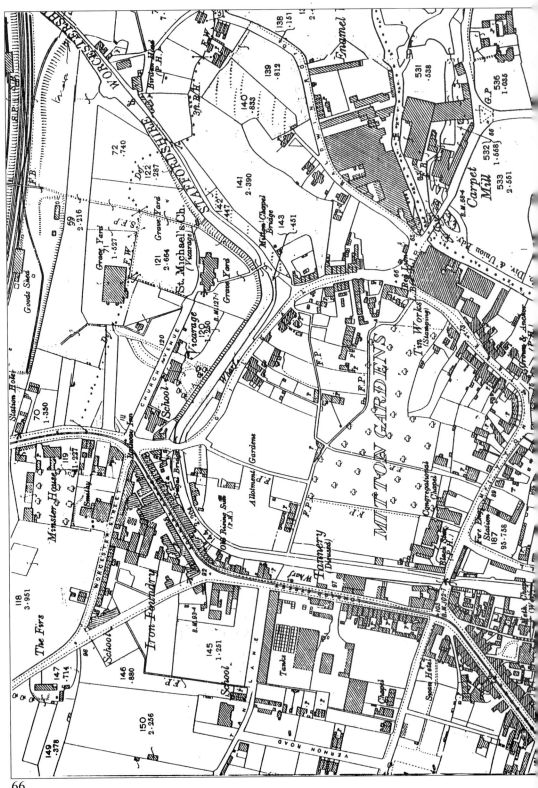

66

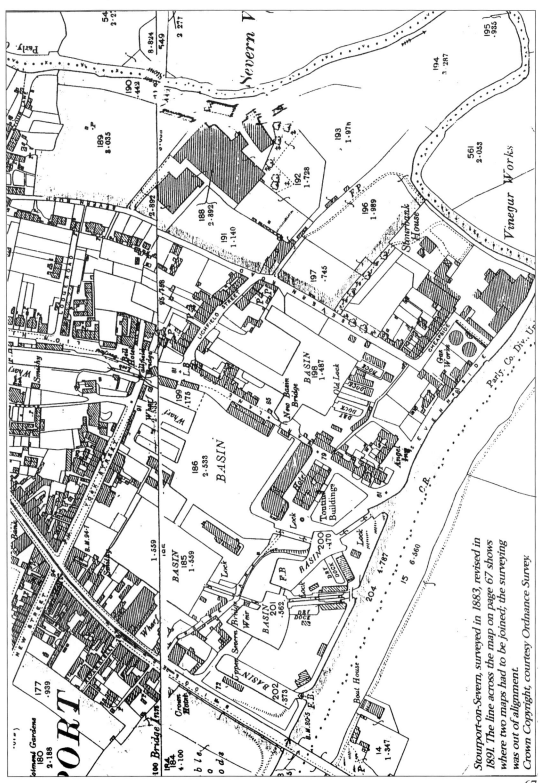

Stourport-on-Severn, surveyed in 1883, revised in 1891. The line across the map on page 67 shows where two maps had to be joined; the surveying was out of alignment.
Crown Copyright, courtesy Ordnance Survey

67

Bridge Street in about 1900. The
Bridge Inn is on the left and the
Crown is on the right.
Courtesy Brindley Arms.
The lower photograph shows
the same scene today.

A song was composed specially for the occasion, as was customary in important events . It contained a tribute to Peter Snider (sung to the tune of 'The Man Who Broke the Bank at Monte Carlo'):

Then a "good word" for "Peter Snider" he's a faithful servant been
For you always had to pay if you wished to cross the stream.
No matter how impatient you was to get away
He would always keep the gate shut till you'd pay
And then he'd let you pass through - right away.

Mr Danks paid the last toll, and then, as Wedley reports:
"Many people who had faithfully paid their tolls over the years gathered, wondering who would be the first to cross the bridge free. The honour fell upon a little old lady of 75, Mrs Jane Lane, quite a character in the village. Seated proudly in her donkey cart, she was escorted over the bridge between the waiting crowds and made a triumphant passage through the town."

Charles Hastings

Not many people know that the founder of the British Medical Association began his career at a chemists in Bridge Street.

Charles Hastings was born in in 1794 in Bitterley village at the foot of the Clee Hills to a family steeped in tragedy. He was one of a family of fifteen, but nine of his brothers and sisters failed to reach maturity. His father was Rector of Bitterly Church, but when Charles was twelve, his father fell from his horse and was brought home in a dazed state. He sat at the bottom of the stairs and, when night fell, refused to go to bed. He would only respond to one person, and that was Charles, his eldest living son. Charles managed to get him up the stairs and into bed. The Rector remained 'a lunatic' until he died at the age of 101.

Whether that inspired Charles to begin his medical career we do not know, but when he was sixteen he was apprenticed to Richard Jukes and Kenrick Watson, apothecaries of 23-24 Bridge Street. After eighteen months, Jukes and Watson persuaded him to take the post of house surgeon at Worcester Infirmary. His life held two great passions, the first was the Worcestershire countryside, the second was the Worcester Royal Infirmary, to which he returned time and time again.

Charles was a tall, handsome young man. Early in his professional life he fell from a carriage which gave him a limp for the rest of his life. His personality was dynamic, one of his colleagues wrote, 'into the meeting came Dr Hastings with the velocity of a steam carriage'. He was said to be a born leader of men, rather assertive, with a keen sense of purpose and social justice, and a workaholic.

Charles worked for a time in Edinburgh and qualified there as a doctor. His first bout of fame came in 1820, when, after writing a learned treatise on 'Inflammation of the Mucous Membrane of the Lungs', he was regarded as a leading authority on diseases of the chest. He pioneered the stethoscope and was one of the first doctors to use a microscope. A prolific writer, he founded a number of medical journals to which his old employers, Richard Jukes and Kenrick Watson, sometimes contributed. These journals combined to become the forerunner of the British Medical Journal. After initiating a number of Medical and Surgical Societies he became a founder member and leader of the General Medical Council. He was fanatical in his belief that the health of the country should become the responsibility of the state, and it was through his pressure that the General Board of Health was established. In about 1847 he became Sir Charles Hastings. He died in 1866.

Riverside lighting

The footpath below the bridge and along the river is now lit by a series of decorative lamps, topped with gold, which were installed in June 1999. One was paid for by Thomas Vale, two were from the Council, one was from the Rotary Club and one was from the Ready family. The first lamps round the barge lock were put there over a hundred years ago, after an old lady had fallen in. This was Sam Drew's mother, who kept a baker's shop with her son, on the corner by the bridge. One of the boatmen owed quite a lot of money and on hearing that he was about to depart, she rushed out one dark night, determined to get payment. In her haste, she fell into the lock. She was fished out and after that it was decided to put a lamp there.

Raven Street (Off Bridge Street)

Raven Street has had four changes of name. It was originally Bennett Street, then the name was changed to Aylesbury Street, afterwards it was White Raven (after the White Raven pub), and finally, Raven. As well as these four names, it had the nick-name of 'Pudding Bag Street'. It was probably originally a cul-de-sac, opening on to Bridge Street.

Although not many people will be familiar with the name of the printer, George Nicholson, most people in the Stourport area will recognise his lovely engravings. He was famous for printing the small wood engravings by Thomas Bewick, and the copper engravings by Mr Bromley. George and his brother arrived sometime during the 1780's and set up a printing press. They lived in the house on the corner of Raven Street and Bridge Street, where he had a book shop. George was a kind man, a socialist and a bachelor, he described himself as a printer, traveller and author. He was really an academic, and wrote 'A Literary Miscellany', in 20 volumes but he paid his way by printing cheap pamphlets on such subjects as fortune-telling, interpreting dreams or telling the lives of saints. These were called 'chap books' and were sold by 'chap men'. He also published a lot of musical scores and was the first person to print the music of 'Drink to me only with thine eyes'. George wrote and printed one of the first guide books in 1808, entitled 'Cambrian Traveller's Guide'. He died in 1825 at the age of 65.

New Street

Lined with elegant gentlemen's residences, New Street was once one of the most important streets of the town.

The present Civic Centre was designed by the architects Andrew and Hazzard, built by Thomas Vale and Sons Ltd and opened in 1966. It replaced an old Town Hall which stood at the opposite end of New Street, on the corner of Bridge Street, on the site of the present Department of Health and Security.

The old Town Hall was erected just before Queen Victoria was crowned in 1837. As part of the coronation celebrations, all four hundred schoolchildren from the Church of England and the Methodist Sunday School had dinner there. They each had to bring a knife, fork and plate and hand it in at the town hall before they went off to take part in a procession. It must have required tremendous organisational skill to return 800 pieces of cutlery and 400 plates to the correct owners! The Victorians loved processions and parades, this one was led by two people holding a banner which said, 'Long Live Queen Victoria!'.

The Town Hall fell into disrepair and, as Fred Rimmel relates:

"One Saturday afternoon in August 1973 Stourport town hall fell down. I had been working at Telford and I came home, looking forward to a nice afternoon in the garden, to find that I couldn't get home! The town was completely blocked. The debris had fallen across the junction of Bridge Street, York Street, New Street and the High Street. Opposite the town hall was a pub called the Hope and Anchor and two people had been sleeping on a bench outside. The rubble landed at their feet. The only casualty was a car, the owners had gone shopping, they were very lucky. In the evening everybody went down to have a look. You met everybody you knew down there."

William Bullock Close

It's not everyone who has a road named after him but this honour has fallen on Bill Bullock. The Close, opposite the Civic Centre, stands on the site of his nurseries which stretched from New Street to the Lickhill Road. They were known as 'Heath Nurseries' because they were in the gardens of what used to be Richard Heath's house. In the mid 1800's Richard Heath left £1,000 to be divided between the National Schools and the widows and deserving poor of Stourport.

William Bullock was famous for his pot plants which he exhibited round the country. In those days, they were called 'stove plants' because they were heated by a stove and hot water pipes. He ran a flower shop in Bridge Street with his brother, Charlie, Pete's Prints is now on the site. Bill is very modest about his contribution to the town:

"I don't see that the nurseries were anything to write about. They were just small nurseries, not even an acre. It was just something to make money - not that we ever made much money at it. My father started the nurseries in 1913 and I went into them when I left school round about 1930. We did bedding plants and all that, with a few lettuces and cucumbers. Our main source of income were bouquets and wreaths - we saw the townsfolk in with the wedding bouquets and we saw them out with the funeral wreaths."

William Bullock Close is a cul-de-sac, leading to the Day Centre. In the early 1960's Jim Perry was asked to investigate and oversee the project despite having just come off the Council because of pressure of work:

"We had to visit other Day Centres to find out what a Day Centre was and how it was handled and it wasn't long before we discovered that a Day

The old Town Hall, built in the 1830's. It fell down one afternoon in 1973.
Courtesy Worcestershire County Archives and Kidderminster Shuttle.

Centre wasn't just a place for people to go for a bit of entertainment and socialising, a kitchen had to be installed and run.

'We must have spent the best part of four years trying to get the place organised, we couldn't find any premises so we were in limbo land. Then we had two pieces of good luck. The first was that suddenly the local authority told us there was a bit of spare land off New Street and they offered it to us at a peppercorn rent. The second was that the boss of the Steatite factory was going to retire in twelve months' time and the new manager was already on the premises, so he volunteered to get the place constructed. Steatite & Porcelain did all the planning and costing and suddenly the building was there. "

Margaret Stringer joined the Women's Voluntary Service in 1951.

"Mrs Moffat, the WVS organiser, provided Home Helps and did all kinds of other charitable work; she was so overworked that I offered to help her. When Mrs Moffat moved away from the district I was left to take over. The Day Centre opened in 1970 and Jim Perry asked me to think about taking it over, this meant looking after the Luncheon Club which provides meals for the elderly. I said, 'Oh my goodness me, they'll have to have bread and cheese and onions if they want to have a hot meal', but I managed, with the help of Jim and many other volunteers.

'In the early days, before the Day Centre was built, we cooked the meals at Steatite and Porcelain and they were taken round on a van provided by the Stourport-on-Severn Guild of Help. We also provided clothing for certain families, for the sixth baby and that sort of thing. In those days people were very grateful, nowadays the kind of clothes we provided would go straight in the bin! When I took over we had no room for anything. I said, 'I have got to have an office, I can't work from home'. We eventually had the top floor of the police station in York Street which is now the dentist's. We had a big clothing store there, you had to go up two flights of stairs to it. We also provided furniture stored in a hut down the road, sometimes it was needed for people whose house or caravan had been burned out. We used to put the furniture in the Meals on Wheels van to deliver it. I remember the phone rang at 6.30 one morning and it was the police. They said, 'Can you provide this family with clothes and furniture? They've been burned out'. There they were, smelling of smoke and they had nothing but the clothes they stood up in.

'The old people are well looked-after here. We have the Darby and Joan, Wardens, Meals on Wheels, and meals are provided in the Day Centres at William Bullock Close and Broomy Close. "

The Day Centre is now run by a Trust.

Moor Hall Lane

Moor Hall (originally Moor Hill) was once a local landmark because of its large tower. Standing between Lickhill Road and Moor Hall Lane, it was a huge, rambling place. An ancient pathway known as Long Lane which went from Lickhill Manor to Hartlebury Common ran past its doors.

It was built by Jonathan Worthington, a boat-builder and wharfinger, and partner of Aaron York. Aaron built his house overlooking the basins but Worthington preferred a rural retreat, and Moor Hall stood in splendid isolation a mile away from the busy docks. The Hall was later occupied by John Brinton, the head of Brinton's Carpets. He improved the house and bought some of the neighbouring fields for a park. He removed hedges, made a drive and planted trees. Park Avenue ran across Brinton's property and the Brintons took toll money at lodges at each end of the park.

At the end of the First World War the estate was put on the market and it was suggested that the Council should buy it as a park. The idea was put forward that it should be a Memorial Park. Mr Charles, then the owner of the estate, offered to sell it to the Council very cheaply providing it was kept as a park for the people. However, the Council argued and debated for so long that in the end Mr Charles sold the estate elsewhere. Since then, the estate has been purchased by the Council but at an increased price.

Galahad Way, Hafren Way and Gheluvelt Court

In Norman times, Layamon, priest of Areley Kings, rescued the tales of King Arthur from oblivion and transcribed them into Anglo-Saxon poetry. These roads are named in old English as a tribute to him. Hafren was an old Hermit and Gheluvelt was an old battlefield. Sir Galahad was one of the knights of King Arthur's round table. Kylemilne (Way), on the other side of the town, translates as 'a mill in the field'.

Moor Hall, from which Moor Hall Lane gets its name. It was built by Jonathan Worthington (1756-1821). He acquired a boat yard and warehouse with his partner, Aaron York, and married Aaron's younger daughter. The house has a tragic history, both Worthington's young wife and his only son died here. It was bought by John Brinton, the carpet manufacturer, and it was probably the Brintons who added the tower, a well-known landmark for many years.
Courtesy Kidderminster Library.

AREA TWO - HIGH STREET, TO THE EAST AND DOWN TO THE SEVERN

The High Street

Most of the houses along the High Street were built in the early 1800's. The shop door had two or three steps in front and the shop windows curved outwards, full of small panes of glass.

Somewhere at the back of the present post office is buried the skeleton of a horse. It once belonged to George Harris, the carpet manufacturer. He had been an old soldier and had fought at Waterloo in the cavalry. He thought the world of his horse and when it died, he insisted on burying it in his garden. As well as being owner of the carpet factory, George was the local bank manager, operating from the front room of his house, 'The Mansion', which stood on the site of the old post office, now taken over by Woolworth's. Before the bank opened in 1866, business transactions were carried out in cash or by a variety of documents known as 'Bills'.

George kept a revolver next to his cash box, and Isaac Wedley says that when a friend of his went to him for payment of an account, he picked up the revolver and said, 'Ah I daresay you'd like some of those (bank notes) but you touch them and I'll blow your brains out'. His friend departed quickly, feeling safer outside. The bank was a branch of the Stourbridge and Kidderminster Bank.

There was a Christian book shop in the High Street, run by Joseph Wheeldon. His wife was eleven years his junior and when, in the late 1800's, Joseph went blind, his wife continued to run the shop. These were the days before sickness benefit.

For many years in the nineteenth century there lived a clock and watch-maker in the High Street by the name of Cork, who bought in clock workings made by Samuel Thorpe of Abberley and encased them in splendid grandfather casings. The ornamentation on the top included the moon and its phases, castles and a ship, and it showed the seconds and the month. Mr Cork operated a type of savings scheme. Everyone who wanted a clock paid so much a week and when Mr Cork had received enough money from everyone to cover the cost of one clock, it was decided by vote who should receive it. Often, someone was still paying for the clock long after it had stopped working.

By the 1870s, the barber's was owned by Jack Goodman. Jack had a second job, that of washing down the streets and while he was doing this he would employ someone to take his place at the shop. To fill his cart with water he had to trail a long pipe into the canal then stand on top of his cart and pump 'for dear life'. He kept his horses in a stable in Parkes Passage and over the stable was a room used for magic lantern entertainments. Jack appears to have been a man of uncertain temperament, for if he was in a bad mood the entertainment had to be rushed through so that the room had been cleared by the time Jack returned.

The Coffee Tavern

Coffee houses were introduced into London in 1652 and for the next 200 years they were popular meeting houses and important centres of information, dispensing new ideas and the daily news with refreshments.

The coffee house did not arrive in Stourport until a week before Christmas 1880. The entrance fee was 1d (1/2p) and after that you could choose between a hot coffee, a punch, a brandy, a pipe of tobacco or merely a quiet read in the Reading Room. It was so popular that three years later it moved to larger premises on the corner of New Street and the High Street and was acquired by Thomas Collyer, a Tewkesbury man with a wife and five children.

One Saturday evening in July 1886, Mr Collyer closed the shop, tidied round and went to bed at one o'clock. An hour later, smoke was seen rising from the ground floor on the side of the house occupied by the family. The alarm was raised but it was an old building, full of wooden timbers, and within a few minutes the whole of the building was ablaze. Mrs Collyer was rescued with the baby and the eldest boy jumped from a window and was slightly hurt. Mr Collyer managed to rescue one boy, but when he returned for his two little girls the heat was too fierce and he was beaten back by the flames.

Living at the premises at the time was the tailor's son. At first it was thought that he had been burned to death but he had managed to climb out of a window on to the roof of the house next door. He had to stay there until he was spotted the following morning. The house was, of course, not insured and Mr Collyer was totally ruined. No-one had the heart to open another coffee house and so this popular and cultivated style of entertainment came to an end.

On the extreme left-hand side of this view of the High Street is the Coffee Tavern which burned down in 1886. Two little girls lost their lives in the fire.
Courtesy: Brian Standish

A church parade in the High Street in about 1900. The banner reads 'Wesleyan Sunday'. This could have been on a 'Charity Sunday'. Courtesy Kidderminster Library.

The Post Office in 1918.
Courtesy Mrs Jean Jones and the
Worcestershire Record Office.

The Post Office

Until Rowland Hill from Kidderminster published his pamphlet on Post Office Reform, the postal service was random and irregular. Letters went by Mail Coach to central points in large towns and had to be fetched by the recipient, being paid for when collected. Some villages employed a messenger to go to the town and collect the post. This would have been the system when the first post office in Stourport-on-Severn opened in 1809 with Ann Hornblower in charge. She left in 1813 and the following year it came into the hands of a member of the Lewty family who owned the Wilden iron mills. The Lewty's would have seen the introduction of the penny stamp in 1839.

At one time the post office was just an opening in the wall, not as large as a railway ticket office window. If you wanted a letter you had to tap at the box and it would be handed out to you through a hole. The accommodation was so small that the postman had to sort his letters out in the street. Letters came in once a day at seven o'clock in the morning, and went out at ten minutes past six in the evening. The letter box was closed at five o'clock and for another stamp you could post up to 5.23.

The Lewty's gave up the post office in 1845. Thomas Wheeldon, the printer, took it over, moving it to his shop in the High Street. Then it settled from 1858 to 1899 at Mr T P Charles, the Ironmongers, Mrs Charles taking it over in 1887. The right hand part of the shop was the Post Office and the left hand side was used to display his ironmongery. Letters were only delivered to the town, other letters were placed in the window to be called for.

It was not until 1897 that there was a free delivery to every home and a number of men were employed to take the letters beyond the town. The Abberley postman had a little dog and if a farmhouse was some way away, down a winding lane, he would put the letter in his dog's mouth for delivery. One day, a farmer wanted to send a letter to the postman for the post but he did not have a stamp so he gave the dog the letter and the penny.

Old letter scales. Engraved on
the tray is:
Rates of Postage
Not exceeding 1oz 1d
  2oz 1.1/2d
  4oz 2d

When the animal reached the postman, the penny was missing. The postman claimed that he saw that the letter had no stamp, guessed what had happened and sent the dog back to find the penny. After a short while, the dog returned with the penny in its mouth.

John Jones was the postman who went to Shrawley. He had such poor sight that he could only distinguish between light and dark, but he was helped by his wife, Hannah. They would sort out the letters in Stourport, then Hannah would walk with him to Woodhampton. John would continue alone to deliver the letters, and at the end of the day, Hannah would meet him at Woodhampton and take him home. There was never a complaint of a wrong letter being delivered.

In 1901, Joseph Ward, who provided the marble carvings in the Methodist church, offered to finance the building of a new post office which would cost £1,800 and include living accommodation for the postman. Plans were drawn up by a Kidderminster architect, and approved by the Council and the Postmaster General. It stood on the site where Woolworth's is now and was demolished in 1969.

Within Living Memory

Some of Stourport's older folk remember the High Street between the two wars. They can recall the trams whizzing noisily along, and the tram lines which threw you off your bike if your wheel was caught in them. By the time the trams disappeared in 1929 cars had begun to replace the horse and carts, although they were so scarce that if the children heard one coming they would wait to see it.

Frank Grinnall says that there used to be such a lot of flourishing businesses in the High Street:

"For example, two gents' outfitters, a saddlers, and a large departmental store, Vickers. It had a long frontage and stood where the Westminster Bank and Boots are now. I can remember when there were seven butchers in the town and they all slaughtered their own animals. Where the Staffordshire Building Society is now once stood a newsagents. It had got two entrances, you could go in one door, round the back and come out the other door which was also on the High Street. The drovers used to take their cattle through the town on market days and a bullock got loose one morning, it went into the shop by the one entrance, round and out the other door."

The High Street seems to have been plagued by escaping cattle. Wedley reports that a cow got loose one day and, seeing a light in the post office, 'made for it with vigour'. Letters were scattered everywhere and trampled into the muddy floor. 'The cow finally fell over with her head under the office table from which position she solemnly rose at last with the table on her head. At last she made for the open door ... and bolted into the street.' As recently as the spring of 2001, a cow raced through the streets of Stourport, to be finally lassoed by firefighters and nature reserve rangers. The cow had been in a nature reserve in the Wyre Forest but had been shot at with an air rifle by children. In a panic she had jumped into the River Severn and had swum half a mile to the town.

The Bickerton family had a shop on this site for 168 years. The first member of the family was a clockmaker and a barber/hairdresser. The barber's pole (now shortened) can still be seen on the extreme right.

Bickerton's

Harry Bickerton arrived in 1832 who was both a clock-maker and a bar-ber/hairdresser. His son, George, had a black waxed moustache with a point at each end. George's son, Bill, who retired in 1991, has a repertoire of entertaining anecdotes about the family business:

"Harry took over a girl's school in the High Street and developed it into a flourishing hairdressing and clock-making business. His son, Thomas, had two sons. One was my father, George Leslie, who had trained on the hairdressing side, while his brother had been apprenticed to a watch re-pairer. When Thomas died, the two sons tossed a coin to see who would take over the family business. I don't know whether my father won or not but he ended up running the business, bringing the family up from Devon to Stourport.

'Thomas was very friendly with Stanley Baldwin, the Prime Minister, who was living in Astley Hall. He would often send for my grandfather to buy little brass tubes from him for his hobby, steam engines.

'I took it over in 1974, when my father died. I reduced the frontage and extended the rear of the shop into the building to reduce the rates. We had six assistants and we were kept busy from morning until night. We had to extend the shop hours from about eight or eight-fifteen in the morning until twenty to seven in the evening. I had also taken on another shop two nights a week and worked there from seven until ten. There was always a queue outside waiting for me when I arrived. Like my grandfather, I had a number of outside contracts and I did about three private boarding schools and an approved school. I have had three bishops coming in for haircuts, one of them used to say, 'Not too short, my wife says I look like a shorn lamb and I'm dining at Windsor in the morning'.

'When the BBC were making the film 'Weather in the Street' they sent a message that, as I was the oldest barber in the town, could I go to the Gainsborough Hotel in Kidderminster, where the cast were staying, and give them all a 1930's haircut. When I got there I discovered that the make-up people had given all the male cast a square back ie the hair at the back of the head and at the base of the neck had been cut straight across.

People didn't have square backs in the 1930's, they had a tapered cut. This was a sign of a good haircut. If it was straight across you had either been to a cheap barber or your mother had done it. I was telling this to Michael York (star of the Three Musketeers etc) while I was cutting his hair and all the make-up people came in to watch

'I was trained to shave with a cut-throat razor and I was always the one who was sent to shave the corpses. Not many people know that the hair continues to grow after death. Nobody else would go. I was told, 'It's not the dead ones you have to watch but the live ones'. The corpses used to be in various stages, sometimes they were almost warm. I leaned across one corpse and it sighed 'Aah!' and frightened me to death, I shot across the room. I once accidentally cut one of the corpses and the fact that it didn't bleed took me by surprise.

'Something curious used to happen every night. We had four chairs in a row in the salon, and every night my father would insist that we shook the gowns out and lay them carefully across the chairs, stretching them across the arm so that the air could get in underneath to keep them sweet. Every morning when we arrived the third chair from the end would look as if someone had sat in it. The gown was pressed neatly against the sides. This used to tickle us pink. My father always joked about it.

The first member of the Bickerton family came to Stourport in 1832. He took over the premises of a girl's school in the High Street and turned it into a flourishing clock-making and hairdressing business. This watch and chain is attached to an engraved metal box with a hinged lid containing matches.

'Just before I retired in 1991 the "crew cut" came in which was a quarter of an inch (about 6 mm) all over. No special skill was required for that, anybody could do it. There was also the American flat top, a much more difficult and taxing job."

Next door to the hairdressers was a jewellery shop in which a young lady by the name of Betty worked. Bill was living on his own after a failed marriage and Betty had been tragically widowed when in her late twenties. Bill said that he had his eye on her for some time before he asked her out and in 1969 they were married. Bill still remarks that it was the best thing he ever did. The family business has been carried on by their youngest daughter who has taken over the florists shop which was part of the original frontage and called it, 'Samantha's flowers'. The same family has therefore been trading in the High Street for 168 years. Unfortunately, Samantha now feels that she wants to spend more time with her family and is selling the shop.

W H Grinnall's

Two of the shops in the High Street have achieved enormous commercial successes. One of them is W H Grinnall's, the popular greengrocers. The W H stands for William Henry, who arrived in 1905 and established the business. Frank Grinnall is his seventh child:

"There were thirteen of us altogether, five girls and eight boys. We were very happy, we lived in a large house in Mitton Street opposite the Holly Bush, known as Mitton House. It has now been demolished. However, I was born in New Street, the family lived there until it became overcrowded.

'My father was a fishmonger by trade and when he married he found that there was a shop available in Stourport with a cold slab for the fish and so he moved here. My mother was a cook and so our family ate very well. We had all fresh food.

'I went into the family business in 1935 when I was fifteen. I was the only boy to go into the business. All the others went off and had their own

careers. My father believed that they should get into the building trade, he never thought there was much future in fruit and vegetables. I was disappointed at first as I wanted to stay on at school and follow another career but I soon got absorbed in it.

'In the early days the shop girls would make up the orders and put them into baskets to be delivered by horse and float. When I was a school lad I would go out into the country with the delivery man. I was sitting on the float in Astley when I was about seven, waiting for the man to return, when a donkey appeared from nowhere and the horse bolted. I grabbed the reins and managed to stop the horse after it had gone about 300 yards.

'My father used to go by train from Stourport station to Birmingham to buy his produce. He could take the whole day over it. He would start off at about six o'clock in the morning, select his produce from the market, load it on to the train, then when he got home, it would be unloaded into his lorry ready for sale the next day. He was one of the first to have a lorry which he parked in a garage near the Tontine. One night, it caught fire and was destroyed.

'The early vehicles had very poor lights and we used to have terrible fogs in the winter. I can remember that when I was only about seven or eight I had to walk from Ombersley in front of my father's lorry because he couldn't see the kerb, but he could just see the top of my head.

'The business had to be progressive, it couldn't stand still. After the war my father extended into dealership, he would buy growing crops locally, sometimes whole fields, and have them packed and sent to Birmingham. We later extended to a bigger shop, invested money in shop fittings and

W H Grinnall's still flourishes in the High Street. William Henry Grinnall arrived in 1905 and established the business. Courtesy Frank Grinnall.

equipment, and diversified into the wholesale side of the business. That's the only way we could survive. My son is a much better businessman than I am. He buys wholesale and delivers to hotels, restaurants, guest houses, elderly people's homes, schools and retail outlets. He gets up about two o'clock every morning to be in the Birmingham markets by three.

'When I was a lad the family grocers was a hell of a lucrative business. People were buying cheap food - tinned milk and even powdered eggs. People have better diets now and eat a lot more fruit and vegetables."

Blunt's Shoes

Grinnall's has developed into a major concern, but Blunt's is even larger. His family and employees have helped to expand his business over the years from two local shops to a series of stores stretching from the South Coast to Yorkshire with wholesale distribution world-wide. Bob Blunt, third generation head of the family shoe firm, was born over the shop which still trades in High Street, Stourport.

Bob's grandfather started the Kidderminster shop in the Bull Ring 135 years ago; he had worked in Mansfield's factory in Northampton, as a clicker, cutting leather uppers for footwear from the hides (a very skilled job) but he decided to set up on his own. He began manufacturing footwear on the premises with a small team of men. He was a well-read

well educated man and a keen cricketer. He played once against W G Grace and he introduced over-arm bowling to Kidderminster. Bob Blunt himself takes up the story:

"During the late 1800s most people of note in the district had their own personal wooden lasts on which their shoes were made. You could go into the back of the shop in later years and see all the lasts still stacked and labelled with customer's names. As people got older they would develop bumps on their joints and grandfather would tack bits of leather on to their lasts. However, by the turn of the century he had ceased manufacturing becoming a retailer, together with shoe repair workshops. His eldest son (also Thomas) took over the business for ten years before handing over to my father during the first world war.

'My father was the youngest of the second generation. Like his father before him, he was a keen sportsman - football, cricket and golf. Both my parents were good people with sound ideas and a strict sense of honesty. When my father returned from the First World War army service, he had about fifteen people working for him, eight in Kidderminster and four in Stourport. My brother Tom joined the firm in the thirties.

'I went into the business straight from Kidderminster Grammar School at the age of fifteen, but had been helping in the workshops from the age of thirteen. I went into the army for two years in 1946, and when I came home I decided not to go back into shoe repairing but moved to the retail side of the business. I had come to realise that working in the repair trade, although very satisfying, would not make the business prosper so I became a buyer and seller and devoted myself to it. I worked for probably eighteen years building the two shops up to what in those days was a high turnover. Towards the end of this period my six children began joining the firm (the fourth generation). From this base, we started opening more shops and also started doing some wholesale business. From there we kept advancing, not planning but just taking opportunities as they occurred.

'Over the years we have had several fires in various locations. One Wednesday afternoon in the 1950s I was with my young family in Worcester when we heard that the Kidderminster shop was ablaze and would I get there quickly. There it was, burning away. The whole of the serving areas were burned or blackened with smoke. In spite of that we opened an hour earlier the following morning selling the damaged stock on the doorstep. We never lost trade for any reason! "

The operation ran from Stourport High Street/York Street until 1982 when newly imposed parking restrictions forced the firm to look elsewhere. Being "Townies" they rejected industrial estates and bought the former CMCO factory in the centre of Kidderminster, where they immediately felt at home - despite the awesome task of dealing with a four-and-a-half acre site of old buildings where 3,500 people had worked - now silent and empty with all the synchronised clocks stopped at exactly the same time. Bob remarks, 'Nothing is for ever!'

Parkes Passage

The Methodist Church and school are here (see chapter 7).

Originally known as Back Alley, Parkes Passage could have been named after a Mr Parker. He probably lived in the old Wharfinger Mansion standing at the York Street end of Parkes Passage. The square in Parkes Passage was originally for pack horses carrying goods to and from the canal basins. When the pack horses disappeared early in the nineteenth century it was used by Methodist ministers for stabling their horses, needed for going round the country on pastoral work.

York Street

The street is famous to Wesleyan Methodists throughout the world as the place to which John Wesley, who founded Methodism with his brother Charles, wrote his last letter.

It happened this way. The street is named after Aaron York, a boat builder and wharfinger from Bewdley who lived at Stourport between 1775 and 1825. He built his own house there, known appropriately as York House. Aaron was a keen Wesleyan and was probably influential in having a Wesleyan Church built in the High Street, for it was Aaron who applied to have it licensed as 'a place of worship of almighty God' by dissenters. John Wesley, then in his late eighties, was on friendly terms with Aaron. His last letter was addressed to him and reads:

"On Wednesday, March 17th, I purpose, if God permit, to come from Gloucester to Worcester and on Thursday, the eighteenth, to Stourport. If your friends at Worcester are displeased we cannot help it. Wishing you and yours all happiness."

The letter was found in Wesley's room after his death in 1791.

Aaron York's house is said to be the first house built in the new town of Stourport. He and his partner, Jonathan Worthington of Moor Hall, owned a boat yard and warehouse along the Upper Basin. The houses on the basins side of York Street have cellars and access to the wharves.

'The Lock Shop' at the end of York Street was built in 1854 and was formerly the Lock Keeper's cottage. It forms a group of buildings associated with the canal, next door was the Toll Office and further along was the canal maintenance yard workship, later occupied by Holt Abbott of Canal Pleasurecraft Ltd.

Wedley has a story about 'a shop beyond the passage', probably the Lock Shop, occupied in 1855 by an ironmonger, Henry Cook. When Cook died, his house was put up for auction. The auctioneer was Richard Baker, who came from a boat-building family living on the quayside but was trying his hand at auctioneering. Richard was on his chair, finalising a bid, and saying, 'Going, once, going twice, going -' when just as he said 'Gone' the floor gave way. Auctioneer and bidders sank into the cellar below. Richard decided to give up auctioneering and confine himself to boat-building.

As a small boy, Isaac Wedley loved York Street. He wrote that the Johnson family kept two shops there, a confectioners on one side of the road and a toy shop on the other. The toy shop had an enormous wooden Noah's ark in the window and Wedley spent much of his childhood gazing at it.

The early residents of York Street in the 1870's followed a variety of trades. John Hickman from the White Gates was a nail and screw maker who had a shop near the Tontine. He kept a team of donkeys which he would lead on a long detour across the common to avoid paying tolls. Mr Griffin went in for tallow chandling, the making of animal fats into such products as candles, oils and soap. When he died his widow married one of his apprentices who became a prosperous carpet manufacturer.

There was a baker, Tom Harding, who kept a pet monkey, named Jane. Jane sometimes got loose and with her chain dangling would climb over the tops of the houses and disappear. On one occasion when she got away she was spotted by a neighbour sitting over a water barrel, the neighbour pulled a chain which released water into the barrel and Jane fell in with a terrific splash. On another occasion she wandered to the back of the houses in High Street and perched herself on the window sill of a man's house

A view of Stourport-on-Severn looking down from Betty Dawes Ridge, at Areley Kings. In the foreground is Walshes Farm, now a public house. The tannery chimney dominates the skyline. Courtesy Ray Franks.

who lay very near to death's door. The poor man heard the chink of the chain, and opening his eyes saw this terrible vision before him. Wedley says, 'You can quite imagine what the poor man thought had come for him.'

Also living in York Street was Mr Anderson, a clerk to a lawyer. Anderson's father had probably been a tailor, consequently he took great care over his appearance and was known locally as the Beau Nash of Stourport. When Anderson decided he needed a new coat, he called in at the local tailors, Edwin Landon's, on Lion Hill. Landon had a coat which fitted him perfectly, but Lawyer Anderson said that he was looking for something more expensive, so he went to the other tailors, Watkins. Watkins said that he had nothing in stock but he would get one. Watkins then went round to the first tailors, Landons, and purchased the coat which Anderson had refused. After a few days, Anderson called back, and Watkins offered him the coat at a greatly increased price, which he readily accepted. The two tailors halved the profit.

The Police Station was at number 19 until the early 1960's. Next door to the Police Station was the Police Inspector's house.

Lion Hill

Lion Hill runs from the basins near to the Tontine, past the road leading to the Methodist Church up to the parish church, consequently it has been known as Tontine Road, Church Street and Lion Hill. The White Lion Inn evidently triumphed. Wedley describes Lion Hill as the playground of the town. In the early 1800's there were only two houses here, consequently it was used by Fairs and the Circus.

Old Jimmy Turner lived down the back of the White Lion, he would stand outside with his roullette-type table, selling numbers with cakes as prizes. He would call out, 'Now then, who'll take two and fours', then he would set the machine spinning and tilt it very slightly so that it would stop on the odd numbers and he would pocket both the money and the cakes.

James Lively, 'the Cheap Jack' sold everything, says Wedley, 'from legs of mutton to mouth organs'. He was so popular that when he had his stall in the centre of the town the trade folk objected. The young men tied ropes round his stall and pulled it to the less populated Lion Hill. However, his trade was not affected and crowds of people still gathered round his stall. Wedley continues:

"The night after he got fixed a number of youths armed with long pea-shooters posted themselves on the wall which then ran alongside the road, and when Jimmy was in the middle of one of his wonderful speeches these boys, at a given signal, shot their peas at his wonderful array of clocks and ornaments with deadly aim. Lively offered a reward of £10 for their capture but they were never caught."

This is where the last of the old pan-pipers played in the early 1800s. An old man had a row of pipes, like miniature organ pipes, resting on his chest and to play them he would blow backwards and forwards across the top. On the floor in front of him he had laid out crossed swords and a pattern of eggs. His pretty little daughter would dance between the swords and the eggs to an admiring audience.

York House, now an up-to-date medical centre.

The entrance to the old police station at 19 York Street. One of the most popular officers was PC Ganderton who was appointed in 1870. He had an endearing habit of giving a warning cough whenever he was approaching a mild misdemeanour that he considered too trivial for punishment.

By the time the Ordnance Survey map of 1883 was published, houses had been built along York Street but there was still a field opposite the memorial gardens, let to travelling shows, theatres and various entertainments. In 1911 the Drill Hall was built on the site.

Mart Lane

'Mart' is an abbreviation of market and this is where much of the buying and selling of canal and river goods took place. The old three-storey houses were built by the Canal Company, probably for staff. A sail cloth maker lived in Mart Lane and there was another one in Foundry Street.

A savings bank opened in a small room on the corner of Mart Lane in the 1830's for one hour every Wednesday. This was before the time of old age pensions and sickness benefit, so a little 'nest egg' was essential. The Bank was managed by a Board of Trustees which included local businessmen and ten Rectors, all giving their time voluntarily. By 1836 £18,250 had been saved by Stourport workers. All the money was invested for the reduction of the national debt.

In 1812, a basin was built between Mart Lane and Severn Road, and part of Mart Lane was rebuilt as a bridge, demolished in the early 1960's.

Lichfield Street and Severn Lane, later Severn Road

The Union Inn once stood opposite the Severn Road end of Lichfield Street. Consequently, Lichfield Street was once known as Union Street. Before the arrival of Severn Valley Carpet Works and the other industries, Severn Road was only a country lane. There were a few houses on the one side while on the other side green fields sloped down to the river Stour. Stour Bank House, home of the Swanns, the vinegar manufacturers, was built on these slopes near to Cheapside.

Thomas Bibb lived in Severn Street who was caretaker of the Methodist Chapel for many years. While he was waiting for their last child to be

Cottages in Mart Lane.

delivered he was reading the Bible and he came across Saint Paul's words, 'Salute Urbane, our helper in Christ'. He decided to call his boy 'Urbane', and, says Wedley, 'until the day of his death he was popularly known as "Erbin", few people knowing how to spell it, or where it came from'.

Cheapside

Fred Rimmel remembers that the vinegar works and the gas works were both at Cheapside. "That part of Stourport was the aromatic quarter, you could tell where you were even in the black of the night."

Cheapside was originally twice its present length and ran all the way to the Stour but then the vinegar works bought the piece between Cheapside and the Stour. The gas works were between the vinegar works and Lichfield Street on the site of the old basin.

Wharfs and boat building enterprises were here, including William Bird's. Numbers 1 and 2 are all that remain of a former terrace of three-storey houses.

In 1842 Income Tax was imposed for the first time by a Tory government. The shop and factory owners were furious. William Stanton was a blacksmith who lived near the Tontine in Cheapside and he chalked on his door in large letters the Biblical quotation 'Tax no man's labour'. When he was canvassed by the Tories during an election he would point to the door and say, 'Look at that, gentlemen, look at that!'

AREA THREE - MITTON STREET, GILGAL AND TO THE NORTH

Mitton Street

Mitton Street is steeped in history. Anglo House is here, so is an entrance to Severn Valley Carpet Mills, the old Congregational Church (now Roman Catholic) is on the corner of Mitton Street and Vale Road, and in this street is the oldest house in Stourport. The pretty half-timbered cottage, number 41, was probably built in the 1600s, predating the canal by a century or more. The house stands at the corner of Stour Lane, once known as Hell Lane. A little square opposite the house was known as Paradise Court. The saying was, 'Keep to the right, for it means Paradise', the other road means —'.

Before the canal arrived, the whole of the Stourport area was known as Mitton, now we have only Mitton Street, Mitton Gardens, Mitton Walk and Mitton Close. John Leland, writing in the first half of the 16th century, describes Mitton village: 'Here doth Stour river break into two or three armalettes, and serveth milles'. Apart from the mills scattered along the Stour there was nothing but green fields and shrubland. The Feathers Inn was the only house between Stourport and Kidderminster except for a turnpike and a row of cottages.

The Stourport area was divided into Upper Mitton (originally Over Mitton) and Lower Mitton, the canal basins being built at Lower Mitton. St Michaels and All Angels, although in the upper part of the town, was just inside the boundary of Lower Mitton. Upper Mitton and Lower Mitton were two quite separate places. Upper Mitton was in the parish of Hartlebury whereas Lower Mitton had been under the supervision of Kidderminster even before the Domesday book was compiled.

The Bridge over the River Stour

About a hundred years before Stourport came into being, a bridge was built across the River Stour, near to what is now known as Anglo Corner. A strange story is told of how it came to be built.

In the sixteenth century, James Wilmot of Hartlebury had built five fulling mills (for the manufacturing of cloth) and a corn mill along the northern bank of the river Stour, on land which he rented from the Bishop of Worcester. The Wilmots were descendants of Elizabeth Woodville, Queen of Edward IV, and distant relatives of Lady Jane Grey. During the seventeenth century they had converted all their mills into iron mills. At some time, they had made a rudimentary bridge of a few planks across the Stour. At high water, the bridge was impassable for horseman, who had to go a mile out of their way to cross the river, consequently trespassing on Wilmot's land, for which privilege they had to pay the Wilmot's a penny. The Bishop received a number of complaints and he decided that a more robust bridge across the Stour was desperately needed.

It so happened that a young man by the name of Philip Tolley, of Hartlebury, was convicted in about 1681 of being the father of an illegitimate child. The Court sentenced him to do public penance in Hartlebury Parish Church, which apparently involved standing in a white sheet with a candle in his hand. However, Tolley came to an agreement with the Bishop, that instead he would pay for the labour in building the bridge if the Bishop would provide the materials. Tolley's bridge served the public for

The oldest house in Stourport, in Mitton Street, predating the canal by more than a century. Before Brindley arrived, Stourport was known as Mitton.
Courtesy the occupier.

about sixty years. It then fell into disrepair because the church and the local council each said that it was the other's responsibility to maintain it

Gilgal

Following the tradition of using London names, the area where the Elf garage now stands used to be known as Piccadilly. The name Gilgal is Hebrew meaning 'circle of stones'. It would have been an appropriate name for this road as the biblical Gilgal is the place where Saul gathered his people against the Philistines and it was here, opposite the Red Lion, that the townsfolk gathered, after a morning in church, for the Mitton Wake and other events.

The Red Lion public house has now reverted to its old name of Steps House. From Gilgal, a flight of steps, known as the 'Hill of Zion', leads up to St Michaels Church. Halfway up the hill were the old stocks. By the Hill of Zion was the coal wharf, where coal, brought by narrow boat from the Staffordshire coal fields, was unloaded.

In Gilgal was once a public house known as the Boat, kept by a Mr Venables. He sold coal as well as beer. He wrote down all debts with a piece of chalk on the back of a door and on one occasion, a dispute over

A very different-looking Gilgal in 1905. The second church of Saint Michael can be seen in the distance.
Courtesy Kidderminster library.

90

a debt landed him in court. The judge demanded proof of the amount owing so that Venables had to take the door off its hinges and carry it into court.

Baldwin Road

Baldwin Road used to be called 'Farm Bed'. It was a ghostly, eerie, desolate place, subject to fogs and floods. There was only one small factory on the right belonging to George Harris and a row of cottages on the left known as 'Weaver's Row'. Right at the end stood the Poor House. By 1890, huge factories had been built from Baldwin Road down to the Stour and continued from the Stour to the Hartlebury Road.

Mill Road

Mill Road leads, of course, to the old site of Mitton Mill. The residents of Mill Road may not know that the one-time Mayor of Philadelphia, city and port of the USA, came from their midst.

John Weaver was the fourth son of Benjamin Weaver who lived in Mill Road. His first employment was as an office boy at Wilden Iron Works, then he became a clerk in the Office of the Severn & Canal Carrying Company. He went to Philadelphia, tried several jobs but wasn't satisfied until he went to work in a lawyer's office. He taught himself shorthand and typing so that he would improve his position, then he decided he wanted to be a fully-fledged lawyer and he studied in evening classes for five years until he was qualified. Although John Weaver was quiet and unassuming he was a man of steel. In a city which was notorious for its bribery, corruption, betting and gambling, John Weaver stood out as an honest, straightforward Christian and he was eventually elected as mayor. One year, he went on holiday in the Rockies and the council took the opportunity of his absence to authorise the sale of the town's gas works which would bring in a large revenue but increase the cost of gas to the townsfolk. Weaver's friends sent him a telegram to let him know what was going on, he rushed back and caught his colleagues unawares. Another time he managed to quell a riot of about a thousand black workers singlehandedly. The townsfolk hailed him as a hero.

Worcester Road

The main road from Stourport to Worcester was known as Buggy Lane because of the number of light carriages travelling across it. A few yards into the road was a toll gate, managed by the Anchor Inn. The Anchor was on the right, together with Heath House and Anchor Farm and on the left were two cottages. These were the only buildings between Stourport and Titton, two miles away.

In about the 1870's an artificial branch of the river Stour ran under the Hartlebury Road, across the Common, under the Worcester road and back to the Stour near the Severn, in order to supply mills and farms between the Worcester Road and the Stour with water. It had flood gates which were worked by the primitive but effective means of a barrel placed on a gate. The water could be used for cleaning and washing, and youngsters bathed in its waters, but it could not be used for drinking. All drinking water had to be fetched from the local mill. The mill closed at eight and if you ran out, you had to go without.

AREA FOUR - VALE ROAD AND TO THE WEST

Vale Road

Between Lion Hill and Gilgal was once an ancient footpath running through the orchard of Springfield House and some allotments. The land was owned by Thomas Vale & Sons Ltd, and in August 1922 they decided to give it to Stourport Urban District Council in order to provide a new road. Vale Road was born. Until then, Lombard Street had been the main route through the town.

One of the older residents remembers that Vale Road very nearly acquired a totally different appearance to its present one:

"A relative of mine was Frank Clarke. When the Council were going to acquire the land he put up to be elected for the Council on the grounds that he wanted Vale Road to be made into a High Street, a wide road with shops along it. Although I was only about seven I was given leaflets to distribute about it. We went to the Parish Room where he was on the platform speaking about it, but he didn't get elected."

Lombard Street

Various explanations have been put forward as to why Stourport roads were named after London Streets. One is that Brindley had high hopes for his town and wanted it to rival London. Another is that an early Town Council decided that the streets should have proper names. Whatever the reason, the town was given Lombard Street, Holborn Street, Drury Lane, Piccadilly and Pall Mall. Holborn Street became Foundry Street and Drury Lane was changed to Mitton Street. Only Lombard Street has kept its original name.

Lombard Street was the home of the Tannery. The works were here on both sides of the road, together with worker's cottages and the home of the Rogers family, who owned the Tannery. The front of the Rogers' house was in Lombard Street, near to the Swan Hotel, where there are now shops. The garden was huge, and went from the Lickhill Road, along Lombard Street, to the Tannery. In the middle was a large mulberry tree, probably brought by the French escaping from the French Revolution of 1789 to 1795 for their silk worms. The Rogers family had two sons, the one moved to The Heath in Lickhill Road, the other lived in Areley House.

The Mulberry was introduced to England in the sixteenth century to feed the silkworms. James I encouraged their planting, hoping to establish the silk industry.

The Co-operative Site

Where the Co-operative Society now stands was one of the tan yards with bark piled into huge ricks. The supermarket building now occupied by the Co-op was built by Jim Perry and his brother. Jim describes how the family came to have the first refrigerator in the area, the first window display of priced joints of meat, and the first privately-owned supermarket in the county.

"Len Perry, my father, was a master butcher in Stourport. His first shop, before he married, was in Mitton Street on what was known locally as the 'Banks of Buggery'. It was a small shared shop in the black and white houses, my father had one half of the front room. Father used to go to Kidderminster, buy a frozen lamb from the ice house and bring it back on the tram. He later married Lilly Ingram and opened a butchers shop in Kidderminster, where I was born. Mother and father left Kidderminster and eventually they returned to Stourport. His next shop, again in Mitton Street, was across the road from his original shop (now a Chinese take-away). Father delivered meat on a motor bike and sides of beef used to hang outside the shop!

'After a while he moved into the town, purchasing premises in Lombard Street (which had been Stones' saddler's shop) from the local building firm Vales, and this was where my brother Robin was born. Father was the first butcher in Stourport about 1933 or 1934 to have a refrigerator on the premises.

'At that time father had his own abattoir situated by the basin in Mart Lane, next to the listed buildings, this was demolished about thirty years ago when the Power Station basin was filled. A butcher was a master crafts-man, selecting his animals in the market and looking after them until they were ready for slaughter, then he killed and hung them, taking great pride in his meat right until it had been sold. Mother often helped him in the slaughterhouse by holding the animals down with a rope looped through a ring in the floor, the animals were poleaxed first to stun them.

'Over the years, my father bought all the adjoining premises in the 'yard' until he had the whole block from the cinema down to Cameo hairdress-ers. After leaving school at fourteen I put the orders up and delivered them on the carrier bike, sometimes they were so heavy I used to fall off. This was during the war years.

'My 'National Service' came and went. I decided to expand the grocery and greengrocery business which brother Robin ran before going into the Army. One day, I went to my Father and said, 'I have heard of a new way of selling grocery called 'Self Service'. Father said, 'What's that?' I replied, 'I don't know, it's an American way of doing business, but the Co-op at Stirchley in Birmingham are doing it, I'll go and find out'. When I ex-plained it to him and said it was the way of the future, he said it would never work. Fortunately, he was far sighted, if he thought you could make something work he would let you do it, but it took him about five months before he agreed to let me reorganise the shop in line with the new con-cept.

'When I got married in 1952 my father extended the shops so that I could expand that side of the business, half the store was to be grocery, the other half greengrocery. My wife, Valerie, and I worked extremely hard in the business. We were the first self-service store in Worcester-shire and had a write-up in a trade magazine describing us as the smallest self-service store in the United Kingdom. Food was still in very short supply and other grocers in the town warned off suppliers from calling on us. Our hard work only began taking off when price maintenance was broken in the late 1950s, we could then pass on the saving of self service to the customer by offering lower prices, as we did not have to cover credit and delivery costs.

'During this time brother John was also out of the Army and developing the butcher side of the business. Father and mother continued in the busi-ness but more in the background, making the sausages and preparing the meat and pies. We had a back yard with access down an entry in Lombard Street. The family all lived on the premises in Lombard Street; brother

Robin had married Barbara soon after I married, we both had flats on the yard while our parents lived in the original home.

'Father and Robin decided they wanted more control over their meat supply instead of being told what they could sell, as rationing eased they built an abattoir in the yard. My father would go to market on a Monday, buy the animals, rest them in pens in the yard overnight and slaughter on a Tuesday. Brother Robin extended the butchery considerably and was the first butcher in Worcestershire and perhaps further afield to have a refrigerated window display. He would cut his meat into joints and display them, individually priced, in the window. Before that innovation in meat selling, customers needed to go into the shop and ask for, say, half a leg of lamb priced about so much and the butcher would cut as they watched.

'Our business flourished, eventually we decided to extend to 2,000 square feet, the size that was required to class the store as a 'supermarket'. The planner refused our first planning application because of parking and delivery problems, so we asked the cinema if we could lease their car park area during the day to ease the situation. Every Christmas the store was getting overcrowded, so we again decided to enlarge the store by taking down everything on the yard, this would increase the area to 6,000 square feet. In those days we were not so mindful of the existing buildings in the town and were only concerned with getting the maximum trading selling space. Looking at the store now I feel we could have built something more in keeping with the existing town architecture. We were, at that time, the largest privately-owned supermarket in the country.

'When I was a small boy, my father was sitting at the top of the table and he said to me, 'One day, we shall have people coming into the shop where I am sitting now, and they will go out by the entry'. Do you know, that came about, all our living premises were turned into the supermarket and the exit was on the site of the entry.

'None of our success would have been possible without the many very good people who worked with us over the years and we are grateful to them all."

Tan Lane

Tan Lane, once leading to the Tannery, was built along the line of an ancient trackway, at least two thousand years old. It ran from Mitton Mill, past the Old Rising Sun public house, along Tan Lane, across the War Memorial Park and down by Lickhill Manor. It finished by the River Severn where there was once a ford before the river was made navigable. It was such an important footpath that when the canal was cut, a wooden bridge was put across the canal so that the route was still usable.

The infant school is here, and opposite is Keith Newnham's pet and gardening shop. Keith was one of the leading lights in the Horticultural Society.

Foundry Street

Two hundred years ago Stourport began at Foundry Road. When coming from Kidderminster, this was the first Stourport road to be reached. And, says Isaac Wedley, 'a more miserable, dingy street it was hard to find'. Baldwins iron foundry ran along the one side and the houses on the other side were black with the smoke from the factory. There were two neglected inns, the Moulders Arms at the bottom and the Rising Sun at the top. The Rising Sun is still there, much improved. When the road was first built it was known as Holborn, later changed to New Road, then Foundry Street.

Thomas Baldwin's old house still backs onto the canal, facing the Fire Station. Next door are the old Foundry warehouses and wharf. The Aquatics Centre was once the Foundry offices, approached by an imposing flight of steps from the road. The works bell hung over the entrance door and the iron framed windows were made in the Foundry over the road. In Margaret Dallow 's *Brief Guided Walk* (along the towpath of the canal) she writes that a tunnel from the wharf to one of Baldwin's furnaces, together with a branch tunnel into the yard, still exists under the road. Pig iron and raw materials were unloaded at the wharf and taken through the tunnel to the factory, then the finished products were taken back down the tunnel to the narrow boats.

The old foundry offices and wharf backing on to the canal in Foundry Street.

Tinker Watson and his wife Biddy lived in a cottage at the bottom of Foundry Street. He went from house to house sharpening knives as he was known as the 'Razzor Grinder'. He was, says Wedley, a fine looking man with long curls hanging on either side of his face and he wore a big old-fashioned straw hat 'that would have fitted no-one else for he'd a grand head on his shoulders'. He played the fiddle and being left-handed, his strings were back to front. Biddy could sing and they patronised the pubs. Biddy's favourite song was 'I know that my Redeemer liveth'. Biddy was the daughter of a rich London merchant and for love of her husband she gave up everything. Then one day, tragedy struck. Tinker Watson was found with his throat cut. With no-one to pay the rent or provide food, Biddy probably spent the rest of her days in the workhouse. The fiddle became one of Isaac Wedley's treasured possessions.

6. Pubs and Publicans

When I was a guard (at Stourport-on-Severn station) we used to have some fun with the trippers. They used to congregate in the Station Hotel, now the Brindley Arms. We used to go in and say, 'Come on, we're ready to go' but you still had to wait for them and some of them were unsteady on their feet when they came out. The train was about three feet off the ground and they had to get up this ladder with only the handles on the train for support. We had to shove them up and into the train. Had they slipped, I would have been responsible.

w

By 1834, Stourport had a population of about 3,000 and 36 public houses, or one pub for every 83 residents. The public houses would have ranged from beer retailers, where you handed over your empty jug and had it refilled, to comfortable hotels and coaching inns for the wealthy. Everyone drank beer or ale, tea and coffee were extremely expensive and water was usually unsafe to drink, therefore ale, beer and cider were part of the staple diet. Even children were given a diluted beer, and children in the Sunday School were given a mug of beer on special occasions.

The question is, which public house was the old Stourmouth, where the Severn bargemen met in the evening before the building of the canal? Wedley suggests that it was the Anchor, which used to stand on the Worcester Road, just south of the junction with the Hartlebury Road. Incidentally, US servicemen were banned from visiting the Anchor during the 1939-1945 war.

THE TONTINE HOTEL

The huge, grand Tontine Building was provided by the Staffordshire and Worcestershire Canal Company in 1788 to accommodate visitors to fashionable Stourport. Here, the wealthy entertained themselves with regattas, parties, and other festivities.

The Tontine was the unofficial business centre of the Canal Company. The Annual Audit Dinners were held here. The directors of the Canal Company, among them Lords Hatherton and Wrottesley, would arrive from Wolverhampton in a private boat. Bill Hughes describes the scene in the 1930's:

"A special boat was kept at Stourport, the Lady Hatherton. It had a black hull and a white top. Once a year all the Directors of the Staffordshire and Worcestershire Canal Company came down and they were taken up the canal in it. Two horses pulled it (although it only needed one) and the horses were all dressed up. The boatmen wore white shirts and a cap. The Lady Hatherton had big tables and white tablecloths and all the best food and wines. When the Directors had finished any food left over was given to the men. We can remember my father coming home with sandwiches and wine. One year the boat was taken into dry dock, beams of wood put through the windows supporting the boat, the hull removed and replaced by a new one. The boat is still in use now."

The Anchor, thought by Wedley to be the old Stourmouth, where boatmen met for a pipe of tobacco and a jug of ale before the canal was built. It once stood on the Worcester Road, just south of the junction with the Hartlebury Road. A toll house stood on the other side of the road.
Courtesy Brindley Arms.

The Tontine, by the basins, named after a popular society using the premises.

Also meeting at the Tontine were the Ancient Order of Druids. Wedley remarks, 'they were fairly influential, judging by the look of the beautiful mugs from which the members drank their ale'.

Only the central section was a hotel, an extension on each side was used by hop merchants. Before Worcester Hop Market opened, Stourport had a thriving trade in hops. The hotel was known first as the Areley Inn, then the Stourport Inn, and finally, the Tontine. This last name came from a popular society using the premises. A Tontine is a system invented by an Italian, Tonti, in 1653, and is a type of gamble on longevity. A certain amount of money is paid into a fund which goes to the person who lives the longest. Tontines were once very fashionable, at one time there were Tontine wills, that is, if someone died, their money was held in trust until only one of the beneficiaries was left. Obviously, this encouraged disposing of your rivals and was not promoted.

The system used at the Tontine gave ten categories of shares but when a share-holder died the shares were not sold but went back to the Tontine to go to the oldest surviving member. Parents put down their children's name at birth and paid an annual subscription. The system also served as a type of health insurance, for club members were looked after financially when off sick from work. They were also promised a decent funeral. On the death of a wife, a club member received £2.10s (£2.50) but no member could receive this more than once in his life.

It guarded the morals as well as the health of its members. There was a long list of rules, for example, members seen drunk or gaming in any public place were excluded. Anyone who cursed or swore or used profane words

or language was fined 2d (nearly 1p) a time. Anyone casting reflections on any person's religion, forfeited 2d. Anyone enlisting for a soldier was excluded. It was rather like a secret society with strange rituals, for example, a little cup was brought with the first carriage of ale and if any member drank out of any other cup he forfeited sixpence.

By 1842 Stourport had lost its popularity, the number of visitors declined, and so the Tontine was subdivided to form twenty separate dwellings. It narrowly escaped demolition in the early 1970's. The hotel had not been renovated since it was first built, and the buildings either side of the hotel had been made into flats, most of which had been empty for some time. By 1971 the whole complex needed drastic repairs, which the owners, the Wolverhampton and Dudley Brewery, said were too expensive to carry out. They applied to the Wyre Forest District Council for permission to reconstruct the Tontine and demolish the flats.

Understandably, the Council were horrified at the thought that one of the areas proudest landmarks was to be demolished and they turned the

The Amo passing in front of the Tontine.
Courtesy Ray Franks.

application down. The Brewery then appealed to the Secretary of State to overrule the decision. Mercifully, a representative of the Secretary of State reported 'the condition of the main building was not bad having regard to its age and defects were not such as to preclude the repair and restoration of the building as a whole'. The Tontine was saved. The Council and the Brewery then met to sort out a solution and the result can be seen in the Tontine buildings today.

In 2001 it was proposed that the building should be converted into flats.

THE SWAN HOTEL

The original Swan was built more than 200 years ago by a Mr Swann, who worked on the boats and built it for boat-owners. Although originally a plain-fronted brick inn, Wedley comments that it was 'looked upon as the premier house, and when, in the process of time, the front was ornamented and embellished with a swan in stone, its position was assured. Besides

The Swan Hotel. During the elections , leading politicians spoke from the balcony to the crowd below..

this, the establishment of a first class bowling green gave it the finishing touch'. The Swan was also important because stage coaches stopped here.

Political feelings ran high in Stourport, and the Swan and the Lion were in direct competition. The Swan was the haunt of the Whigs, or Liberals, and the Lion was the rendezvous of the Tories. Both hotels were provided with balconies over the entrance, from which the speakers could expound their views to the excited and rowdy electors in the street below. Both had good club rooms where meetings could be held under cover in poor weather. At election times the Swan was exceptionally busy as most of the Stourport people voted Liberal and the open space in front of the inn would be full of supporters.

Victor Stout Mitchley was licensee of the Swan from 1958 to 1972.

"The Swan was condemned when Irene and I took it over. It was more or less derelict. When I applied for a licence the magistrate would only give me a temporary one. I was in court with a representative of Allied Breweries, we were just about to leave the building when I said to this representative, 'I'm going back in'. The magistrate was Howard Beard, a relative of Beard's electrical shop. He looked at me over his pince nez and remarked, 'I thought the matter had been finished with'. I said to him, 'I am prepared to leave a good job as Commercial Sales Manager of Rootes, and my wife is prepared to leave a good job as a furrier. We are both prepared to leave our house worth at least £60,000 to go to a rotton old pub in Stourport. If you are only prepared to give me a temporary licence then I won't go and I don't think anybody else will take it on, either. And if the brewery is prepared to spend £25,000 on renovations, then I think you should give them a full licence. I want to put the Swan on the map.' After a bit more discussion he agreed to give me a full licence.

'I married quite late in life and I wouldn't have done so then except that Irene proposed to me. I wasn't enthusiastic at first but it was the best thing I ever did. She was beautiful, chic, full of energy and charming - everybody loved her. She was the Swan much more than I was. Sometimes, at about 10.30 at night, she would bring a silver salver of sandwiches into the bar for anybody who happened to be in there. She was like that.

'We left home in Harborne and we came to the Swan in 1958. The rear car park was two overgrown bowling squares. The builders that were going to do the renovations had made a hole in the hedge in Lickhill Road, they pulled my car and my caravan through the hole and that's where we slept for two years. There was no room suitable to sleep in.

'The bar was completely enclosed by curved panels of stained glass. You had a round window for the customer to look through so that you could only see a face. If you slid another window up all you could see was the feet. We had two regulars, a cockroach and a rat. They used to appear behind the bar when we were serving, Irene used to talk to them. We didn't bother to do anything about them because we knew that the whole lot was coming down in a few months' time.

'We had two other characters as well. These were two Great Danes, Sheba and Buster. They would sit on the stairs at eleven o'clock at night waiting for permission to come in. Each of them would sit in a chair, so high up that, from the back, it looked as if a person was sitting there.

'In the late 1950's we closed for eighteen months and stripped the Swan right down to the cellar. The whole building had no inside, it was just standing on props and we walked on boards across the cellar. We started rebuilding from the cellar upwards. The front door had this beautiful etched glass, I thought it was a pity to throw it away and so it has been used in the lounge bar on the pillar on the right hand side. When a date was given us to open everyone was working right the way round the clock.

'We found a well down the cellar, it was beautiful water. We couldn't bottom it. We have covered it over with a two inch slate and it's under the concrete floor. Down in the cellar was an ingle nook which had been bricked up, I broke it down and at the back were thousands and thousands of cups, plates and saucers with PRHA on them. In the 1930's the hotel had been a member of the People's Refreshment House Association Limited.

'After we were refurbished we entertained many of the owners of local factories. They would come in about ten-thirty and say, 'Right, what can we eat?' and you would go and cook something. I would often work until two o'clock. We used to have Dr Murray, the boss of Worth's carpets, he used to draw his carpet designs on the back of plates while he was having his lunch. He used to say to me, 'I've done another design, can I take the plate?'. We had many famous names, such as the old England Footballer, Jessie Pennington, who captained England a couple of times.

'I used to have people ringing me up from all over the place trying to find somewhere to stay overnight. We only had eight bedrooms and most of these were taken by staff. I went to a Board meeting at Allied Breweries in Aston in 1963 and I said, 'If you only give me half of what we have lost in the area I can manage'. In the end they built a large block on the back and we had 32 bedrooms. When we pulled the cottages down at the back of the Swan to build the extension, the old fire badge was on the wall of one of them and I have kept it. The new wing opened on Friday, December 14th 1964.

'It was a very high class restaurant. If you weren't wearing a collar and tie then you were not allowed in. Irene was a Cordon Bleu cook, when we took over the pub she had done a crash course at the Birmingham School of Domestic Science and had passed with flying colours.

The White Lion, from which Lion Hill gets its name. The ' Society of Females' met here in the nineteenth century. Their motto was Unity, Goodness and Charity.

100

'We had a fire at the Swan in 1963. For three or four days beforehand we had smelt burning and I had gone round, inspecting everything. I couldn't find anything and assumed that, when we emptied the ashtrays into the bucket, some of the nub ends had still been burning. Above the bar were layers of insulating material and an electrical fault had developed which was sandwiched inbetween the various layers. This one Sunday morning the girl behind the bar told me that she could smell burning. I said that I had looked everywhere and couldn't find anything. We closed the bar, then when I unlocked in the afternoon and opened the door the fire just went 'whoosh' and straight up the stairs. We had to evacuate everybody.

'The fire brigade was only in Lombard Street and in those days the High Street had two-way traffic so it was here in minutes. A couple were trapped on the top floor and had to be rescued by the fire brigade with a ladder. A couple of the girls got burned fingers because they insisted on trying to rescue their personal possessions. I told them, 'Leave it, leave it'.

'It burned both bars. The fire was so hot the bottles melted and the smoke and the smell was everywhere. I utilised the bar in the dining room as a makeshift bar and carried on serving. It was three months before we were back to normal.

'We had a ghost at the Swan. Late one evening I went into the office, which in those days was on the first floor, and I had the impression of someone behind the glass panel on the reception desk, waiting for attention. Our largest dog was with me and his hackles rose. I switched the light on, but nobody was there. I happened to mention this to Irene afterwards and she said, 'Oh, you mean the old lady who stands by the window, I've spoken to her several times'. She described her as wearing a bonnet, rather like those worn by the ladies of the Salvation Army.

'We had to leave in 1972 because of Irene's health. The Swan was the only pub that we ever had."

THE WHITE LION

Although the White Lion, from which Lion Hill gets its name, was built mainly in 1820, it has brickwork on the end gables going back to the 1600s. This was the next most important hotel, after the Tontine and the Swan.

The landlord of the White Lion was Samuel Vaughan during the 1800s, who possessed strict Victorian morals and kept a watchful eye on his clients. Mr Vaughan also kept a fly-boat on the canal. In front of the Lion was an open space, used by the circus and other entertainments.

While the Tontine had its men's club, the White Lion had its club for ladies. It began in the middle of the nineteenth century and was entitled 'The Society of Females'. Their motto was 'Unity, goodness and charity'. One of the aims of the club was to afford relief in sickness and another was to provide a decent burial for husbands, if necessary. Not only were the aims of the Society unlike those of the 'Young Wives' or Women's Institutes of today, the membership was also very different. No-one over the age if 40 was allowed to join, nor anyone 'in any way maimed or distempered'. Many of the rules were similar to those of the Tontine. A little cup was brought in with the first measure of ale and if anyone drank otherwise than out of the cup they forfeited sixpence. Gossiping and swearing resulted in a twopenny fine while for quarrelling or fighting the fine was two shillings (about 10p). If any member was 'detected of theft, or murder, or lived a loose, idle or profligate life, or had a child born out of lawful wed-lock' she was excluded for ever. Stewardesses were appointed to see that there was a good clean room, a good fire when necessary, and good quality ale.

The White Lion closed down in about 1974 but it is now being refurbished.

THE RED LION or STEPS HOUSE

The Red Lion stood at the junction of Mitton Street, Gilgal and Worcester Road and the building predates the canal. Built as a house in 1723, it became a public house in the early 1800's and was closed by the public health authorities in 1967. It then remained derelict until it was bought by Mr Ivan Willetts in 1975 who rechristened it with its original name of Steps House.

ROUND O'BEEF

At one time it was the custom to allow regulars a free meal occasionally, perhaps on Sundays or Saints' days, and the public house was then named after the meal that it offered. This is perhaps how the Round o' Beef came by its name. Another possibility is that it was built on a piece of ground which was the shape of a round of beef. The pub stood at the entrance to Stour Lane (then known as Hell Lane) and on the side of Paradise Court, which was opposite. The landlord, Tereh Wainwright, gave the children names to match the location and his grandchildren followed the tradition. There was Abraham, Isaac and Jacob, followed by James, John and Titus (the friend of St Paul) and then Sarah (the wife of Abraham).

RING O'BELLS

The most romantic pub story comes from the Ring o'Bells. It was on the junction of Mitton Street and Gilgal, in an area known as Pall Mall. Isaac Wedley writes that the landlord had five daughters and one son and tells the following story:

Matthew Whittall was born in Kidderminster parish in 1843 and became a carpet works dyer.

He fell in love with one of the daughters, Jane, and had a house built for her in a picturesque spot near the centre of the town. The bridal dress was made but, sadly, before the wedding could take place, Jane died. A gravestone in Mitton churchyard simply states, 'In loving memory of Jane, who passed away on April 27th 1868; aged 24 years. However, only six months later the young man married Jane's sister, Nellie. They sold the house that he had built for Jane to the church organist, and emigrated to America.

For a few years everything went well. They had two children and his business did exceptionally well, then Nellie died.

A third sister was sent for who mothered the children, but this time, when Matthew remarried, he found a wife elsewhere. However, he made sure that this sister was well looked after. He built up the largest carpet manufacturing business owned by one man in the world.

Wedley adds: "Time rolled on, success and honour still followed him, until he became one of the richest manufacturers in the United States. From time to time he came back to Stourport, and before his last visit gave

Steps House, also once known as the Red Lion. Compare this photograph with the one on page 90 which shows Steps House in 1902. Six steps went up to the front door and there was also a flight of steps going up the far side of the house.

some of his wealth to his native town by erecting the beautiful Whittall Chapel attached to the parish church of Kidderminster, as a thank-offering for the blessings of his life."

The Whittall Memorial Chapel is still in St Mary's, Kidderminster. The Reverend Owain Bell, Priest-in-Charge, has checked in the old Parish magazines and discovered that the foundation stone was laid on 23 July 1921. One of the older active members actually remembers Mr Whittall. He died in Shrewsbury, Massachusetts on 31st October, 1922.

THE BRINDLEY ARMS

The Brindley Arms marks the site of the old railway station, for it was once known as the Station Hotel , the station being a few yards to the north. It was in the same family for 93 years, from 1881, when it was built, until it was sold in 1974. It was bought by Thomas Ketley. His grand-daughter used to help behind the bar, standing on an old beer crate to reach the taps.

THE OLD RISING SUN

Built in the early 1800's, the Old Rising Sun was run by three generations of the Hardwick family. The locals called the pub 'The Japanese Embassy'. The husbands used to say to their wives, 'I'm just visiting the embassy, dear'. The Hardwick family brewed their own beer and some locals joked that they used water out of the cut.

THE BRIDGE INN

Previous licensees have claimed that the pub is one of the oldest in England, dating back to 1670, but architects have given it a date of 1790. Beneath the pub is a secondary cellar which is now blocked up but is thought to be the entrance to a tunnel leading to the River Stour. The old timers say that the tunnel was used for smuggling port.

George and Kath Barber were licensees for fifteen years. George had been a licensee for many years at other pubs and he said that nowhere else did he encounter the strange events of the Bridge Inn.

Myke Pryce wrote in the Worcester Evening News of 28th June 1978:

"The Barbers had been at the Bridge for about three years before anything happened. It was a cold winter's night and the last customers had long since left. The fires were damped down and the bars were silent. George had already gone upstairs to bed, falling into a deep sleep almost as soon as his head hit the pillow. Downstairs, Kath was making a final check on door locks and light switches.

'She flicked a switch and plunged the bars into darkness before turning to go down the narrow passageway which led to the bottom of the staircase. Halfway along the passage was a telephone and as Kath passed she was aware of someone standing by it. She carried on for a few steps, thinking, absentmindedly, that it was their youngest daughter, Mal. "C'mon Mal, let's go to bed", she said wearily. Then suddenly Kath remembered - and looked round. Mal was in bed. Instead of her daughter, standing a few feet away, was a woman in a pink crinoline dress. She remained by the phone, motionless, as Kath stared for a few seconds, paralysed by surprise, before dashing upstairs.

'George was still fast asleep and when she told him of her experience the next morning, he laughed. However, something was beginning to click

The Old Rising Sun, built in the early 1800's.

into place. Across the corridor from the phone was a door leading down to the pub cellar. Now although George regularly went into the cellar to deal with the beer barrels, neither the Barber's golden retriever dog, Ringo, nor their cat would set a foot even on the cellar steps. Both refused to have anything to do with the room.

'A few months passed and Kath remained convinced that she really had seen something out of the ordinary that night, while George remained sceptical. Then one evening he changed his mind.

'The barbers were both watching television in their room at the back of the pub when the door to the bar counter opened and into the room drifted the Crinolined Lady. As she passed in front of the television Kath looked at her husband's face which was a picture of disbelief. The dog, which had been asleep, leapt to his feet and his hackles stood stiff as a hedgehog, but he didn't bark or move to attack the apparition.

'Slowly the Crinolined Lady passed through the room and at the opposite end a door into the kitchen opened and she disappeared as swiftly as she had arrived. Neither the kitchen nor the bar door closed

behind her. "Perhaps you'll believe me now" Kath exclaimed to her husband."

Mr Lovelock took over in July 1997. He says:

"I was working in the bar late one night. Some people had stayed on, talking, after I had locked up so I let them out of the side door. While I was doing this I had the feeling that somebody was watching me. I returned to

The Bridge Inn dates back to about 1790. The ghost of a crinolined lady walks the premises.

The Holly Bush, a seventeenth century inn, known to be one of the oldest public houses in Stourport.

the bar and was tidying up when to my amazement I saw this lady walk the full length of the bar. I saw her as clearly as ABC. She appeared at the bottom end of the bar and went all the way through it, into the new part of the building. She didn't walk, she glided across and she didn't look at me. She was in her 30's or 40's, tall with long dark curly hair and she was wearing a creamy-white Victorian costume. It came up under the breast and flared out from the waist. I could only see her top half - the top three feet - because I was behind the bar. When I had got over my surprise I searched the building but, of course, nobody was about.

7. O Come All Ye Faithful!

Every church has its own heartbeat, its own flavour and potential, reflecting the needs and strengths of its members and its environment.

Reverend Andrew Vessey, Rural Dean, Areley Kings

SAINT MICHAEL AND ALL ANGELS

Bishop Philpot, when in residence at Hartlebury Castle, said that Saint Michael and All Angels stood on the most beautiful site in the county for a House of the Lord.

A tiny stone Chapel of Ease stood here, as far back as 1195, when Richard the Lion Heart was on the throne. Incredibly, we have the name of the first priest, Father Philip, who probably trudged all the way from the mother church at Kidderminster every Sunday to minister to his scattered flock. The chapel had a tiny income from a few fields. The present High Street runs across one of those fields, another gave Wallfield Bridge its name. The ground around the church was consecrated in 1625 so that local people would not have to carry their dead all the way to Kidderminster to be buried. In 1707 the church was repaired by the local inhabitants and a loft was added by the Wilmot family who owned iron mills on the Stour.

When the canal was built and the new town arrived it was obvious that the tiny chapel was too small. It was also 'very ruinous and decayed' and so, in 1791 a new red-bricked church was built by James Rose. In appearance it was very much like the present Wolverley Church, which is of the same date.

During the early 1800s a religious revival swept England and the nineteenth century was marked by a seriousness of thought and self-discipline. Family prayers and bible-readings were common, and nearly everyone attended Church. Vicars and Ministers had tremendous power and were often described as 'the Parish Patriarchs'.

The enormous churchyard serves both the Church of England and the Methodists. Most of it is overgrown and a high proportion of the tombstones are illegible. It is probably the largest in the country and contains the foundations of the Rose church. This is where the characters from old Stourport now lie, the men who worked the canal and those who filled the streets - 28 members of the Baldwin family, Aaron York of York House, William Heywood the preacher, Nicholson the printer, Reverend David Davies, Richard Evans of the Baptist Church, Thomas Bond Worth, John Murray (a veteran of Trafalgar), and George Harris (the oldest carpet manufacturer) - all are here, together with reminders of past tragedies. One stone is to the minister's daughter who fell from the rock at Redstone into the Severn beneath. Elsewhere is an 1840's monument to Peter and Mary Groves whose three children predeceased them.

The 1791 church by James Rose, pulled down in 1919. The foundations can still be seen in the churchyard.

The old vicarage, now demolished. Reverend Gibbons decided that this vicarage was not grand enough and moved to Waresley House. Courtesy A T H Baylis and Worcestershire Record Office.

Underneath the name of the first child to be buried runs the strange line:

> *Mother lie by me.*
> Beneath the second the line is:
> *Mother take me away.*
> Below the third the line is:
> *Mother let me go.*

Wedley thinks these must have been the last words of the children.

Reverend Wharton came to Stourport as schoolmaster to the sons of well-to-do classes, became assistant to the Reverend Davies and succeeded him in 1829. He was an energetic, active man. The church was found to be too small under his ministry and so, in 1835, it was decided to widen the aisles so that the church would seat 640. He arranged for more than half the seats to be free, a great step forward. He organised the funding and building of a boys' school, a girls' school, an infant's school and a parsonage. Part of the boy's school was called the Wharton Memorial.

Stourport had been one of the first churches in England to have an organ when a barrel organ was installed in 1806. Revered Wharton persuaded the church to replace it with a pipe organ in 1837 and had the gallery floor lowered especially to take it. He then had problems getting someone to play it for the small salary offered.

Assisting the Reverend Wharton was the sexton, Charles Everton. One of his most important duties was the ringing of the bells, especially so when few people had watches. His daughter, Sarah, married Joe Wakeman from Bewdley who took over as sexton. Sarah was the local post lady, scurrying round in a grey shawl and bonnet. She was the last of a family who were sextons for over a hundred years.

On Sundays, Joe Wakeman had to combine ringing bells with pumping the bellow for the church organ. The old organ was moved into the west gallery in 1888, next to the bells, to make life easier for him. He would give a good few pumps on the bellows, pop out from behind the organ to give the bell a pull, return to the bellows and so on. Joe was meticulous in his time-keeping. In the early morning when the passing bell was tolled from seven to eight, the first stroke was invariably with the clang of the tannery clock, and the sixtieth, one minute before eight. Only once was he known to fail. He had been sitting up with a sick child several nights in succession and was tired out. One Sunday morning, during the sermon he lay down on one of the benches and went to sleep. When the time came for the final hymn, the organ wheezed and groaned but not a single note came out. No-one was pumping the bellows. Joe was found stretched out full length with his arms under his head, fast asleep.

The vicar preached in his black gown and hour long sermons were normal. Wedley tells of the farmer who went to sleep in a sermon. The word 'Commentator' was very popular in Victorian times meaning a person who made a regular series of explanatory notes on the work of an author or a book. An old farmer had become drowsy during a sermon and had just 'come to' as the preacher spoke of the works of 'great commentators'. Next day he was surprised to receive a bag of potatoes from the farmer who said he was sorry that the vicar had to put up with common taters and please accept the bag which he guaranteed as being good.

Reverend Gibbons

Reverend Wharton was succeeded in 1854 by Reverend Waller. However, it was the Reverend Benjamin Gibbons who put his stamp on the town and a road has been named after him. He was given the living of Saint Michaels in 1861, a kind, wealthy man who believed that his wealth was held by him in trust for the benefit of all. Wherever there was need, Reverend Gibbons was to be found. He was tall and broad, an imposing figure made more so because he always insisted on wearing his black gown and mortar board.

He appointed two or three curates, mostly paid for from his own pocket, to minister to his flock. They lived in Saint Michaels Lodge, a large redbrick house standing where the traffic lights are now. The house had huge cellars which were used for storage. Later it was used as a lodging house.

Although Vestry Meetings were held in the church vestry, they covered the general life of the town and anybody could attend. At one of these meetings in 1857, it was decided that a new church was essential for the growing needs of the town. Reverend Gibbons therefore asked one of the leading architects of the day, Sir Gilbert Scott RA, to design one. Sir Gilbert provided two designs, one had a magnificent tower and spire, the other was a modified version costing £11,000 and seating 900. The designs were exhibited at the prestigious Royal Academy in London, where they were highly praised, and the more grandiose scheme was selected. However, the parishioners were rather taken aback when they found that the cost of building this new church would be £29,000.

Reverend Gibbons began asking around for donations. Local businessmen pledged £10,000 but this was hedged around with so many clauses and conditions that most of it was quite valueless. By 1883, £4,000 had been raised and work began on a site to the north of the old church. Mr Smith was employed who was both a church member and a local builder, and the foundation stone was laid on March 25th 1887

Mr Smith was such a terrible builder that only one year after he had been working on the church, it needed extensive repairs and Reverend Gibbons sued him for £150. Mr Smith was not popular. An old manuscript states that 'no-one should molest, slander, roast, spit at or otherwise insult the said Smith'. Mr Smith left the Anglican Church and joined the Methodists.

For some years, the church stood in this half-built state. Darlington's Handbook Advertiser of 1897 reads:

108

"On arriving at Stourport, the first object that strikes us is what at first sight appears to be the ruins of a church, but upon closer examination we discover it to be a modern fabric."

The ruins were christened locally 'Mitton Abbey' or 'Gibbons Folly'. After a few years, work began again, this time paid for entirely by Reverend Gibbons, who probably spent about £15,000 on the building. Reverend Gibbons resigned in 1894 after 33 years at Stourport. Fourteen years later the church was still not finished, by 1908 only the nave was nearing completion. Reverend Gibbons came to an arrangement with the Bishop of Worcester, whereby he sold the building to the Bishop for £1,250, then the Worcester Diocesan offered both church and site to the parish free, on the condition that the church should be completed. The parishioners arranged for each end of the church to be filled in with temporary brickwork so that it could be consecrated in 1910. Reverend Gibbons was therefore able to worship in the building, although it lacked the western tower and chancel, before he died in 1912.

Perhaps the townsfolk preferred their old red brick church. On the last Sunday before it was to be pulled down in 1919 three services were held in the old church, each one packed to capacity.

During the ministry of Reverend Gibbons a long list of developments had taken place. He had built a new school at Tan Lane in Upper Mitton and had enlarged both the boys' and the girls' schools. He had established a Mission Room in Raven Street, installed a splendid new organ by Hope-Jones, enlarged the churchyard, and added Upper Mitton, West Hartlebury and part of Kidderminster to the parish. He could have been behind many of Stourport's other improvements. Societies and organisations in Stourport blossomed while he was Rector. One of his curates, Reverend Barber, had been a member of a University boat crew and trained the Stourport crew.

Wedley tells a story about Reverend Barber who was often in trouble with his peers.

Sir George Gilbert Scott's proposed design for a new church in 1876. It proved to be too expensive, and the chancel and tower, as designed, were never built, as shown in the photograph above. The ends were filled in with temporary brickwork in 1910. A modified chancel was added in about 1966 but the west end was badly damaged in the storms of 1976 and the church was demolished.
Courtesy Kidderminster Library (drawing) and Ray Franks (photo)

"... on one occasion he appeared in the pulpit in a pair of grey trousers which peeped below his surplice. This irreverence was reported to the Vicar who reported it to the Bishop. The Bishop asked for the offending trousers to be submitted to him. After a critical examination, the dear old man assured the offending curate that 'he should be happy if he had as good a pair'."

During the 1930's and 1940's the choir of St Michael's had an excellent reputation. This was partly because the choirmaster was Roland Gregory, teacher and brother of the headmaster at the boys' school in Bewdley Road. As a small boy, Roy Crowe was selected for the choir:

"When you joined the class for music lessons he picked out anybody with a voice and told them to go and join the choir. That's how I became a choirboy. On special occasions we used to sing from the roof, you used to be able to get up into the roof through a spiral staircase in the tower. Bob Evans was Head Boy on our side and Bob Forbes was Head Boy on the other side and we were up to all kinds of pranks. One morning,

Evans and I found a dead mouse in the vestry so we put it in Forbes' hymn book at the first hymn, squashing it flat between the pages. When he walked into the church as choirboy to the congregation we were bursting with anticipation to see what happened. What we didn't know was that the Server had seen us do it so he had taken it out of Forbes' book and put it in Evans' book. Evans looked down and there was the mouse in his book."

The temporary brickwork in the church remained until 1957, when the Bishop of Worcester launched an appeal for £10,000 to complete the West End. The appeal took seven years to reach its target, and then only achieved it because the Reverend Cecil Chesshire made a large donation. His brother had been vicar of the church from 1915 to 1920. Gilbert Scott's design had to be modified to meet costs. Even so, it was the largest Parish church in the country and locals say that it was so huge that it gave them the feeling of being in a cathedral. A sad irony was that Reverend Gibbons lay, with his wife, in the chancel, which he wanted so much to build but which was never completed during his lifetime.

Unfortunately, neither Reverend Gibbons nor the church were to rest in peace. Only ten years after Saint Michaels was completed it was badly damaged in the terrible storms of January 1976. Roof slates and timbers were blown out of the new facing at the west end of the church. Two cars parked nearby were damaged by falling masonry. Health and Safety Inspectors declared the building unsafe and church members were grateful for an offer from the United Reform Church to hold services in their building.

A Parochial Church Council was held to decide what to do. Of the twenty people present, seven wanted the old building repaired and thirteen voted to knock down all but the south wall of the old church and turn the turret into a Bell Tower. The locals were scandalised when they heard that just thirteen people had decided that the church should be pulled down. The battle of old versus new went on for three years. Finally, the Chancellor of the Worcester Diocese Consistory Court gave the go-ahead for demolition. A competition was organised for the construction of a modern church, a number of designs were submitted and the entry from the architects Snell and Thompson was chosen. The estimated

110

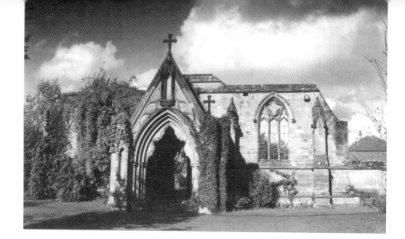

Two photographs of the spectacular ruins of Gilbert Scott's church, as they appear today. The lower photograph shows the new church sited inthe centre of the ruin.

cost was £60,000. The old church was so solidly built that the builders had difficulty knocking it down.

The saga was not yet over. In 1979 Saint Michaels featured in the least likeliest of magazines for a parish church, 'Private Eye'. The magazine claimed that the Vicar had sold the church organ pipes to a scrap dealer for their tin value, ignoring government orders to preserve the church's internal fittings. The Hope-Jones organ installed by Reverend Gibbons had become a collector's item, Hope-Jones being a pioneer in electric organs and Saint Michaels possessing a particularly fine and early example. The Vicar said that he had tried to sell it in one piece but it was so huge no-one wanted it. It had been dismantled, some parts had gone to a Worcester museum and others to a school in Birmingham. The rest had gone to a Birmingham dealer in church furniture.

The foundation stone of a new church to be shared by the Church of England and the United Reformed Church was laid in April 1980 inside the ruins of Scott's church by the Bishop of Worcester, the Rt Reverend Robin Woods, and Reverend Ivor Howells of the United Reformed Church. It had cost £157,000.

John Wesley

METHODISTS

Stourport was one of the earliest and most important centres of Methodism, and it possesses one of the movement's most interesting churches. The Methodist Society was established in the town as early as 1781.

John Wesley himself came to Stourport on 25th March 1787 and preached at a makeshift meeting place at the back of a house in New Street. In those days, anyone who did not worship at the established church was regarded with suspicion and hostility, and John Wesley was attacked by a rough crowd. Mr Hill and Mr Rowley went to his rescue, together with Aaron York (to whom he wrote his last letter).

Members of the Church of England seem to have treated him with more respect. In John Wesley's journals he speaks with delight of a Church of England clergyman named Heath and his charming daughters. When Wesley preached, several clergymen came to hear him, and he remarked that 'they appeared as attentive as the rest'.

On 21st March 1788, almost a year after his first visit, John Wesley was again at Stourport, this time to open a tiny Methodist chapel standing on the present site off Parkes Passage. It was registered for worship the following October and two years later Wesley again preached there. Stourport, therefore, has one of the oldest Wesleyan Methodist churches in England and one of the few where John Wesley himself preached.

The Methodist church in Parkes Passage.

An old oak pulpit stood in the middle of the church, and there were two red curtains, the one hid the singers except when they stood up and the other separated the seats of the paid pews from the free seats. The men sat on one side of the church and the women on the other and there was a great scandal the day that one woman moved across to sit next to her husband.

In the same year that the foundation stone was laid, Stourport was chosen to be head of the Worcestershire Methodist Circuit. This was a great honour as the circuit was 24 miles across and included larger towns such as Kidderminster. Many well-known Methodists were nurtured at Stourport, including three Presidents of Conference. A team of ministers lived at a house in Lichfield Street and, on a Sunday, each minister would walk miles to preach at a church within the Circuit. No matter what the weather, they struggled to fulfil their duty. One nearly lost his life in snow up to his neck on the Clee Hills. Another, John Mantle, walked eleven miles through snow to preach at Frith Common. When he arrived there, the church members evidently thought he could not have made his way through the snow, for the church was locked. He had to turn round and walk the eleven miles back home.

Sculptures from the Ward Memorial, the Last Supper, head of Abraham and the pulpit.
Courtesy Rev Booth

One very dark night, Reverend John Saunders went to preach at Kidderminster. He was walking back home along the canal path when he stumbled and fell into the water. Isaac Wedley writes:

"He succeeded in getting out, and with much disgust and a lot of spluttering, said, 'Just think of it! Three times have I crossed the Atlantic, and then to be nearly drowned in a dirty puddle like this.'"

The Baldwins were enthusiastic Methodists. The father-in-law of Enoch Baldwin, the Bewdley MP, was a Methodist minister who worked on the Stourport circuit. Thomas Joseph Baldwin, born in 1830 and grandson of the original Thomas, was choirmaster. He copied out all the music for the singers into books, arranging it in the correct order and he brought out a book of chants and psalms for the use of the congregation. He also insured his life so that on his death the debt on the Methodist Chapel was cancelled. He died unexpectedly when he was only 50 while on holiday, and the whole town turned out to mourn at his funeral.

The Methodists installed one of the first pipe organs in 1835. Previously, they had sung to a bass viol, occasionally accompanied by a flute.

The church was altered and enlarged in 1812 and 1857, taking on its present appearance in 1874. The interior is unusually decorative because of the Ward Bequest. Joseph Ward lived in Bridge Street and was a stonemason, a surveyor to the local Government Board and he owned a building company. He built the first new houses in Mitton Gardens, the great chimney stack of the Tannery and another at the textile works. He was one of

the pillars of the church. He had innumerable responsibilities, among them that of Sunday School Superintendent. Originally, the chapel was a plain square building with three galleries, then in 1894, Joseph Ward decided to create a memorial to his father, Thomas Ward. He ordered a number of alabaster panels and, over the next few years, devoted his liesure time to carving them for the interior of the church. The pulpit and the entire front of the chancel has carvings of scenes from the Bible, various Biblical characters, John Wesley, Passion flowers, etc. Joseph Ward died in 1902.

In the church is a window dedicated to Thomas Henry Ganderton (1856-1943). His father had been a popular police constable at Stourport. Thomas owned several houses in Prospect Road and lived at number seven. For over 40 years he was Stourport's rate collector, not a popular occupation but this kind, gentle, intelligent man was regarded with affection by everyone. He was a Borough Councillor for twelve years and at one time or another he held an official position in at least six local societies. He was a co-founder of the Guild of Help and he helped to nurse the Literary Institute through its development into the Workmen's Club. When he reached his eightieth birthday the club held a great surprise party in his honour, with a telegram from the Prime Minister (Stanley Baldwin) and a cake with 80 candles. He married twice, his first wife was Sarah Ann Landon (1856-1921) and it was his second wife, Mary Maria Ganderton - a cousin (1873-1963), who arranged for the window to be installed. In the year 2000, the print shop in York Street decided to clear the attic where they discovered boxes of photographs and memorabilia from the Ganderton family. A descendent, Sylvia Young, was traced who had been working on the family history for four years. She said that the discovery was better than winning the lottery. 'It's the kind of thing you dream about but which rarely happens'.

During the 1980's, disaster struck. Fred Rimmel explains:

"My wife and I attend the Methodist church and in the early 1980's we were evicted, owing to what I call 'The Stourport Blight'. When the town was first developed, most of the land had a leasehold of 200 years. Nobody bothered about it very much but then, in the 1980's, a lot of people discovered that they didn't own the land that their buildings were standing on. Some of the shopkeepers in the town were put out of business because they couldn't afford to buy their leases. We discovered that the land on which the Methodist Church stood belonged to a local family. They, naturally, hoped to realise their assets and we were evicted. They offered us the freehold but we couldn't afford to buy it. Fortunately, the church is a listed building and the owners of the lease were unable to sell the site for any type of development. Three years later the site had still not been sold so they reduced the asking price by two-thirds. In the meantime, we had been frantically fund-raising which meant that by that time we had sufficient funds to purchase the freehold and we were able to move back into the church."

PRIMITIVE METHODISM

A group broke away from the Wesleyan church in 1812 and founded Primitive Methodism. Wesleyans were thought of as being 'High Church' and dominated by the clergy. A second chapel was built by the Primitive Methodists in Lickhill Road. In 1932 most of the various branches of Methodism united and the Lickhill Road Chapel joined the same circuit as the Parkes Passage Wesleyan Church. Later, the Circuit decided to close the Lickhill Road Chapel but some of the members objected and they established a free Church nearby called Vernon Hall, which is still a place of worship today.

CONGREGATIONALISTS

A little later, in about 1865, Congregationalist doctrine became popular. First they met in Mr Bickerton's cottage (the barber) near the Round o' Beef, but as their cause grew they transferred to the Woolpack in 1867, then to a house in Raven Street. Finally, the first church was built in about 1877 on the site of an old barn on the corner of Mitton Street and Vale Road. The MP for Kidderminster laid the foundation stone in which were various artefacts representing the 1870's. Despite the torrents of rain and the absence of Reverend Gibbons who disapproved of the new church, an enthusiastic crowd made the event one to remember.

The Congregationalists devoted a great deal of time, energy and money to their Church. They managed to raise the funds to pay for the building of the church in five years. An organ costing £160 was paid for in two months. The organ blower's salary was met by each church member giving one penny per month which was more than adequate to cover the salary of thirteen shillings a year (65p).

They were not able to afford a minister for thirteen years. During the early years a Mr Potter from Kidderminster used to come and give Tonic Sol-fa classes. Then Reverend Ellis Davenport arrived. Not only was he a knowledgeable theologian but he was also famous for his bees. He lectured on bee-keeping and was asked for advice from all over the country. Wedley says,

"He would put his hands in a cluster of bees as if they were blackcurrants. Reverend Davenport was asked to move a swarm of bees from Burlish House to Great Witley but instead of taking them himself, he asked a local green-grocer, Mr Jones, to do it. When Mr Jones reached Dick Brook, just beyond Dunley, a sudden swerve upset the trap, breaking the hives and releasing thousands of infuriated bees. Mr Jones was quickly enveloped and was a pitiful sight but the donkey was worse and they stung him to death."

They also built a Temperance Hall on the Bewdley Road. The old Congregational Church was purchased by the Roman Catholics in the 1970's.

Reverend Richard Evans

BAPTISTS

Halfway through the 1800s the first Baptists arrived in Stourport. Richard Evans had worked in the tannery at Leominster and moved to Stourport-on-Severn when he was offered a post in the tannery here. He and his wife arrived at a house in Tan Lane with a wagon load of furniture. Perched precariously on the top was a twelve-year old boy, Richard Evans Junior.

They managed to make contact with a few Baptists in Bewdley who tramped across three miles of empty countryside each Sunday to worship with them. Three years later there were ten of them, enough to hire the corrugated iron Temperance Hall in Bewdley Road, built by the Congregationalists and seating 300. After some years, their flock had grown to such an extent that they decided to build their own church and with this in mind they bought a piece of land on the corner of Prospect Road and the Minster Road.

The Temperance Hall stood on a piece of land owned by John Brinton. Mr Brinton decided he wanted to use the ground, therefore the Temperance Hall had to be removed. This meant that the Baptists had a piece of land but no hall and the Congregationalists had a hall but no land. It was agreed that the Temperance Hall was to be put on the land bought by the Baptists.

Mr and Mrs Evans guaranteed the continuity of the Baptist Church by encouraging their son to take over the ministry. Richard Evans Junior became leader of the church in 1875, when he was 36 years of age, and remained as pastor for 53 years. He has been described as a big man with a big black beard and a voice to match. An honorary pastor, he never received a penny for his work. He paid his way by running two businesses, a grocery shop with a large bread round in the High Street (where Barclays' Bank is now) and another store and post office in Baldwin Road. Reverend Evans was very highly regarded in the town, he was a Justice of the Peace, a member of the local council, and was elected Chairman of the Stourport Urban District Council (a position equivalent to mayor) in 1911.

In 1882, two young men, Mr Goodman and Mr Price, asked for baptism and church membership but the Temperance Hall had no baptistry for adult baptisms. The two members said that this didn't matter, they still wanted to be baptised in their home town and would be baptised in the Severn. It was pointed out to them that the river was far too dangerous so they settled for the canal.

Saint Wulstan and Saint Thomas Canterbury Roman Catholic church buildings.

116

The Baptists finally managed to build their own church and the foundation stone was laid in 1883. An organ was provided by Roland B Worth, the carpet manufacturer, who had installed it in his home but later, understandably, decided he wanted to sell it and offered it to the church for £200.

A few years later the Baptists decided that they needed a schoolroom so, in 1895, they held a bazaar in the Town Hall which was opened by Stanley Baldwin. The school was, of course, built by Vales.

Reverend Evans remained as pastor until he was 87 years of age and enjoyed six years of retirement before he died.

ROMAN CATHOLICS

Nora and Kathleen were born in the last years of the nineteenth century and wrote this account of the origins of the Roman Catholic Church before they died a few years ago, aged 99 and 94 respectively.

"We lived with our parents, James and Bridget Thomas, in Swan passage (off the High Street), Stourport-on-Severn, where we were all born. There were three of us, two girls and one boy, Norah, Kathleen and James. Our garden is now the Swan car park.

To get to church at St Ambrose's, Kidderminster, we had to walk both ways as the trams did not commence in time for us to get to communion at 8 am. It was compulsory in those days for monthly confession and communion and we were not allowed even a drink of water before we went.

'We cannot remember a Mass in a pub but our parents did speak of some sort of meeting in the Raven pub, Raven Street. The room was called a mission room and served all sorts of gatherings.

'The first Mass in Miss Randle's Tea Rooms (in Bridge Street) was some time before 1911 as our mother attended and took us three children, and she died in December 1911. The tea room was always crowded in the summer months with visitors to the town needing tea. Afterwards we had to clear the room for Mass the next morning. The altar was an ordinary table standing on blocks to make it high, with a curtain at the back and a small square of carpet in front. A couple of vases for flowers, chairs to form pews and the room was ready. The parishioners, all 25 of them, were able to hear Mass on Sunday mornings at 9.30 am once a month."

Nora and Kathleen's two daughters (the third generation) add the following comments:

"Miss Randle's tea rooms were in Bridge Street, next to Bufton's and at the back of a cake shop. They were probably once stables but they had been turned into a tea room, they're now derelict. A priest used to come visiting Catholic families in Stourport and he walked from Kidderminster. Although the families had nothing, they used to club together to find him the tram fare to go home.

'Our grandmother, Bridget, had severe asthma and on her walk to St Ambrose she often had to hang over a gate to get her breath back. The nuns would give Bridget and her three children a cup of tea and a thin slice of bread and butter to prepare them for the journey home. James Thomas (our grandfather) was not a Catholic but when Bridget died he made sure that the children were brought up in the faith as she would have wished. Father O'Dowd paid for Kathleen to go to school at Saint Ambrose in Kidderminster so that she could teach Nora and James the catechism.

'We weren't a parish then, not until 1948. Our first church building was in Lodge Road, built in about 1935, and it had 72 seats. A house was given for the parish priest by Mrs Morris. After the war, the Polish and the Irish came and we had to extend it to take 100 seats."

The Church continued to grow. Mr F W M Raybould, a member of the Roman Catholic church, continues:

"The Archdiocese therefore purchased in about 1959 a building in Vale Road that had previously served as a school, a public library and (during World War II) as a British Restaurant. Congregation sizes continued to grow and eventually a new church was built on the Vale Road site, being officially opened on 22nd December 1973. The church authorities then bought from the County Council the adjacent Weights and Measures Office, which they linked to the main church to serve as living accommodation for the parish priest, who had previously lived in a house in Minster Road.

'The next major development in the parish's history was the purchase of the nearby Congregational Church building on the corner of Mitton Street and Vale Road, built in 1877. In 1982 it was opened as a Parish Community Centre. Then in 1992, a new presbytery was built on the side of the church, the old County Council unit servicing now as office and kitchen facilities. A Roman Catholic school was opened in Lickhill Road during the 1980's catering for children aged from five to eleven. From there they go to Hagley High School"

WILLIAM HAYWOOD

Of all the new denominations, none met the evangelical standards set by William Haywood.

William Haywood was such a forceful and earnest character that some of his ideas reverberated through the Midlands. Charles Hadfield mentions in his canal books that Stourport in 1839 rebelled against Sunday working. This was no doubt because of our William.

He was born in West Bromwich in 1795 and came to Stourport as a young man to work in the cast iron hollowware factory. He had a fine physique, tall and well-proportioned. He was a member of the Methodist church and no-one dared go to sleep during the sermon when William Haywood was there. He would march over, prod the offender with a knobbed stick and tell him off. Yet he was a very likeable person. He had a disagreement with Isaac Wedley's father and at midnight, there was a loud knocking at Wedley's door. The family scrambled out of bed and opened the front door to find William standing there, asking for a reconciliation. The Methodist church must of been a little suspicious of him because he was never allowed to become a fully accredited preacher.

And preach he did - all the time! His one thought was that of saving his fellow men from hell and damnation. He was often arrested for preaching in the streets or for standing outside a factory preaching against Sunday working. Once, when he was before the court and the magistrate asked him to show his preaching licence, he held up his Bible and, in his powerful voice which rang round the court room, he boomed: ' Isaiah 58, first verse, Cry aloud, spare not, lift up thy voice like a trumpet'. The magistrate told him to go away. On another occasion when he was in the cells he sang all his favourite hymns so loudly that he was set free. Often, on Sundays he walked to Birmingham and back so that he could preach in the streets there. He was known right across the Black Country.

One of his favourite topics was against working on Sundays. He stopped the Bishop driving to church and reminded him that he should not work on Sundays. Joseph Rogers of the Tannery once opened on a Sunday and William wrote to him so forcefully that he never opened on a Sunday again.

People were a little afraid of William as he was said to have divine powers. Mitton Mill began working on Sundays, so he held a service outside and the owners threatened to let their savage dog loose on him. William was undeterred, and the next Sunday stood outside the Mill singing 'I'll praise my Maker when I've breath'. The dog was let loose and shot out ferociously but when it saw William it wagged its tail, lay at his feet and licked his shoe. After that, the factory closed on Sundays and a large joint of meat mysteriously arrived at the Haywood household, evidently as a peace-offering. The village wake at Rock was held on both a Saturday and a Sunday. William went on the Sunday and prayed that God would send something to convince the people of their sin. Immediately a great storm arose, which blew down tents, overthrew stands and scattered the items on sale. The people were terrified. From that day onwards there has been no wake held at Rock on a Sunday. His favourite walk was along the towpath from Bewdley to Stourport. He came across a gang of workmen cursing and swearing because their barge had stuck in the shallows at Blackstone Ford in low water. He said that if they stopped swearing, he would drop on his knees and pray, and at the same time they must all heave together. They did this and the boat glided into the water.

In May 1868, William's wife died. Every night he stood over the grave of his wife and sang a hymn. In the September he went to work as usual but didn't feel well. His son took him home and put him to bed where he died, aged 74. In those days there was no retirement age and no state pension. Ordinary people worked until the end of their days.

8. The Happiest Days of Your Life

Most pavements had hopscotches chalked on them. Every group of houses had its own hopscotch and there was an unwritten rule that you only played on your own, never on anybody else's. We played marbles, conkers, top and whip, we bowled hoops and we played tippet, a stupid game where you had to hit a little stick with a big stick and make it jump. When we got fed up with playing in the road, we could go off to the park. The mysterious thing was, nobody ever said when it was time to put away one toy and get out another one but one day everybody would be playing, say, marbles, and the next day top and whip.

People didn't worry so much in those days. My family moved to Kidderminster for a few years and I was only about seven when I used to come back to Stourport on the tram all by myself to stay with my grandmother. I had my sandwiches in a little sixpence-halfpenny bag made of cardboard from Woolworth's, together with my nighty and my spare money tied up in a handkerchief. I had stern instructions not to touch the money. The conductress used to look after me and make sure I was alright. The terminus was outside the Crown Hotel and I had quite a long walk to my grandmother's from there.

Retired resident

James Brindley has sometimes been criticised for his lack of written instructions but the fact is that when he surveyed, designed and supervised the building of his canals, probably only about half of his employees would have been able to read. There are now eleven schools in the Stourport area offering free education. When Brindley built his canal there were none. All education had to be paid for, consequently many children never attended school

Here was an opportunity for the spinster, the disabled and the elderly, to earn a living. Almost anyone could open a school. Hardly any qualifications were required and there was virtually no inspection of premises. Nearly every street had its school, seminary or, in one case, academy. For a few pennies each week a teacher took charge of young children, usually from three to eight years old. Betty Purser in Parkes Passage was a cripple but 'a good and patient soul'. She held her school on hard benches in her front room under a row of geraniums on the window-sill. Miss Eliza Smith Rutter had a ladies' seminary in the High Street, later moving to York Street. Elizabeth Gissack educated 14 girls in New Street. In describing Lionel Stanton's "academy" in Raven Street, Isaac Wedley remarks 'Here the young and well-to-do hopefuls received chastisement of such a nature that the master's very name was hated and his terrible birch frequently drew blood'. Occasionally a school was of a high standard, Reverend Davies of Saint Michaels educated gentleman's sons at his house, Belle View, in Sion Gardens.

The Church had a centuries old tradition of providing education, and, a few years after Stourport came into being, it devised a system by which it could provide free education - Sunday Schools. Every Sunday, children would be taken to or from church services to be crammed into a room where a voluntary worker (often of dubious educational standards) would teach them to read and write.

As there were two denominations in Stourport, the Church of England and the Methodists, there were two Sunday Schools. Religious principles were taught as well as the 3 R's. Children received lessons on piety, chastity, thoughtfulness and other Christian virtues, as well as those characteristics which the upper classes found convenient in the lower classes, such as obedience, discipline and loyalty. Any form of decoration, ostentation or individuality was frowned upon. Two of the teachers of the girl's Sunday School were Miss Barnett and Mrs Joel Brown. One Sunday, to their horror, a little girl appeared with a few white daises in her hat. Miss Barnett gently took the child aside after school and putting her arm round her suggested that she did without them as it was such a bad example to the other children.

The Methodists used a building in front of their church in Parkes Passage. The boys were taught downstairs and the girls upstairs, reaching the schoolroom by an outdoor staircase. The scholars from Saint Michael's C of E had to make do with a room in Raven Street catering for both boys and girls. Every Sunday the scholars would walk two by two in a long crocodile all the way through the town from Raven Street to the Church of England to take part in the service. They sat in the galleries, boys on one side, girls on the other. William Horton was one of the church officials and when one of the boys caused a disturbance William would wait at the door, then as they filed past him on the way out it would be 'whack' under the left ear and another on the right to keep him from falling.

During the 1800's education for the poor became one of England's major charities, and funds were raised to build day schools. They usually came under the auspices of the Anglican National Society and were therefore known as National Schools.

Thomas Shaw, of Burlish, died in the 1830's. He happened to have a wealthy brother, William, living in Worcester who decided that, as a memorial to his brother, he would build a National Girl's School in Church Avenue, near to the Parish church. The ongoing costs were met by public subscriptions, payment by the children and a small endowment from the will of Richard Heath. By the middle of the century it had 100 scholars.

1839 saw the beginning of state grants to primary schools. Encouraged by the prospect of state funding, National Schools blossomed. The Reverend Wharton built one in 1840 near to Baldwin's Foundry for the children of workmen. The first schoolmaster was William Eaton who held his post for more than thirty years. Schoolmasters were only paid a pittance and Mr Eaton augmented his salary in a number of ways. He kept a stationer's shop on the corner of New Street which afterwards became the disastrous Coffee Tavern. He was also an officer in the Volunteer Rifle Corps, a first secretary to the Gas Company, secretary of the local Book Club and churchwarden.

Pigot's Directory of 1841 also lists a National School in Bridge Street.

Primitive Methodist Chapel Class in Lickhill Road, about the 1920s.
Courtesy Kidderminster Library.

123

By the time the Reverend Wharton retired as Vicar in 1854, he had managed to raise enough funds to buy a piece of ground in Bewdley Road (opposite the present police station) from the Rogers family and had built a boys', girls' and infants' school, complete with a house for the headmaster. By 1860 there was an infants school and a National boys' school at Bewdley Road and a National Girl's school in Church Avenue, with 300 scholars between them.

The state grant was tiny and extra funds were needed for the running of each school. This was usually raised in three ways: First, scholars paid an average of 2d (nearly 1p) each week, secondly by various donations and bequests and thirdly, by Charity Sundays.

Charity Sunday was one of the most popular events of the town. The children were paraded through the town, hopefully to win the hearts of the local people so that they would continue to support the schools by voluntary donations. The Methodists' Charity Sunday was in May, while the Church of England Schools usually held theirs on Mitton Wake Sunday.

The children would be dressed in their Sunday best, the girls with new bonnets. Usually a choir with a first class reputation would arrive from another town to entertain and a special preacher would be brought in to drive home the claims of the children. Often, too, gifts were handed out to the children, the girls would be given a pinafore or a frock and the boys would receive either a pair of shoes or a shirt. Whenever the Methodist children sang at a charity concert, the choirmaster lined them up at his house before the service and dosed them with rum and eggs to make sure that their throats were clear.

The slate at the front reads: Stourport Junior Girls, Standard II. The photograph may have been taken in about 1910. From Ray Franks' collection.

In 1870, state grants to the school for each child was doubled. Reverend Gibbons founded Tan Lane School. He was very interested in its progress and often paid the school a visit. This was in the days of Payment by Results, when the School Inspector arrived to grill the children. On one of these visits the Inspector asked the children 'Who is it who is always with us?' expecting to hear the answer, 'God' but the children all replied: 'Mr Gibbons'. Although kind and generous, Reverend Gibbons held strong views and did not hesitate to enforce them. When the School Board wanted to appoint someone whom he thought unsuitable, he threatened to close the school.

The Methodists acquired their own school in 1875 through the generosity of Thomas J Baldwin. He made the largest donation in the history of the town by paying £1,000 for the building of a new school near to the church. His brother, John, became sole superintendent. School began at a quarter past nine when children were marched from their classroom to the chapel to start the day with hymns and prayers. One of the great annual features of the school was the 'March Tea', a combined Parents' Evening, Speech Day and communal tea. Staff and parents mixed and the latter heard how their children were progressing (or otherwise). The Victorian school building is still there.

Apparently, the educational environment was a happy one, as Wedley reports:

"The Parish Schools of Mitton have been singularly fortunate in their headmasters ...There was a clannishness among the teachers of both the girls and boys school which resulted in several of the second masters carrying off to their new homes those who had been with them in their work."

Methodist school in Parkes Passage, built in 1878 through the generosity of Thomas J Baldwin. Still standing, but no longer used as a school. The photograph below was found by Ray Franks in a sale of old post cards. The slate at the front reads: Stourport Infants School. This is probably Tan Lane School.

Compulsory education did not arrive until 1880, and then only for children between the ages of five and ten. Parents had to wait another ten years before school fees were reduced or abolished.

By the mid 1930s Stourport had four schools all housed in old buildings. There was the Girls' School situated in Church Avenue, the Boys' School at the lower end of Worcester Street, and the two Infants' schools - one in Tan Lane and one in Minster Road. The nearest grammar schools were at Kidderminster and Hartlebury.

Tan Lane Infants is the only one of t[..] old national schools still standing.

TAN LANE SCHOOL

The school is still used, although it is now known as Stourport-on-Severn First School. One elderly Stourport resident went to school in Tan Lane when she was only three:

"The babies had their own classroom with a swing attached to the beam and the teacher used to push me in it. We wrote on trays of sand with our fingers then we shook the tray to clear it. It was very efficient. I don't suppose we learned much but it kept us amused."

Margo Addison started when she was four and remembers:

" It seemed huge to me in those days although I suppose it wasn't really. You had to go up steps to get to your desk, I always remember climbing up those big steps. They were arranged in tiers, as in a theatre, and the desks themselves were in pairs. The room was divided by drawing a big curtain across, then when there was singing or music the curtain was drawn back to make one big classroom. First of all we wrote on slate board with a chalk then when we were older it was pencil and paper. The teacher had a huge blackboard at the front of the class, she wrote the letters on this board and you had to copy them.

'My father started going to Tan Lane school when he was only two. His family lived in the house which is now Keith Newnham's Pet Store, and when his mother was eight months pregnant his father died. She had four or five older children, and because my husband was the youngest, Miss Drew, who was headmistress at the time, used to let him go over to the school and she would give him pencil and paper to draw with. Later, he was very good at drawing and passed his exams to go to Art School but couldn't afford to go."

For many years, Elizabeth Mills was Chairman of Tan Lane School:

"I have seen a lot of changes over the years. A friend of mine had two boys and she taught at Tan Lane before Learning by Discovery came along. When her two boys were old enough to go to school, she came back to Tan Lane to teach. Later, I met her and asked how she had been getting on. She told me that on her first morning she had been given the five-year olds. She had been used to the children sitting down and not moving until they were told and she was appalled to find them all over the place. She concluded, "Shall I tell you something? At the end of the morning, one little boy was sobbing his eyes out. I said to him, 'Whatever is the matter?' and he said, 'Well miss, if I had known it was going to be like this I wouldn't have come'. I told him, 'Neither would I!'""

THE NATIONAL GIRLS' SCHOOL

Conditions were very primitive, as this resident testifies:

"Before the last war, if you were a girl, you went to the primary school until you were eight, then the girl's school, and then you moved to the Secondary Modern at eleven.

'The girl's school was at the Foundry Street end of Church Avenue. It had two classrooms each divided into two by a curtain with about twenty or thirty in each class. The heating was provided by a 'Tortoise' stove which had to be regularly stoked with coal and had to have the ashes raked out. During the winter the daily entitlement of a small bottle of milk was put on the stove to warm through. The 'Top Class' had a smaller separate classroom and when you were in that classroom you were allowed to go to the better toilet which was a single cubicle under the old chestnut tree on the bottom yard and near the canal. Once a week we went to the Vicarage for a lesson and once a week we went to the Baptist chapel for one. This eased the shortage of classrooms.

'If you had taken sandwiches and you wanted a drink, you had to ask permission to go to this tiny room about six feet by three feet (about 180 cms x 90 cms), where there were some slate sinks, some cold water taps and one tin cup fixed to the wall on a chain. It was a terrible place and even then, permission was only grudgingly given.

'In those days you had a ruler on the hand for the slightest misdemeanour, such as talking or giggling. I was an awful giggler, I often had the ruler.

'I got the cane once in front of the whole school. Our teacher was Miss Mason, she was a burly lady who sat on a little platform so that she was above us. She kept asking us questions and I kept putting my hand up but I didn't get picked so I got frustrated. Then she asked us a difficult question and no-one put their hand up. I said to my friend, 'She should know the answer, she's got the book'. It had suddenly all gone quiet and she heard what I said. I had to stand up and repeat it to the whole class, then she sent me to the headmistress. The headmistress said, 'I don't know what I'm going to do with you. I'm not going to tell your parents but I'm afraid I shall have to cane you.' After prayers the next morning she called me up on to the platform and gave me a stroke across my hand in front of the whole school. I was determined not to cry. When I got back to my seat I held on to the iron legs of the chair and this took the sting out.

'I left school on the Friday and I ran all the way home full of happiness.

The girls' school was pulled down many years ago.

THE NATIONAL BOYS SCHOOL

Originally built by Reverend Wharton and enlarged by Reverend Gibbons, it stood in Bewdley Road on the site of the present police station. Until the 1930's, an infant school was attached. Roy Crowe attended the boys' school:

"If you were a boy, you went from Tan Lane to the boy's school until you were fourteen, unless you passed your eleven plus in which case you would go to the grammar school.

The headmaster of the Boy's School was George Gregory, he was a real character who earned the respect of the boys. He was a guy who would throw chalk at you. If you were due for the cane, you would try and get under a gas lamp, then when he raised the cane the end would get caught in the chain of the gas lamp so that it wouldn't come down. It didn't save you because you would get another one for that.

'He must have been in his forties when he was a member of the Workmen's Club. I still called him Mr Gregory. One evening he said to me, 'When I was sorting the drawings out, I kept some which caught my eye and there's one done by you. Would you like it?'. He gave it back to me and I've framed it and put it on the wall. I did that when I was ten years old. It was good schooling in those days."

The old school records reveal that poor George Gregory made many applications for his salary to be increased, which were ignored.

Frank Grinnall says that there was only one master he disliked:

"When we were only six years old this master made us read a chapter of history and he said that he would give us ten questions afterwards and anyone getting less than five correct answers would get the cane. I was terrified, and I got the cane."

A so-called 'improvement' of 1885 gives some idea of the primitive state of the Bewdley Road schools. The School Board wrote to two building contractors, to 'enquire the probable expense of sinking a well and providing a pump for the boys' and infants' schools'.

In 1939 the Board of Education blacklisted all the buildings. The cost of bringing the buildings up to standard was horrific, and, in addition, a playing field was required for the boy's school. The Church of England had no alternative but to hand the schools over to the Local Education Authority. The Board promised the Local Education Authority that both schools would be closed after eighteen months. However, the boy's school was not closed by the Board of Education but by a Heinkel III, more of that later.

THE FIRST COUNTY HIGH SCHOOL

The government decided in 1920 that all children between the ages of eleven and fifteen should receive a secondary education. There was great excitement in Stourport in 1936 when a new High School was to be built, the first school not to be under the influence of the local Churches. One of the older residents looks back with nostalgia:

"In 1936 a posh school was opened up - a modern place by the park and that's where I went after the Girl's school. It was all modern and lovely. The classrooms were round a big quadrangle. A gentleman came up from London to be headmaster, Mr E J Jones, and he was wonderful. He played the organ and piano and was highly thought of. He lived until he was over ninety. He was very strict but fair and he always had time to talk to you. If one of the boys was naughty he would call all the pupils together in the assembly hall and cane the naughty boy in front of the whole school. For a minor misdemeanour you had to stand outside the classroom for half an hour. I remember standing outside the classroom one day when he happened to come along and I felt so ashamed. He organised all kinds of events for us, one year we went on a school holiday to Sandown in the Isle of Wight. That was quite a thing for Stourport. About thirty of us went, boys and girls and we stayed in a nice hotel."

Mr E J Jones arrived at the beginning of January to be the new headmaster. In his memoirs, written for the Anniversary of 1986, he stated that the school opened with 323 pupils on the roll, and added:

"My salary was £396 per annum and out of that I had to pay my income-tax. I was soon informed, when ordering equipment for the new school - only the second of its type in the County - that head teachers had to pay, out of their own pockets, half the cost of all school games equipment, the school piano, and any other musical instruments required; yet the school was forbidden under any circumstances to purchase a wireless set in that comparatively new age of radio. When I contacted head teachers over a wide area they confirm that this was the accepted over-all practice in the county. Well, I suppose everything has to end sometime! Suffice it to say that these unacceptable customs ended there and then so far as Stourport was concerned."

Roy Crowe remembers Mr E J Jones coming to a reunion in 1986. He was 85 years old but still knew everyone's names.

STOURPORT-ON-SEVERN HIGH SCHOOL-LANGUAGE COLLEGE

The 'posh' new County High School had only been opened for nineteen years when it was converted to Lickhill Middle School. Mr E J Jones transferred to the new High School as headmaster. A brand new Comprehesive was opened in 1955 for pupils in Stourport-on-Severn between the ages of thirteen and eighteen. Every year, between 200 and 250 thirteen year olds (90% of the total) are absorbed by the school as new pupils.

The school was one of the first schools in the West Midlands to get an Investor in People award, and it has also received a Sportsmark award and a Quality Mark for Careers Education. The Deputy Headteacher, Mr Humphreys, remarks:

"Our claim is that we never let a child fail through lack of support. We have the best sixth form centre in the Wyre Forest as far as ordinary comprehensives are concerned. For expressive and creative arts we are the best in the county. The level of teaching expertise here is so good that we teach other people and we take other students in to show them how to perform. We have a production event every year - the last one that we had was Guys and Dolls which we performed at the Swan at Worcester and was a complete sell-out. We are also the host school for Worcestershire Youth Music Theatre.

'Individual students have done some remarkable things. At the moment we have got a student in year 13, Ted Baylis, who has played cricket for England and is currently being assessed to play football for England. Students from the school have represented England in gymnastics, hockey and cross country running and the county in Rugby, basketball, bowls, cycling and football. Louisa Murphy has won one of the first Princess Diana of Wales Memorial Awards. She has been battling against illness but she has never disappointed her teachers and she always comes in with a bright smile. She is an inspiration to others.

'Mrs King was headteacher from 1986 to 1999 and during her headship the government was keen to set up a series of specialist schools. It had this grand vision of a link between education and commerce, where business people would bend over backwards to invest in schools. It was a philosophic approach as well as a practical one and it so happened that we had a good claim to be demonstrating it. Our aim has always been to widen and develop the aspirations of students and make sure that they are not limited by their ambitions. We were therefore holding such events as workshops,

RULES

OF THE

ARELEY KINGS NATIONAL SCHOOL.

1st. Hours to be 9 a.m. to 12 p.m., and 2 to 5 p.m., or 4:30 p.m. in the winter half-year, except on Fridays, when till 4 p.m. always.

2nd. The large bell is to be rung at 9 a.m. and 2 p.m., and the doors not to be closed for five minutes afterwards.

3rd. No children are to be admitted under the age of 5 years in future, except specially allowed by the Secretary. Those children not in attendance without satisfactory reason, at the calling over of the names, shall be liable to be reported, and to have their names struck-off by the Committee. Payment is 2d. weekly for each child eldest of a family, 1d. the others. Children not bringing their money by Tuesday afternoon in any week, may be sent back for it.

4th. Parents are not to be permitted to visit the School premises, in or after School hours. Any complaint must be made to the Secretary, or to the members of the Committee, and not to the mistress.

5th. Refractory children are to be punished as at other National Schools, and a journal kept of punishments, for inspection ; the children are not to be retained in School longer than three--quarters of an hour after time.

6th. Fire to be lighted between Michaelmas and Lady-day before 9 a.m. in the School Room, and afterwards as the weather and temperature require.

7th. Washing of the School-floor is to be done on Fridays at the cost of the Committee, viz. 3d. per week is to be allowed to the Mistress for two head scholars, who are to be fixed upon by the mistress to wash the floor, and the School is always to close on Fridays at 4 p.m. for the above purpose.

By Order of the Committee.

MAY 13th, 1869.

M. EATON, PRINTER, STOURPORT.

These school rules for Areley Kings provide an interesting insight into school life in 1869. They were printed by Eaton's in the High Street when a member of the Eaton family was the headmaster of a Stourport school.
Courtesy Areley Kings School and Worcestershire Record Office.

focus days and focus weeks. Our application was accepted and we had the full support of the government together with matched funding; they said that if we could find £100,000 from sponsorship they would match it. This enabled us to establish a Language College. We have five part-time foreign language teachers including a Japanese teacher. We have all the latest technology including a video link on a Friday morning when we have a live link with an Italian class. The Italian teacher gives our class a lesson in Italian and vice versa. It's quite impressive.

'We can't do many of the things that we would like to do because of our finances. One of our biggest problems is that Worcestershire gets so very little money from the government

'Our biggest challenge is preparing kids for the 21st century. These days they have got to have so many different skills, they need to be extremely numerate and literate, and have high levels of communication skills and information technology. We believe languages are important too. We don't know precisely what's going to happen in the future, we can only teach them how to be adaptable in order to cope with new ventures as they arise."

9. The Pace Quickens

Everything moved slowly. Imagine today seeing six, and sometimes eight, donkeys hauling undergrowth from the woods, to be used for bean sticks, crate wood, etc. Some went by canal into the Black Country for packing cases, and quite a lot was sold in Stourport at the foundry and screw works for making boxes, and the gypsies also had some for pegs and other gypsy work. The donkey team went once every day, or sometimes twice if the wood was near.

There were many donkeys kept. One very fine black, curly-coated donkey was a parcel carrier at the Swan Hotel, which was the G.W.R. parcel agent for the town. Many a drive have I enjoyed behind it! The "boots" from the hotel drove it, and kept everything very clean - brown harness and varnished sprung cart.

The above is an excerpt from the memoirs of Herbert Richard Pheysey (1869-1961). He was a distant relative of the Pheysey's of Pheysey Ltd, the ironmongers' and builders' merchants of the late 1800's.

Water transport has been described in chapter two. In the early days, public transport inland was usually by means of a coach of some kind. Most local coach services only lasted a few months because of the heavy costs involved. There were horses to keep in good condition, road tolls, duty to be paid to the government, coach hire and the wages of coachmen and guards.

By about 1820, the springing on coaches had been improved to make them more comfortable and legislation had been introduced to ensure that the horses were changed regularly. The golden age of coaching had arrived. In 1841 coaches, mail carts and horse-drawn buses were calling at the Swan on their way to Bewdley, Wolverhampton, Worcester, Dudley and Kidderminster. The morning coach to Wolverhampton was named the 'Bang-Up' and the afternoon one was the 'Everlasting'. The fares on the Bang Up and Everlasting were five shillings (25p) for a seat outside and ten shillings (50p) for a seat inside.

In Foundry Street old Mr Williams had a coach and 'two fine greys' which travelled at six miles an hour. The story goes that he asked someone if he wanted a lift and the pedestrian replied, 'No thanks, I'm in a hurry'. Sometimes small boys would hang on to the back for a free ride. Then Mr Williams would leave the horses and creep across the top of the coach to leather the small boys with his whip.

There was such competition between the various coach companies that sometimes passengers were asked to stay on the coach until the staging post at the Swan so that a rival company would see the high number of travellers they carried.

From the late 1800s onwards, bicycles were a popular method of transport. Going up Gilgal from Bridge Street was quite a pull.

132

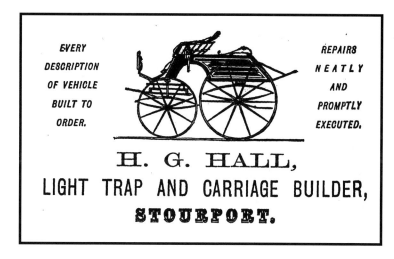

EVERY
DESCRIPTION
OF VEHICLE
BUILT TO
ORDER.

REPAIRS
NEATLY
AND
PROMPTLY
EXECUTED.

H. G. HALL,
LIGHT TRAP AND CARRIAGE BUILDER,
STOURPORT.

TRAINS

When news broke in 1845 that the Railway Company was planning a railway running parallel to part of the river Severn and the Staffordshire and Worcestershire canal, many canal users objected strongly. The Railway Company needed to get an Act through Parliament to allow the building of the railway, and so, to placate the users of the canal, they guaranteed to make up the canal tolls to £14,000 a year. The four locks built between Stourport and Diglis were built on money from a £180,000 bond from the Railway companies.

The first train came through on 7th February 1862, when the station was packed with a cheering crowd. George Griffiths wrote a poem to mark the occasion, one verse of which read:

> Stourport is all alive today,
> The flags are flying bright and gay,
> The dusty miller's left his mill;
> The anxious tradesman's left his till;
> The tanner's left his pits and skins;
> The ploughboy ope's his mouth and grins;
> The boatman's filled with jealousy;
> The coachman, guard and boots, all three
> Declare the world is filled with evil,
> And going headlong to the devil,
> Since steam, grim conqueror, spoils their trade,
> And causes all their hopes to fade.

The line passed along Great Western Way, just north of St Michaels and All Angels and had three stops at Stourport, described by Mary Rose Benton as follows:

"There was Burlish Crossing, which was a level crossing with just a house there. The gate was opened by hand, the guard lived in a cottage next to the level crossing and you would see him rush out and open the gate every time a train was coming. Then there was Burlish Halt, which was a Halt Stop in what is now Burlish Close. If no-one was there the train didn't

133

stop. After that was Stourport station where there were enough stables to hold half-a-dozen horses. From the station you would go down a bank, vehicle drivers would throw a kind of brake under the wheels and it would leave skid marks all the way down the road.

'In later years a lot of traffic used the Minster Road and by the time the gates opened there would be a long queue of cars, especially when trucks were being shunted. Several nasty accidents occurred so the Railway Company dispensed with the old-fashioned method of opening the gates by hand and substituted new gates worked from the signal box. Later they provided a footbridge for pedestrians."

The first stationmaster was Isaac Hunt who lived in the railway house on the station, it was then surrounded by green fields. Ron Matthews was the son of a driver, in the late 1920's and 30's he had the curious job of

134

The Minster Road level crossing in 1970. Bank Holiday excursion trains would block the level crossing for five or ten minutes.
Courtesy Kidderminster Times and Kidderminster Library.

going round at four or five o'clock in the morning knocking on bedroom windows with a big stick to get the railway staff out of bed.

Sam Keenan, who was born in a little cottage in New Street, worked on the railways for 47 years and was eventually elected as Vice Chairman of the National Union of Rail Workers. Sam is an expert on the local railway and says:

'By the 1880's, the Great Western Railway had built a network of railways across England. Part of one of the lines went from Worcester to Birmingham via Hartlebury and Kidderminster while part of the Severn Valley branch went from Hartlebury to Shrewsbury via Stourport, Bewdley and Bridgnorth. Therefore, if you lived in Stourport and wanted to go to Birmingham or Worcester by train you had to change at Hartlebury.

'The railway at Stourport ran to the north of Saint Michaels, along Great Western Way and up into Burlish with a station near the Brindley Arms.

There were two platforms and a loop so that trains could pass each other. Burlish Crossing takes its name from the level crossing once there with a footbridge. All that remains now is a large bump in the road.

'At Stourport there were a number of sidings and little branches. Between (what is now) Great Western Way and Brindley Street was a huge grain store and cold store. Everything used to arrive frozen - sides of beef and so on. Another branch went to the basin (opened in 1885) which is still in Longboat Lane. Iron, coal and steel were transferred to barges there and taken to Wilden Iron Works. There was a siding between Stourport and Hartlebury at a place called Leap Gate, where the petrol was pumped during the war. That's where the army and the petrol tankers used to come and fill up.

'I started working on the railway in my mid-teens on 15th July, 1940. During the 1940's there was no railway line to the Power Station and we used to take the coal there by tractor and trailer. The chap standing between the tractor and the trailer as it travelled to and fro was called 'The Vanguard' and that was my job (see page 52). We had two tractors and there were two sets of us. We had to fill the trailer with slack kept at the station, take it along to the power station and tip it into their hopper. I was lucky because my father worked on the hopper and he used to wind the trailer up for me. We had to take seven loads apiece during the day and three on a Saturday up to dinner time.

'When the siding to the power station was installed we used to go to Alveley with the empties, pick the slack up from the colliery there and take the slack engine from Hartlebury to Stourport. We did three loads a day to the power station then we took the empties to Droitwich. The two engines I worked with were the Pannier Tank Engine and the Priarie.

The 4613 train at Stourport-on-Severn station in 1958. Courtesy Stan Lane.

A page from a 1939 timetable. Printed by the Great Western Railway and aimed at the fishermen and weekend travellers from the Midlands. Courtesy Ray Franks.

The impressive old railway viaduct crossing the River Stour at Wilden.

n to SEPT
(INCLUSIVE)
after SEPT. 30th, see SUBSEQUENT ANNOUNCEMENTS)

OKINGS . to
DDERMINSTER,
RY, BEWDLEY,
— AND —
RT-ON-SEVERN

FROM	To Kidderminster Bewdley and Stourport-on-Severn Depart	To Kidderminster and Hartlebury Depart	To Hagley Kidderminster Bewdley and Stourport-on Severn Depart	RETURN FARES—THIRD CLASS				
				To Hagley	To Kidderminster	To Hartlebury	To Bewdley	To Stourport on Severn
	a.m.	a.m.	a.m.	s. d.	s. d.	s. d.	s. d.	s. d.
Earlswood Lakes	6 40	—	—	—	3 2	—	3 8	3 8
Grimes Hill and Wythall	6 44	—	—	—	3 2	—	3 8	3 8
Shirley	6 49	—	—	—	3 2	—	3 8	3 8
Yardley Wood	6 52	—	—	—	2 8	—	3 2	3 2
Hall Green	6 55	—	—	—	2 8	—	3 2	3 2
Spring Road	6 58	—	—	—	2 8	—	3 2	3 2
Tyseley	7 1	7 19	7 19	2 1	2 8	2 8	3 2	3 2
Small Heath and Sparkbrook	7 4	7 22	7 22	2 1	2 8	2 8	2 8	3 2
Bordesley	7 8	7 26	7 26	2 1	2 1	2 8	2 8	2 8
BIRMINGHAM (Snow Hill)	7 15	7 35	8 0	1 7	2 1	2 8	2 8	2 8
Hockley	7 19	7 39	8 4	1 7	2 1	2 8	2 8	2 8
Soho and Winson Green	7 23	7 42	8 7	1 7	2 1	2 8	2 8	2 8
Handsworth (G.W.)	7 27	7 47	8 12	1 7	2 1	2 8	2 8	2 8
Smethwick Junction	7 32	7 52	8 17	1 7	2 1	2 1	2 8	2 8
Oldbury and Langley Green	7 36	7 57	8 22	1 4	1 7	2 1	2 1	2 1
Rowley Regis and Blackheath	7 40	8 2	8 27	1 3	1 7	2 1	2 1	2 1
Old Hill	7 45	8 7	B 8 32	— 9½	1 6	1 7	1 7	1 7
Cradley Heath and Cradley	7 49	8 12	8 37	— 7½	1 4	1 7	1 7	1 10
Lye	7 53	8 16	8 41	— 5½	1 2	1 7	1 7	1 7
Wolverhampton (Low Level)	7 23	7 23	8 0	1 7	2 1	2 8	2 8	2 8
Priestfield	7 27	7 27	8 4	1 7	2 1	2 8	2 8	2 8
Bilston (W.M.)	7 30	7 30	8 7	1 6	1 7	2 1	2 1	2 8
Princes End and Coseley	7 35	7 35	8 12	1 4	1 7	2 1	2 1	2 1
Dudley	B 7 44	B 7 44	8 22	1 1	1 7	2 1	2 1	2 1
Blowers Green	7 47	7 47	8 25	1 0	1 7	1 7	2 1	2 1
Brierley Hill	7 52	7 52	8 31	— 8½	1 4	1 7	1 7	2 0
Brettell Lane	7 55	7 55	8 34	— 6½	1 3	1 7	1 7	1 7
Stourbridge Junction	8 5	8 25	8 55	— 3½	1 0	1 7	1 5	1 7

B—Change at Stourbridge Junction.

RETURN ARRANGEMENTS—SAME DAY.

From Stourport-on-Severn at 6.23 p.m., 8.5 p.m., 8F20 p.m. or 8D39 p.m. ; Bewdley at 6.37 p.m., 7.35 p.m., 8F34 p.m. or 8D55 p.m. ; Hartlebury at 6.15 p.m., 8.18 p.m. or 8F44 p.m. ; Hagley at 6.58 p.m. or 9F6 p.m. ; Kidderminster passengers return by any train giving a service to destination.

D—To Stourbridge Junction and all Stations to Birmingham (Snow Hill) inclusive only.

F—Not to Priestfield.

The signal box at Stourport in 1963. Sam Keenan is on the left.

'Looking back, the best bit was shunting during the war in the middle of the night with no lights. Every time the fire door was opened so that we could put more coal on, the light shone straight up in the air. We had to pile the slack on and close it quickly. All the lamps were blacked out, we just had a little slit. When it was foggy it was terrible, especially at night. As soon as the sirens went we were supposed to stop work and get out of the way but after a bit we got used to it and kept on working.

'One day, I was shunting at the Park (the coal siding), I had hooked all the wagons and I'd told the head shunter the train was ready. The train was puffing along nicely when I noticed a horse and cart racing alongside the engine. The horse had been tied to the buffer to stop him from moving and when the wagon moved, it took the horse and cart with it.

'In November 1948 I was disciplined by the Railway Executive (Western Region) and had to go in front of the inspectors at Shrub Hill in Worcester. Fly shunting was not allowed but we sometimes did it for speed. You would attach the wagons to the engine then, when so many wagons had gone past the points, you would change the points so that the remainder of the wagons went on a different load. I was doing this and one of the vehicles was derailed. We had to send for the breakdown van to come and put it on the line again.

'25 MU at Hartlebury was at the back of the railway station where the factory units are now. When George VI paid it a visit during the war I had to unhook the Royal coach and leave it in a siding. The place was swarming with half-a-dozen bodyguards.

'I took early retirement in 1987. If I had my time all over again I would still do it, I enjoyed it, but not today, not the state of the railways as they are now."

TRAMS

In 1898 the first trams clanged noisily into Stourport, sparks flying from the overhead wires. Wedley says that on the first day, everyone went wild. Immense crowds waited and queued all day long. Youngsters ran alongside trying to outrace them. It was impossible to impose a timetable as the trams were crammed to capacity as soon as they arrived back at the Kidderminster terminus. The trams filled up at Kidderminster, and as no-one got off at the Stourport terminus, those waiting for a ride at Stourport couldn't get on. In the afternoon two trailers were added to cope with the crowds. During the first year the Electric Tramway Company carried 753,500 passengers.

The trams ran from Kidderminster to Stourport, a distance of four miles. The Kidderminster terminus was near to the present Charles I High School. They went into Kidderminster town centre and out again, travelling along the Stourport Road and Minster Road. At Stourport they went along Foundry Street, Lombard Street and High Street to the terminus at the bottom of Bridge Street. Each tram had a driver and a conductress, there was no heating on the tram and in winter it was bitterly cold.

In their book on the Kidderminster trams, David Voice Associates describe the trams as having bright orange-yellow and white paintwork. "Fares were affordable but not cheap, it cost 3d (or about 1p in today's coinage) to ride from Kidderminster to Stourport, when a skilled man was earning about 30 shillings a week (£1.50).

A delightful photograph from Brian Standish of one of the first 'toastrack' trams.

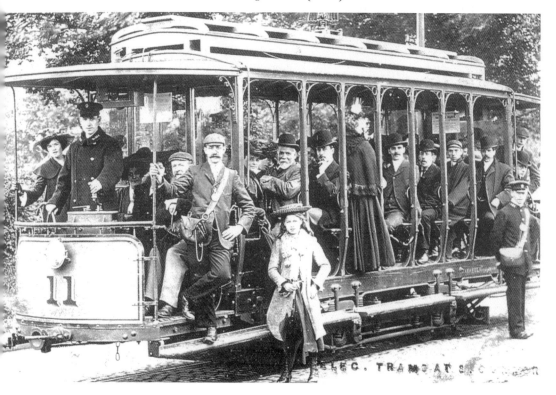

139

'At the weekend the trams were full of trippers and ... when the day trippers were in transit towards Stourport, touts would board at Kidderminster and try to sell steamer tickets as they travelled along. There were two rival river boat companies, and, with no love lost beteen the touts, it often ended with a punch-up at the Stourport terminus and the possibility of a dip in the basin!".

By 1929 the track was in need of repair and competition was growing from the Midland Red buses and so it was decided to close the tramway.

Another photograph of the early trams, taken in about 1900 and printed as a Christmas card. The white rectangle on the street wall near the right-hand edge of the photograph is a wall clock supplied by Bickerton's.
Courtesy Mrs Jean Jones and the Worcestershire Record Office.

10. Fun and Games

**Posters announced the visit of the travelling theatre. The
wagons and caravans arrived drawn by horses and the tents
were erected in no time. Sweeney Todd, the Demon Barber of
East Lynne and the Murder of Maria Marten in the Red Barn
brought the worked-up audience to its feet as we booed and
hissed at the villains who betrayed her, and her death. It was
3d in the gallery - a rickety tier of planks right up to the roof,
and 6d in the pit for those of a high degree. On a Saturday
night they would have prizes and a singing competition. As
thirteen year old school girls we got to know all the actors,
they were a close-knit crowd and all ages from two years old
to 80 and all took part. It was staged in the yard of the Station
Inn, now the Brindley Arms. The yard is still there, but it is
now a car park for the Station pub.**

**This was in the early 1930's and one of the last visits of the
travelling theatre company, which vanished with the coming
of the cinemas.**

Retired resident

ANNUAL EVENTS

Travelling Entertainments

Once a year, George Sander's circus would arrive and pitch on the field at
Lion Hill. Often, the performers and circus-followers would repeat their
acts in the road outside the main tent, then pass the hat round. Crowds
would be standing watching fire-eaters and sword-swallowers. There was a
blacksmith's on the hill and outside the shop the circus performers would
be rotating red hot bars with their feet.

Even in Victorian times many people were against the idea of a circus,
not so much because of any cruelty to animals but because of its sensation-
alism and base humour. To cater for this group, Wombwells Menagerie
stood next to the circus. It was simply a variety of wild animals on show
inside a large tent and was considered to be educational. The elephants
gave penny rides to the children.

Reg Hughes went to the more educational events:

"Before the war we had a visit from Alan Cobham's flying circus.
They were in a field off Wilden Lane and were using a little two-winged
plane called a flying flea. I think there was a lady aviator. I cycled up
Wilden Lane and across the field to see it and everybody shouted at me
to go back. I was cycling across the field that the plane was taking off
in.

'Stourport Station was by the Brindley Arms (previously the Station
Hotel) and just before the station on the right was a piece of open ground.
One year a huge tent was erected there and in it was a stuffed whale.
There were also planktons in jars. You had to pay to go and see it and the
owner told you all about it."

Mitton Wake

A Wake in England was originally a celebration, commemorating the birth-day of the Saint to whom the Church was dedicated. As time went on, the Wakes lost their religious significance and became the opportunity for a boisterous festival.

Mitton Wake was once one of old Stourport's most popular days. The townsfolk would dress up in their finery and attend Church in the morn-ing, to be entertained by a visiting choir and a 'Charity Sermon'. For the rest of the day, it was one long community party. In front of the Red Lion (now Steps House) was an open space, and most of the Wake would be held there. One of the most popular entertainments was 'Dancing for the Pumps'. A large, low cart was pulled onto the site to form a stage and dancers took it in turns to perform in front of the crowd. The prizes were pumps (plimsolls) and corduroy trousers, which were hung on a pole from the Lion. The music was supplied by a double bass, a fiddle and a flute. Wedley remarks, ' The squeaking of the fiddle and the tootling of the flute, punctuated by the grunts of the double bass, was as delicious to our ears as any modern band'. The Wake would spread into the town. There was bull baiting, until it was banned in 1835. Donkey races started from the Red Lion and went over the bridge and back. Biting at the treacle roll was also popular, a very sticky treacle roll pudding would be suspended in the air, contestants would have their hands tied behind their back and try to take bites at it.

An old man used to come from Kidderminster with sweets and gingerbreads and put his stall against the wall of the Red Lion. The Charity Sermons seem to have had little effect on the small boys, as the old man was plagued by them. On one occasion, they tied a rope to one of the legs of the stall, waited until he had a crowd round then pulled the stand over. Everybody scrambled for the sweets for which nobody paid while the old man cursed and swore.

A great scandal occurred on one Wake Sunday concerning the Church organist, Mr Halmshaw, a tailor by trade who lived in Gilgal. Wedley tells the story:

"He was a fairly good musician, but his chief claim to fame was not his playing but his failure at the crucial moment. It was Mitton Wake Sunday, otherwise the Dedication Festival: the lasses all wore their new bonnets and cloaks and boys their caps and shoes, for it was the great day of the Charity Sermons, when Mitton did its best. In the early morning, rumour gathered, quickly followed by certainty, that the organist could not be found, neither could the wife of one of Stourport's great men and a warm sup-porter of the cause. A message was sent post haste to Kidderminster and Mr Fitzgerald, well known in bygone days, was persuaded to come over and officiate. The service was a success and Mitton Wake duly celebrated but the organist had fled, none knew where, and thus ended the career of Mitton's "Master of Musick"."

The Carnival

The present carnival is always held on the first Saturday in September. In the days of the great depression Stourport, like many other towns, was suffering from poor trade and general unemployment. A police superin-tendent and a few other town officials decided that something had to be done and in the 1920's they formed a Guild of Help. The Guild was such an asset to the town that in 1925, it was decided to stage a Carnival to help their funds. It has been held every year since then except during World War II and for four years in the late 1960's. Mr Ready Senior reckons that it is one of the best in the Midlands:

"It's held in the first week in September and is both a land and river carnival. It starts off with a land parade at lunch time, then the parade comes down on to the fields by the play area at the riverside. In the afternoon there's the river parade and in the evening the illuminated river parade. In the early years the Carnival Queen was a man in drag but in later years the queen and her attendants were the girls who had collected the most money, irrespective of looks and personality. The carnival had to stop for a few years then when it started up again it had the conventional carnival queen."

Reg Hughes says that the evening parade of illuminated and decorated boats is quite a sight:

"One year, before the war, the organisers of the carnival decided to introduce a new feature and let off fireworks from a boat in the river. Something went wrong, perhaps a spark landed in the boat, and all the fireworks started going off at once. The man in the boat had to jump into the river."

Until recently, a platform was erected in Vale Road outside Lidl's supermarket and the mayor took a salute.

FAIRS AND MARKETS

Three years before the first part of the canal was officially opened, while it was still under construction, Stourport was considered to be so important that it was allowed to hold a weekly market on Wednesdays and Saturdays and also fairs on the first Tuesdays in April, July and October.

On fair days, rows of horses would be tethered in Lion Hill, while sheep and pig pens would be erected in York Street and New Street. Iron sockets were let into the pathway and the pens were fastened to them. York Street was chaotic, it was filled with cattle from end to end a with men shouting and animals adding to the noise. When they had gone the mess was indescribable, and the townsfolk spent the next day scrubbing and swilling to get the streets clean again.

CLUBS AND SOCIETIES

Stourport-on-Severn now has many lively clubs, groups and societies. The following is a selection of those which are over fifty years old.

The Literary Institute

Today, when newspapers and junk mail arrive through our letter boxes regularly, it is difficult to imagine the lack of reading material in the 1800's. The Stourport Reading Society, founded in about 1845, came like a breath of fresh air, even though it was only based on six magazines and a few religious or educational books. No fiction was in stock and a book had to be returned within six days. The boy's Sunday School was opened twice weekly so that books of an improving nature could be borrowed. Another twelve years went by before newspapers were allowed and then they were of the most respectable kind, such as the *Illustrated London News*. By then, the monthly circulation of books had increased from 50 to 90. Two years later Charles Harrison, the carpet manufacturer, introduced chess and draughts to the Reading Society and Rev Gibbons, the wealthy and popular minister of the Parish Church, read aloud from various books and magazines and charged 1d (1/2p) per person for the privilege of listening to him.

In 1866 the Stourport Reading Society was allowed to use the Town Hall for a small fee. Now that it held its meetings in such a distinguished environment it decided to upgrade its name and became the Stourport Literary Institute. It had a reading room, a library, a classroom and another room for occasional use. From then onwards, it blossomed. It held penny readings, lectures, exhibitions, parties, flower shows, outings, and founded the Young Men's Reading Institution. Members increased from 96 to 171, and when the Institute Committee organised an outing to London by train, 470 turned up. This was very embarrassing, as catering had been arranged by Lord Lyttleton at the Grosvenor Club and only 300 had been expected. There were 170 extra mouths to feed.

An insight into 'Penny Readings' is given by the *Kidderminster Shuttle* on the 23rd January, 1909, where 'Stourport Jottings' complains that 'the behaviour of a section of the Penny Reading audience is 'execrable in the extreme':

"... the person who goes to the Penny Readings and gives a song not exactly of the comic variety meets with a reception more surprising than welcome. Before the poor wretch has time to open his mouth - aye, actu-

The Workmen's Club outside the Holly Bush.
Courtesy Kidderminster Library.

ally at the moment his vocal item is announced, what the Vicar calls "audible disappointment" is manifested in the room. ... we are afraid that "Ta-ra-ra-boom-de-ay" and "Put me among the Girls" have a greater attraction for the majority than "My Pretty Jane" and "The Land of the Leal".

From the Stourport Literary Institute sprang other Societies, such as the Horticultural Society, the Music Society, the Glee Club, the Instrumental Society and the Chess Club. In 1890 it merged with the Workmen's Club in Lombard Street where a book club had been running for many years. By 1900 the Stourport Workmen's Club had a library of 1,000 books, a library catalogue of 1887 lists 644 books of science and general knowledge, 179 novels and 40 periodicals. The first librarian was an enterprising man by the name of Thomas Parker. He was one of the few working men to own his house which he did by insuring himself with a company who built his house for him, on the understanding that it became free at his death. Parker was long remembered in Stourport, not so much for his admirable work in the library, but for having a dog which could jump off the bridge into the water 40 or 50 feet below.

The Workmen's Club hit a crisis in 1965 when it had to vacate its traditional meeting place at the Outback pub in Lombard Street because the Council were considering widening the road (all the newer buildings in Lombard Street are set well back). Roy Crowe was then president, he has been a member for over fifty years. He says:

"We desperately needed our own premises. R P Vale & Sons were kind enough to provide us with a plot of land at the rear of the Swan Hotel but at that time we only had a membership of about 200 or 250, not sufficient to provide funds for a new buildings. We had to increase the membership. We put on cabarets, big concerts and gentlemen's shows. Everything was free of charge with free refreshments. Members could bring a friend, the idea was that the friend would then want to join. Membership increased to about 700 and we were able to build the new premises."

The Horticultural Society
The Horticultural Society began in August 1889 as an offshoot of the Stourport Literary Institute. Keith Newnham's story illustrates the fact that you can be successful even if, at the start, you know very little about your subject, providing you have drive and enthusiasm.

"The society was revived in the 1930's when it was known as the Stourport and District Horticultural Society and Poultry Keepers Association. After more than 70 years of existence it started to fail.

'I went in the army for two years; when I came back I married a local girl and her father was into dahlias. He used to take them to shows on his pushbike. You couldn't do that today! The secretary of the committee was trying to hold the Horticultural Society together. At the first annual general meeting I went to, the committee said that they wanted to wind up the offices and close down. Most of the committee were getting a bit long in the tooth and had been running the society for years, so they all resigned.

'There was such expertise in Stourport that some friends and I decided it was a great pity that the society should close, so about a dozen of us decided to keep it going. When we looked at the accounts we found

they were so much in the red that the trophies had been put in the bank. When we got the trophies out to insure them we discovered they were solid silver and virtually irreplaceable. We had to insure them just for the scrap value.

'We had to raise lots of funds. We had whist drives, beetle drives, bring and buys - you name it, we had it. We had cheese and wine parties where the ladies served the wine - they wouldn't let the men get near it!

'I was made chairman. We decided to arrange a meeting and get a speaker. Only the committee turned up. We tried it again and the same thing happened. How could we get people's interest?

'Ralph Belsom was a keen amateur photographer and he followed the progress of the plants throughout the year on slides. Alan Hill, who was a specialist on Chrysanthemums, and Geoff Philips helped us. We got slides together on the year of the Chrysanthemum, so we decided we would give a talk on growing them. We filled the room. That's when our fortunes turned and we started to get extra members. We went round promoting the Society by giving talks about it to various other clubs. We not only had evenings on gardening but also invited speakers in - from the gas board, the MEB, even Percy Thrower. Sometimes we asked them to judge competitions, such as the best sponge cake.

'We decided to have a flower show. Can you imagine it? We had no experience in growing or showing flowers, and no experience in running a show. Joan Belsom, who had been secretary when she was a young lady, saved us. She knew from taking the minutes what happened during the various months of the year. We decided to try and tap all the expertise that was around us by talking to local people and asking them how they grew these prize dahlias or whatever. Everybody said, 'They won't tell you, it's a secret' but they did tell us.

'In the early days, finding a place for our committee meetings was a problem. First we used the parish room which used to stand in front of the police station. Then we were in the Catholic hall, which is now the church. We paid a fee for the rent of the hall but then the priest used to come in and buy the value of the rent in raffle tickets so that we got our money back.

'With Stourport-on-Severn being twinned with Villneuve-le-Roi, Roy Crowe in 1971 arranged for us to throw down the challenge as to who could grow the biggest onion, the English or the French. Everyone said we were mad, they told us that the French grew loads of onions, they pedalled round on bikes with them hanging round their necks. The onions we took over weighed 3.1/2 lbs. We also took leeks and Chrysanthemums. Their onions were tiny compared to ours. We won an international medal and the Villneuve Vase.

'As well as the trophies we had the Vase which we put up every year and any class could win it, even the children's classes. The membership went up to about 500.

'In the Queens Jubilee year we decided that we would hire a marquee. We hired one and put it up by the Old Beams in Areley Kings. It cost £1,100 so we thought, instead of having it for the one day, let's have it for two. Cyril Fletcher, the comedian, opened the show for us and it actually made a profit.

'At the annual show we usually had a section for eggs. One of the older gentlemen always used to take part. When we read the rules we discovered that one egg must always be broken. When we broke one of his eggs, we discovered that he had been polishing and exhibiting the same eggs year after year. The broken egg stank the marquee out.

'One year, Ruth Jacks did a wonderful floral display using old records, but there was a heavy wind that night which went through the marquee and blew the display over. At two o'clock on the morning, three of us who knew nothing about art were desperately trying to recreate the floral display. Ruth never found out and it won first prize.

'The Committee had thirty members and innumerable helpers. One of our better-known members was Bill Milner who kept the hardware shop. He was such a notable begonia-grower that he has had one named after him by Blackmore and Langdon, the international begonia growers. Then there was William Bullock who had a nursery on the site of the old house, the Heath, which has now been demolished.

'The society went to national gardening events such as those at Wisley and Kew. We started travelling around in personal cars and eventually went in coaches. The society featured in the *National Garden News* in December 1978 and March 1983. The *Kidderminster Shuttle* has run features on us more than once. The radio programme, *Gardener's Question Time*, was held at Stourport High School in the 1980's. Geoffrey Smith came and he was a real gentleman. We had a note from him thanking us for our hospitality before the official letter arrived.

'I had been involved with the Horticultural Society for more than 40 years when I decided to retire in 1986. Two years previously I had decided to convert my hobby into a business. I had left my job and taken over a Gardening and Pet Shop opposite Tan Lane school. A friend of mine owned the business and he gave me first option when he was selling it.

'I still enjoy all things to do with gardening. My shop and involvement with the talks keeps my knowledge up to date. I still have much to learn!"

Some of the Keith's inspiration for the Horticultural Society came from old newspaper cuttings saved by his mother from the time when the Society was at its height in the 1930's. At the Jubilee Garden Party of August 1939, the 'bonny baby competition' was won by a little chap by the name of Keith Newnham.

Musical Entertainment
When the Penny Readings finished, a number of Musical Societies began.

The Music Society
There's a happy ending to the story of Mr Halmshaw, the eloping organist. He was succeeded by Alfred Quarterman who became well-known in the musical world and raised the music society to new heights. Mr Quarterman was friendly with Edward Elgar, the great composer, and for the Jubilee in 1887, Elgar was persuaded to play the violin solo in 'The Erl King's Daughter'. Elgar at that time was thirty years

Edward Elgar, 1857-1932, composer of the Enigma Variations, Dream of Gerontius, etcetera.

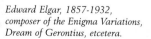

of age, already a well-known composer and the violin was an instrument on which he was expert. Yet Wedley reports:

"Upon returning to the ante-room after his solo, which was one of his own compositions, he shook like a leaf from his intense nervousness and highly strung feelings. I was standing near, having been sharing in the concert, and expressed my surprise at such a competent player being so nervous. My companion, a lady who was a great friend of Elgar's ... immediately replied, looking me straight in the face: 'Ah! my boy: All 'artists' are nervous'. I never more criticised nerves."

Stourport's enthusiasm for music produced two well-known composers. Julius Harrison's Mass in C was performed at the Three Choirs Festival in 1951 and was one of the principal musical attractions at the Festival of Britain. Born in York Street in 1888, he was the son of a grocer, was educated at Hartlebury Grammar School and studied at the Birmingham Midland Institute School of Music. He immortalised the music of the two Spragg brothers. The Spragg family was a large one and every one of them had a physical defect. Abel Spragg was blind but he was very musical and played the fiddle while Bob Spragg accompanied him on the banjo. They earned a living tramping about, playing and singing in pubs and village fetes around Stourport and anywhere that they could earn a coin or two.

Julius was best known as an operatic conductor, specialising in Wagner. The Covent Garden Syndicate sent him to Paris in 1914 and from 1922 to 1927 he was attached to the Royal Opera House. Occasionally, he conducted Elgar's works and the two men were great friends. In 1930 he settled for a post as conductor to the Hastings orchestra. Ten years later, tragedy had overtaken him and he was forced to leave because of his increasing deafness. Instead of conducting, he threw himself into composing with great passion and vigour.

Another Stourport musician achieving national fame was Martin Easthope who was born in Stourport in 1882. He attended the boy's school at Stourport and later studied at the Trinity College of Music. Martin was best known for his songs such as 'Songs of the Fair'. When George Jackson retired as headmaster of the boy's school Martin travelled especially from London to make a presentation to him on behalf of past pupils. He died when he was only in his early forties.

Glee Clubs
Wedley refers to the Stourport Glee Club -

"The first practices were uphill work for they had neither piano or harmonium to give them a lift, only a tuning fork which sounded "C", and their attempts to get it into the right key as well as find their individual notes can better be imagined than described. "

The Glee Club lasted for 30 years.

The Instrumental Society
By the 1880's Stourport had a good reputation for singers but a poor one for instruments so, in an attempt to improve on the situation, a little group of music lovers met in an old school room at Lion Hill. At first the noise was so terrible that the fishermen complained that the fishes wouldn't bite so the Society moved to the coffee house. One instrumentalist persistently drowned the others until it was discovered that he thought pp meant pretty powerful. After practising for a couple of years, they were so proud of the result that they decided to go on a busking trip to Portsmouth, hoping that by busking they would recover their expenses. Every time the train stopped they rushed out and played but unfortunately, their efforts were not appreciated by the general public and very few pennies were thrown into the hat.

Musical Evenings
Many of the townsfolk simply enjoyed a musical evening in their own home: Nora and Kathleen Thomas, when referring to the time between the two wars, wrote:

"Here and there people had a piano and sometimes a member of the family played the violin so one was sure of a musical evening. Some families even had a gramophone and that was another treat."

The Stourport-on-Severn Apollo Glee Union.

149

Sporting Activities

The Boat Club

A popular sport at Stourport-on-Severn was, of course, boating. Only a few years after the canal was completed half-a-dozen young men clubbed together and bought an old four-oar, inrigged heavy tub, with narrow-bladed oars and hard-fixed seats. The first team wore blue caps and white cotton jerseys and they were followed by a team wearing white caps.

Their phenomenal successes began when an Oxford University trainer arrived and stayed for a couple of seasons, bringing with him an eight-oar boat. The trainer wore a red coat and the team changed to red caps. At their first regatta in 1892, when competing against clubs from other towns, the Stourport Boating Club won every event. The locals were ecstatic and ran along the riverside, shouting themselves hoarse. The Boat Club won the town plate, presented by the local vicar. The Bridgnorth regatta was next on their itinerary and they won everything there, but because they had won the Stourport town plate, they were disqualified.

Success followed success. Two years later, in 1894, they won the West of England Challenge Vase, valued at £120 and prizes to the value of 30 guineas (£31.50). Three years after that they were winning the Victoria Challenge Vase valued at 350 guineas (£367.50). The crew were so good that many boating clubs refused to row against them.

The successes of the Stourport Boating Club were scarred by the memory of a fatal accident. Five members of the boat club were out for a trial spin in 1889 when the old tug 'Enterprise' met them and they were overturned by the wash. In the boat were Thomas Smythe and John Beech who could both swim a little and they managed to get to

A Regatta held by the Stourport Boat Club, probably around the turn of the century.
Courtesy Ray Franks.

the bank but were exhausted. Mr Baylis could not swim, neither could his young son who was with him, but he managed to hold on to the boat and grab his son as he struggled past, holding him until help arrived. One of the Baldwins had been coxwain. He could not swim and was carried down river by the current and drowned. He was buried at Areley Kings.

Reg Hughes was a member of the Club in his younger days:

"A family named Glover revived the Club and I became a member after the last war and rowed for the club. We were a crew of four: myself, Jim Perry, Ivor Bird and Phil White plus the cox who was quite a small lad, known as Mousey. We were rowing upstream one day in 1949 when this speed boat swamped us and we had to jump out. Mousey couldn't swim. Ivor grabbed Mousey then found he could stand up in the water. Ivor said to Mousey, 'You'll be alright, you can stand up here' and he let go of him. Mousey promptly disappeared, Ivor was standing on a ledge - there are a lot of those in the river. Ivor had to dive down and grab him.

'Phil White had been a local hero when he was in his mid-teens. On the weekend of February 14th 1943 he was walking near the bridge over the Severn when he heard a commotion and noticed a person in the water. The river was in flood, quite high. He dived off the bridge and pulled him out. He was in the local papers and the Royal Humane Society gave him an award."

The Boat Club House was one of the finest on the banks of the Severn when it was built in 1901 and it is still used by the Boat Club.

Swimming

For many years, officials had been concerned about the small number of young people in Stourport who could swim. Only a few months before the boating accident in 1889 which cost young Baldwin his life, a boat builder of Shrewsbury had built a swimming pool at Stourport. It was moored to the side of the river near to where the putting green is now and floated on air-tight petrol barrels.

This rudimentary contraption was still there before the last war and remembered by many a senior citizen, here described by a lady from the Walshes:

"It was between two barges fastened to two telegraph poles which were hooked into the bank. There was a shallow and a deep end with a plank across the middle. A lady was supervising and when you were proficient she would allow you out into the river. I was about ten or eleven when I was allowed out into the river for the first time. I swam to the other side and looked back and it seemed miles, I thought I would never get back. When I reached the pool I just hung on to the telegraph pole. I was so relieved to get there."

Bill Harper comments:

"One side of the swimming baths was for the ladies and the other side was for the gents. The roof was made of tin and when the sun came out it used to get really warm so the lads would lie on it. There were gaps in the tin sheets so that you could see partway into the girls' cubicles, the lads would lie on the roofs and whistle at the girls.

'From the inside of the swimming baths, boards projected out into the river so you could dive off these boards. I used to swim in the river every night. There was a lamppost in the centre of the bridge with a crossbar and I used to stand on the arm and dive into the river. You had to know where to hit the water because the foundations of the old bridge are still in the river."

When the pool first opened, Thomas Matthews was employed as swimming instructor. He was a local man who had taught swimming on the Irish coast. Strangely enough, he was the first person to drown because of it. During the first week in January a flood loosened the mooring chains and the pool floated down river. It stuck at Lincombe Lock and the authorities decided to let it stay there until the water subsided. Matthews thought that, in the meantime, he would try to retrieve the mooring chains. He asked two fishermen to help and roped a punt near the bridge. The two fishermen got into the boat but when Matthews went to climb in, it capsized. The two fishermen managed to hold on to the iron bars of the bridge, but Matthews was swept away. He was wearing a thick winter coat which weighed him down and although he managed to keep afloat for some time, he eventually sank from exhaustion. His body was not recovered for some days, even though a steam tug went up and down the river in the hope that the wash from the paddles would send the body ashore. He left eight young children, and in later years one of his children unveiled the town's war memorial as three of his sons had been killed in the Great War.

The need for a swimming pool was so great that, in the 1950's, the pupils of Stourport High School set to work building one themselves in the school grounds. They dug an enormous hole, carted away barrowloads of

Stourport bridge, crowned by the Tontine. The white shed-type building on the left-hand river bank is the old swimming baths. Courtesy Gordon Ward.

soil and saved silver paper, jam jars and newspapers to raise funds for the building work. This received national publicity and one day the entire BBC Lunchbox Team, hosted by Noel Gordon, descended upon them. Margaret Cook, an old scholar, writes:

"Finally the beautiful day dawned when the blue pool nestled amongst grassy banks on which it was planned would later be landscaped with shrubs and trees. The area alongside the metalwork and woodwork rooms and in front of the caretakers house was packed to capacity with staff and pupils, notability from the local Council, School Governors, T.V. cameras. I well remember Mrs. Rose, one of the School Governors, resplendent in pink silk dress and bedecked with a floral cartwheel hat sitting demurely on a chair alongside the side of the pool. The opening ceremony was to be performed by the very popular sports commentator of that time, Peter West, and to swim the first length was Bill Pickering from West Bromwich who had just completed swimming the channel. A man of very ample proportions he dived into the pool and completely showered the notability sitting in the front row around the pool. How we laughed at the soaking they received, I well remember poor Mrs. Rose's look of astonishment."

Unfortunately, the pool proved impracticable, maintenance was time-consuming and expensive and the days of the year when it was warm enough to swim in an outdoor pool were very few. Eventually it was filled in and a new sports hall was built on the site.

The town now has a modern swimming pool, largely thanks to Roy Crowe who worked hard on the project:

"The Council had talked about building a swimming baths for fifty or sixty years but they hadn't put a plan forward to develop one because they thought this would mean a possible increase in rates. I thought, 'We have all this water all round us and there's no swimming baths!'. When I became Trustee of the Sports Association I was able to urge forward the development of the riverside swimming pool. We had a five-year rolling programme so that we could spread finances. We had to rush the preliminary agreements through because we knew that the work of the Urban District Council was to be handed over to the District Council. If we didn't get one then, we never would.

'We planned to have a learner pool there and squash courts but at that point the Wyre Forest District Council came into being and this has not been done."

Cricket

Cricket was first played on the top of Hartlebury Common in 1834 and it was evidently a thriving club because 600 to 700 people attended a Field Day held four years later to commemorate the coronation of Queen Victoria. The club had moved nine times before settling in the Memorial park in 1925. Jack Stringer has been associated with the Club for over 70 years and was president from 1968 to 1989:

"I first watched the players when I was standing where Stourport-on-Severn High School is now. Then they moved to the Memorial Park. After we had used the Park for 48 years Stourport Urban District Council allocated 30 acres down by the riverside for field sports, and so we moved there. The fields adjoining those of the cricket club are used by the 'Swifts' football club and Stourport-on-Severn Rugby club. Cricket club members and their wives went to a lot of effort to raise funds for a pavilion which was opened in 1976 by Reg Perks, the county cricketer.

'We had problems when Bond Worth formed their own cricket team. Most of our first team players left. Then Steatite formed a cricket team and we were down to eight players, but we recovered. We were unbeaten in the 1962 and 1975 seasons but our best year was 1980. We're doing very well at the moment, Clive Hutton is president."

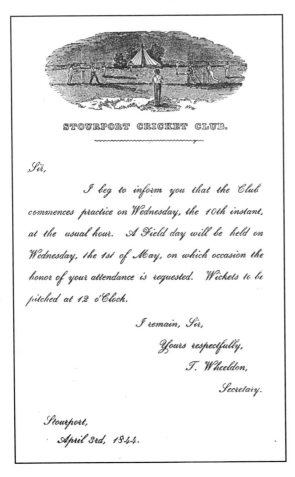

STOURPORT CRICKET CLUB.

Sir,

I beg to inform you that the Club commences practice on Wednesday, the 10th instant, at the usual hour. A Field day will be held on Wednesday, the 1st of May, on which occasion the honor of your attendance is requested. Wickets to be pitched at 12 o'Clock.

I remain, Sir,

Yours respectfully,

T. Wheeldon,

Secretary.

Stourport,
April 3rd, 1844.

Football

The first club meeting on record is way back in 1882, when football enthusiasts met for practice in a field near to the Station Hotel, now the Brindley Arms. The team wore dark blue jerseys with a white swallow on the chest and white knickerbockers, and so the promoters christened them 'Swifts'. Rules were strict in these early days, if any member used bad language first he was cautioned, secondly he was fined a shilling (5p), then he was expelled from the team. Two team members were sent into Kidderminster on foot to purchase a new ball. Going home, they couldn't resist the temptation of giving it a 'warm up' and lost it twice.

The Swifts, like the cricket team, were plagued by the loss of their grounds and moved several times until, in the 1970's, they settled in the 30 acres allocated by Stourport Urban District Council for field sports. Despite not having a permanent ground, in 1912/13 they won both the Worcester and Bromsgrove charity cups. Play was suspended during the first world war but they returned with a vengeance when the war was over, winning the County Cup three times between 1925 and 1927. Twenty years later they lifted the trophy again, and in 1982 they reached the County final but lost 1-0 to Metal Box. Since then, the team has been constantly near the top of the table.

The trainer, Mr E Baines, is on the extreme left and Mr Gregory, the headmaster, is on the extreme right. Reading from left to right, the boys on the top row are J Westwood, W Chamberlain, F Knight and R Price. The middle row comprises R Hutton, W Harper, R Drew, D Thomas and V Carradine. J Shepherd and H Southall sit on the grass.
Courtesy Florence Wilson.

WINNERS: CHARLES AUSTIN CUP, 1933.

Bowls

The bowling green behind the Swan Hotel dates back at least to 1884, perhaps earlier. Originally, it was larger than the present site, the Co-op supermarket has taken over part of it. The Squirrel at Areley Kings was so popular for bowls that folk from miles around would walk there.

Scouts and Guides

By an extraordinary coincidence, Stourport-on-Severn has provided County leaders for both the Scouts and the Guides. Betty Webb was the first female District Commissioner for the Scouts in the county, perhaps the country, and Elizabeth Mills was County Commissioner from 1970 to 1982

Over the fireplace in Betty Webb's house is an illustrated framed Citizens Award. It was presented in 1994 by the Stourport-on-Severn Rotary Club and reads:

In recognition of her many years involvement in the Scouting Movement, rising to its highest rank, furthering the movement in its endeavours to mould & create good citizens of the future.

Mrs Webb became District Commissioner in1981, in1986 she became one of the very few Scouts to receive a Silver Wolf award. She says:

"In the 1950's, my sister was running a cub pack at St Michaels and my husband was involved on the Lay side, so when my sister asked if I could help, my husband said, 'Why don't you do it?'. I helped her for four years, then we moved to Halesowen. Ten years later we moved back to Stourport, and I restarted the cub pack at Areley Kings. I also helped on the County Training Team. Eventually I became Assistant District Commissioner in charge of Leader Training. I really enjoyed it. I had a wealth of experience and it was nice to feel you were handing it on to other people.

'My husband was well-known in the Scout movement, in fact we were invited to attend the Queen's Garden Party in about 1979. At one time he was District Commissioner but he gave up this post to become County Secretary. When he died, I took over both posts for two years. I was one of the first ladies to be a District Commissioner in Worcestershire and probably in England. I thought I would get a reaction but everyone was very supportive, perhaps because they had known my husband and looked up to him a lot."

The Electric Theatre in Lickhill Road, later The Haven, taken in about 1920. The cinema was built in the Tannery garden.
Courtesy Kidderminster Library.

An attractive photograph of the Wilden Girl Guides, dressed for a garden fete in 1934. The girls made the dresses themselves.
Flo Wilson, who supplied the photograph, is in the centre.

156

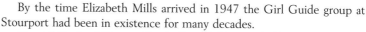

By the time Elizabeth Mills arrived in 1947 the Girl Guide group at Stourport had been in existence for many decades.

"An All-England Ranger Guide Round Up was held in 1968, a very prestigious event at the Royal Albert Hall. As Ranger Captain, I was given the honour of carrying the County Standard. Immediately before the march past, I lost it! You have never known such a panic! I said to my friend, 'I know they're going to send me to prison!'. We found it just in time, it was hidden away in the bowels of the Albert Hall.

'I was appointed County Commissioner in 1970 and retired in 1982. I was determined, before I went, to secure a camp site for the Guides and Brownies. The Council leased us a lovely piece of land at Hanley Swan, which looked up to the Malverns. First of all we had it on a 25-year lease, then we raised the money to buy it.

'Stourport-on-Severn District has four Guide packs and five Brownie packs. There are also a number of Rainbow groups catering for four-and-a-half to seven year olds, and a Trefoil Guild of ex-members of the Guide movement, for any age from eighteen to eighty-plus."

Mrs Mills is still County President of the Girl Guide Association and, as she joined when she was eleven years of age (living in Staffordshire), she has therefore been in the Guide movement for 77 years. During the 1980's she was awarded the MBE.

CINEMAS

Between about 1910 and 1950 cinemas were enormously popular. On a Friday and a Saturday night there would be a queue outside as long as fifty yards. The main cinema for the town was in Lickhill Road, opposite the Swan. Built as a Biograph picture house in 1912 on the present site of the mall, it was known as the Electric Theatre in the 1920's and later became the Haven Cinema. Reg Hughes was once forcibly ejected:

"I remember seeing Al Johnson there in the first of the talkies, 'The Jazz Singer'. The commissionaire was Mr Drew, an ex- sergeant, resplendent in his uniform with the stripes down one side. I once took my clappers, which were a pair of bones held between the fingers and shaken to produce a clattering noise. I decided to enhance the sound of horses' hooves in a cowboy film by playing them but Mr Drew dragged me out by my ear.

'Stourport was fortunate in having two cinemas. Bill Osborne was the foreman electrician for Vales and ran the electrical shop in Lombard Street. He was connected with the air cadets and built a cinema in his garage to show instructional films for air cadets. It was in Woodbury Road, off the Bewdley Road and was a proper theatre, with curtains that opened and two projectors, everything."

After using the cinema for the air cadets, Bill Osborne began showing films to his friends which proved to be so popular that he expanded until it held more than fifty people. Known as the Woodbury Cinema, it was 3d (approximately 1p) to go in the pits and 9d (approximately 4p) to go in the balcony. Saturday Matinees cost 1d. It closed in September, 1976 and flats have now been built on the site.

11. A Holiday Town

Most people come for the boats, the steamers, the funfair or the children's play area. Tourists need somewhere to eat and shop and for that they go up into the town. It's an important part of the town's economy. Stourport has something for everyone. If you like quiet countryside you can walk along the canal. If you like noise and excitement Shipley's is here for you and you will have to go a long way to find a fair which is so well-managed. If you like something in-between, then the play area, the putting green and the radio-controlled vehicles are ideal. The beauty of Stourport is that it's very flat. It's good for the elderly, the disabled in wheelchairs and mothers with pushchairs.

Margaret Ready

Stourport's long-term residents all remember the holiday-makers. Fred Rimmel says:

"The railway suffered in the Beeching cut-backs of the 1960's. It was a great pity because the trains were very popular for excursions. Stourport was a focal point in the summer. Excursion trains used to arrive from all over the Midlands: Dudley, the Black Country and other places. It was the only place for an outing in those days. There were no cars and not even buses for some. When one of the trains disgorged, the streets were solid with people advancing to the riverside. There really was a terrific number of people. You had to battle your way through to get to the other side of the town. The trains would stay in the sidings all day then take everyone back at night. The pubs used to get full and, in those days, trips on the steam boats were popular. You could go five miles for sixpence. Then there were rowing boats that people used to take out on the river, occasionally somebody would be drowned."

Many holiday-makers arrived on bicycles, and, later, cars began to make an appearance. In the Thomas Memoirs we read that 'the first car was like an armchair for two on four wheels, no cover of any sort and the noise was terrific'.

In Carole Ann Stafford's touching book, 'Us Kids', about growing up in some of the worst Birmingham slums, she writes:

"It was about this time (late 1950's) that Dad passed his driving test and started to take us on weekend camping trips to a site by the river Severn at Stourport. We slept in a big canvas bell tent that our Tony bought from old man Clements' junk shop. The old wind up gramophone came along with Tony's pop records and we had a great time. Telly, car, and now holidays. Before we went, Mom would give Mrs King half crown to keep an eye on the house and she would wave us off from the kerb, tears streaming down her face as though she never expected to see us all again."

Some holiday-makers came on motor bikes, as described by one Stourport resident:

"In the middle to late 1920's the young men would come out from

From the era of comic postcards.
Courtesy Brian Standish.

A recent photograph of the funfair
by the side of the River Severn.

ARRIVED SAFELY AT
STOURPORT

'Weary Willie and Tired Tim fishing
at Stourport'. Another comic
Stourport postcard.
Courtesy Ray Franks.

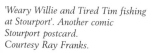

Birmingham on their motorcycles and the city girls would be with them riding pillion, all legs and make-up. They wore rouge and a lot of lipstick, not always carefully applied. They had very short hair, long necklaces and mini skirts - yes, miniskirts - hitched up as high as they could get them. At the top of their stockings they would be wearing fancy garters. They looked the cat's whiskers. Although I was only somewhere between seven and ten years old at the time I was very impressed."

A trip on a steamer was a great attraction, at one time there were five steamers such as the Beatrice and the Amo.

Bob Blunt says that the whole town population doubled at the weekend during the summer months:

"They stayed for one or two days. The steamers used to ply up and down the river; these were the lovely old steamers with varnished wood and polished brasses. They had a piano on board with a pianist playing by ear, he rattled out the music beautifully."

Frank Grinnall paints a more colourful scene:

Passengers from Stourport arriving at the Holt Fleet Hotel in 1905. The steamer is either the Beatrice or the Amo.
Another lovely photograph supplied by Brian Standish.

DINING & TEA ROOMS

"From the bridge up to the far end of the putting green were four huts of wooden construction, about the size of a large room, where visitors were catered for. They sold novelties etc. On bank holidays there used to be anything from five to ten trains arriving loaded with visitors (before anyone had any motor cars) and there would be crowds on the riverside, literally crowds, mom and dad and the kids and they would really enjoy the day out. Dad would get plastered and the kids would get pop and crisps. When they returned to the railway station it was a sight to behold. The kids were tired out, mother was at the end of her tether, father very grumpy. And the young men fought over the girls just as they do today.

'In the 1920's there were a lot of one-up and one-down cottages off little courtyards with a pump in the middle of the courtyard. The tenants would put a bowl of water outside their front door with a towel and holiday-makers could have a wash and brush-up for 2d."

CARAVAN PARKS

Stourport-on-Severn now has eleven parks holding about 1,250 caravans. One of the oldest is the Walshes Caravan Park, sited within easy walking distance of the town. Two brothers manage the site, Chris and Steve Robson. Here Chris gives an insight into the world of the Caravan Park Manager:

"This caravan park probably started after World War II when the farmer at Walsh's farm diversified and allowed campers to pitch their tents by an old orchard. He probably found it quite lucrative and extended it to caravans.

'During the 1970's the Council were running the park which, by then, had 200 privately-owned caravans. The Council had neither the expertise nor the manpower to run the site and it was in a terrible state. The dustbins were only emptied occasionally, the grass wasn't cut and the lavatory block wasn't kept clean. It was so bad that one day all the campers marched from the site to the Town Hall to protest. The Council found managing the site a bit of an embarrassment and they invited tenders to buy it.

'It so happened that my brother, Steve, and I had just been told that the savings bank, which we had spent ten years building up, was going to move to Manchester in three years' time. We could either move up north or find alternative employment. We put in a tender for the caravan site and came second. Then the number one tenderer disappeared, so a few weeks later the Council asked us if we would still like to get involved. We jumped at the opportunity. They asked us if we would like the farmhouse as well, now the Old Beams pub. It was then in a very dilapidated state and we thought we had taken on enough so we turned it down. We have regretted that ever since!

'We took over on (dare I say) April 1st 1978. We worked hard. There was a terrific amount of work to do. We emptied dustbins and kept the place tidy. Our long-suffering girlfriends cleaned the toilet blocks five times a day and even put flowers there. Campers remarked that they could eat off the floor. One of our first jobs was to erect a perimeter fence. Anybody could have walked through and caravans were often burgled.

'The caravan owners were delighted when they saw that we were doing something and they helped. They gave us a hand with the fence, tidied the place up and cut the grass with the machinery that we provided. It started to look a bit more like a caravan park. We even installed street lights. All this time we were also working eight hours a day in the savings bank.

'My brother and I moved from our parent's home in Lickhill Road and lived on the site in a small caravan which had been given to us. We had only been there a week when disaster struck. On April 7th I broke my leg in three places playing football. I was on crutches. I did as much as I could, I would drive the mower sitting on it - but I was largely office-bound. I learned to do the paper work and it became my job from then on. I still run the office, a converted cowshed. I moved back home with my parents, but then my brother got married and moved off site so I lived in the caravan again, still on crutches. In those days the caravans were only small and they had no electricity, water or drainage. I upgraded as soon as I could and when I was married a few years later I moved to an even better caravan.

'The local holiday makers, especially the teenagers, had been used to doing exactly what they wanted on the site, and Steve and I needed to instil some kind of authority. This was very difficult as Steve was only 21 years of age and I was 24. On day one we were given a large long-haired Alsation. She was not very well trained and the first time we took her for a walk, we let her off the lead and didn't see her for a week. When she was eventually caught she settled down and helped police the property. The problems in the park we were experiencing stopped almost immediately. When she produced a litter of puppies, I kept the pick of the litter and Steve's wife felt sorry for the small one so we ended up with three Alsations.

'The majority of the holiday-makers in the 1970's were from Wolverhampton, Birmingham and the Black Country. It was very difficult to understand their accents. I was often saying 'Yes' and I hadn't a clue what I had said 'yes' to. That was a bit of a shock. Over the years the accent seems to have faded out.

'Most of the campers came at the weekend. Not many people had cars in the early days and they would come by bus. The Birmingham bus ran every hour in those days, it stopped by the cafe and you would always know when they arrived on the Friday, they would come flooding in - a bus load of them. They were a fairly mixed lot, some families, some young couples, some retired people.

'Six months later, in 1978, Steve and I acquired our own self-drive boats on the river. It had been Steve's life-long ambition to own the boats. Most of them were on the bottom of the Severn. The Birmingham partnership who owned them thought they would be OK over the winter and had just left them there. The frost had set in and they sank. We had to get them up from the bottom, that was quite a challenge. There were about 30 boats all built by Ron Ready, he had also built the landing stage.

'We were required for safety reasons to monitor the boats and so our girl friends ran the caravan site while we ran the boats. They were very popular. The powers-that-be in Stourport-on-Severn used to encourage Sunday fishing trips and part of the trip was to have a go on a boat.

'The boats kept us busy. Young people tended to get very excited and would try to have as much fun as they could by rocking them. We had a patrol boat on the river and we had to deal with that. Sometimes they would run aground, and at other times they would bump into one of the expensive boats moored by the side of the river, either by accident or on purpose. Very often we had to apologise to a boat-owner and calm him down.

'We had a floating caravan as a workshop and rest room but in one of the winter floods that sank to the bottom. The Fire Brigade tried to refloat it and failed. Then my brother and I had another go at putting pumps under it and eventually succeeded. We got rid of it after that.

'We had three very good summers and we enjoyed working down there, but we were still working eight hours a day with the savings bank and we realised we were doing too much. We had to decide which direction to go in. The boats were sold to Dave Darby who did a first class job in restoring them to their original condition.

'We always enter a carnival float and we have won a prize every year for the last fourteen years. We hold an annual sports day, and, as this is very popular, in 1985 we decided to organise a football match between the caravan-owners of Redstone caves and ourselves. Both teams were anxious to win and the players got over-excited. There were a lot of fouls but, as it was only a friendly, the referee didn't send anyone off. Due to the behaviour of the teams the game was never played again. It should have been a nice annual event.

'In the winter floods of the year 2000 we lost fourteen caravans but all were insured. Some have their own insurance policy but we offer a block policy which most caravan owners take up. Three months afterwards we were back to normal.

'We are now licensed for 250 caravans, all privately-owned except for twelve which are for hire. The hire vans attract an international clientele, in one week recently we had families from Holland, Denmark, Australia and South Africa. These days we have got security cameras and a barrier system. Each caravan is alarmed and has central heating and double glazing while some even have washing machines and air conditioning.

Chris Robson's floating caravan which served as a workshop and rest room but sank in one of the winter floods.

THE RIVERSIDE DEVELOPMENT

Margaret Ready (nee Pickett) has been carnival queen twice, in 1971 and again in 1977. She married John Ready, grandson of the founder of the building company constructing many houses in Stourport-on-Severn. He arrived in the 1930's and one of his interests was the renting of a piece of land on the riverside to the west of the bridge. At that time it was a marshy swamp used as a council tip, with an open sewer running through it. This is Margaret's story:

"You will notice that the putting green by the bridge is about three feet lower than its surroundings. About 200 years ago, when the canals were built, it was discovered that the soil here was ideal for brick-making and so it was dug out to make bricks for puddling one of the basins.

'When the building trade slumped in the 1970's the Ready family were not the type who could sit idle, they liked to work. Various sections round the edges of the putting green and go-cart track were overgrown, so John decided to clear and develop one of them. He first built a pool with re-mote-controlled boats. It just took off, and was so popular that the following year he took over another patch and did remote-controlled tanks. The third year he developed the LGB trains, then tiny little bumper cars. Nothing was planned, it just developed as the building trade declined and the leisure side became more lucrative.

'A small children's zoo used to stand where the model arena (go-karts etc) are now. It housed monkeys, squirrels, snakes, goats and a baboon. My father-in-law was in charge and the baboon gave him quite a lot of trouble, she could be quite violent. Once, when he went in to clean the cage, she leaped onto his back. He also had a donkey which liked a drink of beer and was taken to the Crown every night for a pint. The donkey rides were stopped by Health and Safety officials because of the donkey droppings. The zoo ran for many years but was developed into the model arena in 1976.

'Where the model boats are now was once a tea garden, where John's grandmother sold tea and scones. Senior citizens will remember the long blocks of Lyons Maid ice cream, sliced and laid between two wafers. As the years went by a children's boating pool, miniature railway and trampolines had been installed. John took these over from the previous owners in the Spring of 1996. For safety reasons he reduced the height of the trampoline and made the miniature railway more compact."

In the play area is a bench in memory of George Jones (1921-1997). He worked there and loved it so much that when he died his family asked permission to place a bench in his memory.

In 1966 Roy Crowe was elected to Stourport-on-Severn Urban District Council. He decided that the whole of the riverside should be improved:

"The one thing I was always interested in was sport which led to my becoming Chairman of the Parks and Recreation Committee. We had a problem in that much of the riverside in the centre of Stourport had been covered with black ash. When the weather was dry it was black dust and when the weather was wet it was black mud. Where the car parks are now was rough grass and weeds. I thought it would be a good idea to get the area developed. We used to have a travelling fair come down on bank holidays which was very popular, also we needed to provide more car parks.

Plans were eventually agreed to make the meadow by the river into a large picnic area and to convert the grass and weeds into car parks large enough to hold a travelling fair and still provide plenty of car parking. The girls in the netball league were always asking us for netball courts and so we had the idea of marking out courts on the nice new tarmac of the car park. In the winter, when it was quiet, the girls could play netball."

The bank of the river between Mart Lane and Bridge Street early this century. Note the swing bridge used to cross the basins. In later years the ground was covered with black ash from the power station. The modern development is evident in the photograph on page 158/9 which is taken from a similar viewpoint. Courtesy Ray Franks.

12. Emergency!

The floods were part of Stourport and you just took them in your stride. In 1947 there was a terrible winter with everything buried in snow, then when the snow melted in the February there were very bad floods, the water was well over our wellies in our cottage. After the floods had gone the smell stayed in the furniture, you never got rid of it, it was terrible. I had just bought new carpets and when I hung them on the line they went stiff. My husband said, 'The best thing you can do with those is throw them out'. I had to use my savings to buy new ones. You never had any compensation. Nobody did. If you were flooded that was just your bad luck. The terrible winter was followed by a very hot summer and when it got hot, all the creepy crawlies came out of the furniture. We had newts running across the floor and little jumping frogs, all kinds of things. I went out one day and when I came home my neighbour said, 'Have you seen your window?'. It was black with flying ants.

The local drainage system has been improved so that the cottage has not been flooded since about 1950.

Retired resident

THE FLOODS

Reservoirs at Trimpley and Chelmarsh have now been built so that when the level of the Severn is high, water can be extracted and stored, reducing the risk of flooding, then when the water level is low, water can be released. In this way the water should be kept at a moderate level. Before these modern flood control systems were in place, all the land beside the river Severn was liable to flooding, from Moor Hall and Lickhill Manor to Redstone. Mr Ready Senior remembers that, before the last war, there was to be a big funfair at Redstone caves, due to open on the Easter Monday, "However, there was a great flood and everything was carried off - stalls, funfair - everything".

Stourport is fortunate in that most houses have been built above the flood plain, but factories on the riverside have had their problems, as Fred Rimmel relates:

"The floods before the 1980's were terrible. I worked at the oil depot down on the riverside near to the present Marina for sixteen years and we were often flooded. I have been called out in the middle of the night over that. Outside the office was a fishpond and the lads in the office used to take a lot of care of these fish, there were golden carp and all sorts. Every time we had a flood the fish used to go missing. The depot hands used to spend quite a lot of time trying to rescue the fish

'For some years I was in charge of the distribution of heating oil. It would be the middle of winter, we would be flooded out and everybody would be screaming for supplies. I remember one Christmas we had a particularly bad flood and about a fortnight after the floods subsided there

was a severe frost. Everything was frozen. Supplies ran out and everybody was going mad on the telephone and I was going mad in the office trying to cope with it."

Another business to suffer in the floods was that of the Ready family's Putting Green and Playland. Mr Ready Senior says:

"I was here in the floods of 1947. The floods took the putting green hut, the mower hut, the mower and all the tools. We had brought young trees from West Bromwich to plant on the edge of the putting green and the floods pushed them over. If you look at the trees now you will see that they are growing at an angle. One of the worst things about the flood is the mud that it leaves when the water goes down. You daren't let it dry out or it sets just like concrete, you have to swill it off before it goes hard. But I will say that the floods are responsible for the lovely piece of grass which is the putting green. The mud makes a good fertiliser.

'On the night of the flood, water got into the cellars of the Old Crown at the bottom of Bridge Street and the locals reckoned that afterwards the beer was the best they ever had."

The River Severn celebrated the millennium with the worst flood for fifty years. It was almost as severe as the 1947 floods. Lickhill Manor, which is now a retirement home, was surrounded by water. and the staff had to be ferried in by boat. Even the school had to be closed by the Deputy Headteacher, Mr Humphreys:

"The school has only closed twice in the twelve years I have been here but we had to close on Thursday, 2nd November 2000 due to flooding. The Stour had flooded through Gilgal, and the Severn had flooded the car parks on one side and the Old Beams on the other. The river was rising and due to peak at 3.30. We could not get assurances from the Environment that the road leading from the High Street over the bridge would not be flooded. We could not risk the possibility that we could be sending the children who lived in Areley Common home through flood-water."

The Franks' family own the Redstone caravan site, Ray Franks lives with his young family in one of the bungalows on the site and helps to run it:

"In the early autumn of 2000 the site was running smoothly and I thought that when we closed for the winter I would have a nice long holiday and carry on with some of my hobbies but instead, I have never worked so hard. I came to Stourport in 1969 and I never before seen floods like the ones in October and November 2000. We lost 250 caravans but they were all insured so most people have had new caravans. The new ones are raised so that they will be above any future flood levels.

The site was flooded three times. On the first flood alert we just had to leave everything and go to stay with my father. The flood level was 5.6 metres above the normal river level and it came right to our doorstep, another few inches and the house would have been flooded. When the water started to go down two days later I came back and I stayed here by myself. Fortunately, we have a big electric generator which is raised off the ground so I was able to rig up a light. The gas tank floated but the connections held. I just slept on the settee.

'I packed everything up and moved it all into the attic. That was a job, that was! All the pictures and plaques off the walls, everything out of the cupboards, it all went upstairs. I brought in some old cupboards out of the veranda and put furniture on top of these. The car was flooded but it started up, a gallon of water came out the exhaust. I have had to have a new alternator and some rewiring but nothing much.

'At the end of that week the water rose again. Fortunately, the predictions were very accurate, they said it would be 5.4 metres and it was. I knew that we would be in trouble if it was anything over 5.6 metres.

'We moved back in and were starting to get sorted out in the bungalow when just over one week later the river flooded again. This time the water was 5.2 metres. We had a boat moored to the front of the house and I had to take the children to school by boat.

'Over the winter the caravan site has just looked like a bombed site but it was all in order for the opening in the spring. It has taken us until the end of May 2001 to get straight in our bungalow."

The caravans have now been raised above the flood level

There have been worse floods in Stourport. The most severe were in 1947 and 1886. The bridge was swept away in 1795, while the storms of August 16th 1879 were the worst on record. There had been heavy rain for at least two days and the wind had been so strong that it had blown down thirty yards of wall at Hartlebury. The canal had turned into a rushing river. The paddles of the locks in York Street were not opened until after the storm had raged for some time, with the result that, when they were opened, the water rushed into the locks and overflowed. A raging torrent roared down Lichfield Street, carrying with it bricks and stones from the locks. One of the houses below street level was occupied by the Congregational pastor. The water poured in at the front door and out at the back, taking most of his furniture with it.

Titton Brook is a tributary of the Severn, and runs from Charlton Pool at Hartlebury, under the Hartlebury Road, across Hartlebury Common to go through the little village of Titton and under the Worcester Road to the Severn. On the night of the storm the drain or culvert which goes under the road burst from the pressure of the water. On the other side of the

168

Worcester Road was Mr Cooke's builders' yard. Mr Cooke heard a terrific crash and he sprang out of bed. The raging waters had brought down most of his outbuildings.

An old mill stood at Titton, and at the time of the storm it was a flour mill occupied by the Wheatley family. Mr Wheatley saw that the mill was surrounded by water and tried to pull the sacks of flour out of the water's reach, but by midnight the water was twelve feet up the walls and coming through the bedrooms. He managed to get a boat and rescued his wife and child through a window. They all landed safely on Hartlebury Common.

Perhaps the most frightening experiences were those of the Smith family. They occupied a small cottage on the Worcester Road. Early on Sunday morning, while it was still dark, Mr Smith was woken up by the sound of one of the children crying. Getting a light in a damp room in 1879 was no easy matter, and when he finally managed to light his lamp he saw water coming through the bedroom floor. He grabbed the weight from the bedroom clock and knocked a hole in the chimney but couldn't manage to get out, so he turned his attention to the thatched roof. By the time he had managed to hammer a hole in it and get out, the water had risen by three feet and the beds were floating. His wife stood on the bedroom table and handed the children out to him, but when she went to get out the table collapsed and she fell in the water. Mr Smith had great difficulty pulling her out. The house was on a bank so they managed to scramble on to Hartlebury Common. They were all wringing wet and although it was mid-August, the night had turned cold with the storm. Fortunately, they managed to struggle to the next farm which was only 200 yards away at Pansington.

By Monday morning a gigantic gorge 50 yards wide had been made from the pool at Hartlebury to the river Severn, through which water pounded. The dam had gone, so had the blacksmith's shop, the cider mill and the wheelwright's shop.

THE FREEZE-UPS

In 1890, eleven years after the great flood, came the great freeze-up. The frost and the cold was so severe that the River Severn froze with thick ice from Stourport to Blackstone (about a mile south-east of Bewdley) and the canal froze from the Vinegar Works to Kidderminster. Stourport folk treated it as an excuse for a great festival, everyone went down on to the ice and sometimes there were as many as 3,000 people walking or skating along the waterways. Peels of laughter echoed across the ice as people tried to find their feet. Wedley describes the scene:

"There were groups of young skaters, married couple going round arm in arm gingerly feeling their way, and old ladies pushed in wheelchairs ... The snow fell but the boatmen were idle and with their sou'wester capes and caps they kept (by sweeping) the ice clean."

The great freeze-up lasted for about six weeks, from the closing weeks of 1890 until the end of January. Then, at Bewdley, the river rose rapidly, the ice bulged in the centre and one evening there was a great explosion and hundreds of little pieces of ice flew into the air. People at Stourport were concerned and wondered if their part of the river was going to thaw in the same way. At last their turn came. There was a low rumbling, the noise of ice cracking like pistol shots, and the river burst out through the cracks. It carried away the floating swimming pool, a steamer launch, ferry

The top photograph from Kidderminster library is labelled 1914 but is more likely to be 1922. The bull-nosed Morris Cowley belonged to John Coleman. Sitting in the car is Miss Cattell, daughter of the landlord of the Swan. The lower photograph from Ray Franks' collection is dated 1917.

boats and innumerable other goods and chattels. For days afterwards, great blocks of ice could be seen floating down to the sea.

Other freeze-ups have occurred down the years but they have not been so severe. Florence Phillips (formerly Mrs Abbott) remembers skating in the basins in the early 1950's and says that in those years, they were often frozen over. Bill Hughes can remember two little children on the ice sometime during the 1950s walking towards York Street lock.

"There the water is running and the ice is not so thick, it broke and they fell in. Fortunately, an electrician from Areley Kings was passing in his van and he had a ladder on top. He was able to put the ladder on the ice and rescue them."

THE FIRES

Fred Rimmel says that until just before the early 1930's, the one fire engine at Stourport was horse drawn:

"The fire engine was stationed opposite the Congregational Church and the horses were kept in the field where the Parsons Chain factory is now. It was the standing joke that when the horses heard the fire bull (hooter) they thought, 'We'll make ourselves scarce'. By the time the firemen had caught the horses, tacked them up and got to the fire, it had burned itself out.

'After that, the arrangement was that the local dust lorry dragged the fire engine out. Wherever it was in the district it had to drop its load and go hurtling off to the fire station to attach itself to the fire engine. Wooden wheels and steel rims being dragged along the road at 50 mph was quite a sight. We did acquire a proper fire engine during the war.

'In the late 1950's there was a huge fire at the Regent Petrol Depot down at the riverside. I got involved in that as I worked immediately next door at FINA and I was called out during the night. It was really spectacular. All the fire engines were there from Herefordshire, Worcestershire and Shropshire. Luckily they had got a driver who managed to get all his petrol tankers out, some were full and they could hold 20,000 gallons. One of our tankers was very close to the fire next door and although the firemen were playing their hoses on it all night we lost a third by evaporation. When I went back home in the morning my wife had to hold her breath when she got near me, she said that I stank with the smell of oil."

Stourport had another major conflagration in the early 1960s. Victor Mitchley, Licensee of the Swan Hotel, had a first class view of a fire at the Tannery:

"We had a request from the National Wire Company of Kidderminster asking if we would entertain a Belgian who had come over to sell or buy wire. We couldn't understand him and he couldn't understand English. We used to have to take him into the kitchen and ask him to point at what he would like. It was hard work. One night at about twelve-thirty he came through the front door, got hold of my arm and kept flicking his lighter. I thought he wanted a cigarette but he shook his head, no it wasn't that. He kept pulling me and so I allowed him to take me out of the front door, then I looked across the road and the whole of Lombard Street was on fire. Henry Beakbane's tannery was ablaze. He had these drying sheds where he dried the leather, they were barns made with wooden lathes so of course they had gone up in smoke. I was worried because my car park is only just across the road. Ketley's garage was opposite and the firemen drained the canal tipping water on to the garage. One of my cameras had a film in it so I took a photograph of the fire, I still have it - it hangs in my lounge."

The Regent Depot fire in 1956. Courtesy Kidderminster library and Kidderminster Shuttle.

The horse-drawn fire engine outside the old fire station in Mitton Street. Courtesy Gordon Ward

13. Poverty, Sickness and Death

The 1920's were hard times. Jobs were so scarce that one man cycled to and from Bromyard to work at Vales every day. When the men were leaving the Power Station the kids used to stand at the gate and call out, 'Have you got any sandwiches left mister?'.

Retired resident

POVERTY AND THE POOR HOUSE

As far back as 1601 each parish had been made legally responsible for the care of its invalids and aged people, for providing work for the able-bodied poor and for making sure that pauper children were apprenticed. Overseers of the poor were appointed with power to levy a poor rate and build workhouses. The wealthy of Stourport held a meeting in 1803 to discuss the situation.

It was decided to build a Poor House and twelve months later it had been erected at the end of (what is now) Baldwin Road, between the road and the canal. It was a Georgian-style building, facing the town, three storeys high, with stone steps leading up to an impressive entrance. The garden was the length of Baldwin Road, with an orchard and piggeries. The inmates, if not sent to the sick ward, were usually divided into seven groups: infirm men, infirm women, able-bodied men fifteen years of age and over, able-bodied woman fifteen years of age and over, boys between seven and fifteen, girls between seven and fifteen, and children under seven. No communication was allowed between the classes except by special permission, so that children were separated from parents and husbands from wives. The only exceptions were old and infirm married couples. In Stourport Poor House in 1841 there were 94 males and 102 females.

This was a new venture for the Board of Guardians and so they modelled the Stourport Poor House on the one already in existence at Chaddesley Corbett, about five miles away. Their first task was to appoint a governor. The first applicant refused to accept the post when he saw the terms and conditions, but eventually Thomas Davis was appointed. The Board of Guardians were not happy with Mr Davis and complained that he only attended their meetings when he felt like it.

Two years later it was decided to provide the inmates with a uniform. When inmates arrived, their clothes were taken from them and held for them until they left. The uniform was a claret suit for men and a claret jacket and petticoat for the ladies. First of all they were supplied with boots but this was found to be too expensive and so they had to make do with clogs. Every inmate had to wear a button, probably a badge, with MP on it.

Inmates were expected to work at tasks such as digging, scrubbing, washing, ironing, needlework and so on. In 1805 the Poor House began taking in work from outside. Their first assignment was that of pulling apart the fibres of old ropes and boiling them down to form oakum, used for filling in the seams of ships. This was not pleasant work and the fingers were soon raw and bleeding. One of the inmates, John Lee, objected and was asked to leave. In later years, more agreeable occupations were found, such as straw hat making.

At the back of the Poor House was a mortuary and a prison. If one of the inmates swore or otherwise misbehaved he was removed to the prison. The Poor House Governor was given the authority to punish the inmates. A great scandal arose in 1821, when Mr Partridge was the governor. He was accused of cruelty towards one of the children. A young lad by the name of Perry had been throwing stones at other children, and when Mr Partridge disciplined him Perry began 'cursing and abusing Mr Partridge in a most scandalous manner'. As a punishment, Perry's wrists were tied together and the cord thrown over a hook in the kitchen. A 7 lb weight was attached to the other end, which did not reach the floor. One of Perry's legs was, for some time, tied behind him.

In 1817 the Poor House was painted on the outside and white-washed on the inside, and the largest room in the house was decorated and fitted out to serve as a Sunday School. The Board asked the local vicar, the Rev Davies if he would preach there every Sunday for £30 a year. However, the Board already owed Rev Davies five guineas (£5.25) so the Rev Davies decided not to reply. The Board again wrote to Mr Davies, reminding him that it was legally his responsibility to look after the poor of the parish, also, he received a collection from the parishioners for preaching the Sunday sermon at Mitton Church, which was a great deal more than £30.

Four years later, for some unknown reason, the room at the Poor House could no longer be used, consequently it was decided to provide a Sunday School in Raven Street which the Poor House children could attend.

Poor Houses, later known as Work Houses, existed for almost a century, and were only abolished in the early years of the twentieth century. Then came the First World War, and after it, 'The Hungry Twenties'. The 1930's were not much better. Stourport was fortunate in that its great industries kept unemployment levels lower than in most other towns. Nevertheless, some families lived in poverty as described by a retired resident:

"The Police Station was in York Street and opposite was a pawn shop. A lot of people used to use the pawn shop - there was no disgrace in it but it was just the kind of thing you didn't tell anybody. I used to go with my friend to the pawn shop. She used to be given her father's suit to pawn.

'My friend came from a large family and they were very poor. They used to have two thick slices of bread with mashed potato in-between or bubble and squeak. They used to come out of the house eating it, they never sat down at the table. But they were all nice kids and their mother had the most beautiful white washing. At the top of the street where the market is now there was a shop on the corner run by Evans, the Baptist preacher. If you were very poor you had a yellow card and you were given a loaf free of charge."

SICKNESS

The Victorians, and those before them, walked with death. All kinds of fatal diseases occurred which have now been eradicated; cholera, diphtheria, scarlet fever, poliomyelitis, tuberculosis, infant diarrhoea etc. Many women died in childbirth. The good work carried out by Medical Officers of Health did not take effect until the 1870s. Superstition and home remedies were widespread and used until recent times. Until the 1930s it was considered unlucky in Stourport for a pregnant woman to wash her feet.

Quack doctors did a thriving trade. One by the name of Sequah regularly visited Stourport, accompanied by his brass band. He specialised in extracting teeth and curing rheumatism. The conductor of the band would watch Sequah at work, and when the patient began to yell he would work the band up into a loud extravaganza to drown the cries.

Cholera can strike and spread quickly and in 1836 an outbreak resulted in 23 deaths. Many people fled from the town. The tiniest microscopic spec of the uncontrollable diarrhoea which symptomises cholera can spread the disease, consequently no-one could be found to burn the bedding and clothing of the victims until a local man, of strong body but low intelligence, was persuaded to take on the job. He soon became a victim himself. The bodies of the cholera victims were buried in a grave just outside the boundary of the churchyard, and a large flat sandstone was placed on top of the mass grave with the words cut into the stone in large letters, 'Not to be removed'.

A worse plague hit the town in 1869. Its symptoms were unrecognised, it was never diagnosed and remains a mystery sickness to this day. There were 70 deaths, three-quarters young children. Wedley says that in the August a death took place every day and each morning the townsfolk were greeted by the mournful tolling of the church bell.

Before the National Health came into being, townsfolk registered with a doctor and paid him a shilling (5p) a week to cover all their medical bills. There were two doctors serving a population of about 10,000. One retired resident comments that they attended all the births and if you rang them in the middle of the night they would pay you a visit. Dr McKay used to live in Hafren Way, he had two cars and if he had to do a call in the middle of the night he would choose to go in his old 1954 Morris Minor. He could put a crank handle in the front to start it, he said that it had never let him down.

Stourport now prides itself on its up-to-date medical centre in York House, In 2000 it became the first in the country to establish a group to provide information for patients, and receive feedback from the patients, known as 'Friends of York House'.

A funeral procession in York Street in about 1927. The wording on the postcard reads: CDF Hodges, Undertakers, Stourport. The Hodges' brothers also provided horses for the Great Western Railway and the local fire engine. Courtesy Ray Franks.

FUNERALS

Some of the many traditions regarding funerals have lingered on to this day such as the wearing of black, the sending of wreaths, the funeral party entering the south door of a church, and so on.

In the days before refined sugar, when housewives relied on honey for sweetening, it was considered important to tell the bees when someone in the household died, or when any important event took place, otherwise the bees might take offence and swarm away. You had to rap three times on the hive with the front door key and say something like, 'Bees, bees, my husband is dead. Will you stay and work for me?'. Some bee-keepers have carried on this age-old custom.

176

Reverend David Davies died in 1832 when he was 81 years of age. He had been the curate of St Michaels for 45 years. He lived in Lombard Street, directly opposite Tan Lane, in a quaint ivy-covered cottage backing on to the canal once known as Belle Vue, demolished more than a century ago. Between the garden and the street was a long high wall, in the middle of which was a doorway. From the doorway, steps led down into the house.

At his death the strange custom of attendant mutes took place. Wedley describes it as follows:

"On either side of the street doorway these silent messengers in tall hats and long black cloaks tightly fastened under the chin and reaching nearly to the feet, stood silent and grim until all that was mortal of the old man had been carried to his last resting place. This was probably the last time this weird, awe-inspiring custom was observed in the neighbourhood."

The funerals of the well-to-do was an event not to be missed. The hearse was a large, heavy-looking ebony carriage, its front decorated by eight black ostrich plumes. When the body was carried to the grave a rich, heavy pall, bordered with white was used. The bearers were each supplied with black hat bands reaching to the waist, long black silk scarves to drape across the shoulders and hang down the side, and gloves to match.

14. Stourport-on-Severn Goes to War

One of my favourite places was the Memorial park. It had been part of the Moor Hall estate but by that time, Moor Hall was in ruins. Because it was a memorial to the war it was considered to be more or less hallowed ground. I was first taken there by my grandmother. It was a lovely open area and well-tended. Before the war it was the social centre of Stourport on a summer evening, everybody used to meet everybody else. It was a bucolic scene. The Stourport people didn't bother about the riverside, in the same way that people who live by the seaside never go to the beach. You had the old Stourport band doing its stuff in the bandstand, its expertise as limited as its instruments. They used to have cricket and football matches there and the carnival but it's used very little now.

Fred Rimmel

Throughout the centuries, Stourport (or Mitton) has been involved in many wars. The Civil War of 1642-1648 came to its doors, partly because of nearby Hartlebury Castle which was an important Royalist garrison. In the Napoleonic wars, John Murray was present at the battle of Trafalgar (1805), and George Harris, the carpet manufacturer, fought at Waterloo in the cavalry (1815). Henry Court, the shoemaker and licensee of the 'Lord Raglan' lost a leg in the Crimean War of the mid 1850's. No doubt at least one of the regulars from Stourport took part in the Boer war of 1899-1902.

In 1859 a placard appeared stating:

> Men of Stourport -Enrol!
> And form at once the first company of
> Stourport Rifles
> God save the Queen

It was signed by no lesser a person than Enoch Baldwin.

178

The possibility of war with France had emerged and the government had decided to set up a Volunteer Corps throughout the country, managed by paid adjutants and drill instructors.

Enoch Baldwin assured potential recruits that conditions and drills were not of a difficult kind and the times of the drills would be fixed to fit in with work. The Stourport Rifles would only be called out if England was invaded. When assembled for active service two guineas (£2.10) was paid to each man. Pensions and sick pay were offered and anyone could leave at any time giving fourteen days notice. The Rifles needed 100 recruits, they received 102. The Captains were local factory owners - Messrs Baldwin, Harrison and Worth. They even had a band comprising five side drums, a bass drum made in Kidderminster and 24 flutes. Crowds cheered as the band first marched through the streets. They used the huge warehouse of Danks, Venn and Sanders for drill and practised rifle shooting on the Hartlebury Common across the Worcester Road. If anyone was approaching, a bugle was sounded as a warning.

It was not a passer-by on the Worcester Road who was the first victim of their lack of expertise, but an bystander at the docks.

During the first year a trip was arranged to a mass assembly of all new Corps at Gloucester. The Stourport Rifles were travelling by trow, pulled by a tug. The Volunteers made a spectacular show, in dark green uniforms with cock's feathers in front of their caps. The brass band, about a dozen strong, sported scarlet plumes instead of cock's feathers.

It had been decided to fire a cannon when they were all aboard to celebrate the event. The gun was placed on an old tug, 'The Enterprise', but as the cannon was about to be fired the tug rolled and the cannonball went into the watching crowd. One man was killed.

In 1911 a Drill Hall was built by Vales for the Stourport Rifles on the site of an old rickyard in Lion Hill. It became the TA barracks for the Worcestershire Regiment. Neil Johnson joined the Regiment in 1975 and tells the story:

"One hot, balmy Tuesday evening in the middle of June in 1974, three regulars from the Worcestershire regiment decided to go over to the barracks early to set the place up for training. These were level-headed, sensible people. As they walked into the office, they noticed that it was uncannily cold. Looking over to the desk they saw, facing them, a sergeant who was 'doing his fruit', wearing an expression of great anger and shaking his fist as if they were late on parade. He was a big man in his thirties with a moustache and obviously from the first world war, in full dress with sash and pace stick, and puttees up to the knees. Joe said, 'Who the hell's that? and as soon as he said it the apparition disappeared."

The ghost was seen many times over the years and The *Worcester Evening News* of 2nd October 1981 suggested that it could be Sgt Isaac Nunney who had died 12 years previously. Mrs Dorothy Cook, of Church Road, Areley Kings, claimed that the description of the ghost fitted that of her father who died in 1969 at the age of 82. She explained, 'We lived in the house attached to the drill hall from December 1931 to December 1933, My father was in the Territorial army for 29 years, I don't know if I believe in ghosts but if there are such things it could well be him. He was a stickler for discipline and could well be keeping a special eye on soldiers using the drill hall at Stourport.'

Empire Day, held each year on the anniversary of Queen Victoria's birthday, May 24th. The custom began in 1904.
Courtesy Gordon Ward.

This lovely photograph of the celebrations in Stourport High Street was donated by Frank Grinnall. He thinks it must have been taken in 1918 because the family greengrocery store is closed. The only time the shop closed in its entire history was during the years of the First World War. It can be seen slightly to the right of the centre of the picture.

THE FIRST WORLD WAR

By 1914 Stourport had acquired a reputation as a holiday town and each weekend thousands of campers and nature-lovers flooded in from Birmingham. All this came to an end at the outbreak of war. The population of Stourport had, by then, risen to about 4,700 and from these young men, 200 conscripts were raised. They trained at Malden in Essex and one Sunday evening on a cold, raw night, they returned home for a few days before leaving for the battlefields. At 2.30 prompt one afternoon they lined up outside the Drill Hall then marched to the station, led by the town band, through streets lined with cheering crowds. Employers gave their employees a few hours off to say goodbye. As the train went away the young men

'Of the 200 conscripts

could be seen leaning out of the windows, waving frantically until it disappeared from sight. The band played 'Should Auld Acquaintance be forgot'.

Of the 200 conscripts, more than half were killed and of the remainder, many were never the same again.

Peace came one misty grey morning in 1918. Wedley says, 'A Union Jack was seen floating over the Foundry Works and the news quickly spread that peace had come at last'. Hundreds of flags came from nowhere as people rushed into the streets. One woman appeared with a saucepan and bucket which she banged together 'as though hiving a swarm of bees'. The Chairman of the District Council asked the residents to meet him at the Town Hall at 3 o'clock and the inevitable procession toured the streets. An unusual occurrence was that the leaders from the three denominations in Stourport, the Church of England, the Methodists and the Baptists all stood together and said a prayer from the balcony of the White Swan.

The demobilised men came home on a beautiful summer's day. The procession to celebrate the end of the war was led by the police and the town band, then the demobbed men walked in file. Afterwards came the Volunteer Corps, followed by the wounded on a wagonette, the nurses (known as the 'Angels of Mercy' who had tended the wounded without fee), the land girls and the clergy. After the walking groups came three streets of decorated wagons and rows of girls dressed in the colours of the various nations.

The memorial to the 113 men who had lost their lives was made by the skilled craftsmen of the Bromsgrove Guild. First of all, the local Council could not agree where it should be situated. Mitton Church was considered, then the Minster Road. Finally it was set into the wall of the High Street, where the Midland Bank now stands. In the mid 1970's it was

Celebrations in the High Street at the end of the First World War. Courtesy Mr Hancox and Worcestershire Record Office.

1914-18

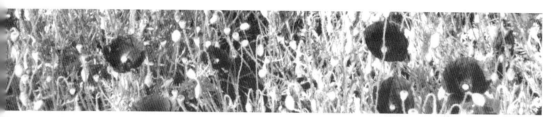

nore than half were killed ...'

During the First World War, Vale House was converted into a convalescent home. Matron is sitting at the front, with a wounded soldier on each side. Florence Wilson donated the photograph, her father is on the right.

moved to the corner of Mitton Street and Vale Road, opposite the old drill hall, and set in the memorial gardens. The stone edging is from the gardens of Great Witley Court.

A Memorial Park was purchased for £400 between Lickhill Road North and Bewdley Road. The bandstand in the park came from Abberley Hall where John Joseph Jones had hoped to form a local band with estate workers and villagers. Unfortunately he had died in 1882 before his dream could be realised. Twenty years later, the unused stand was sold to Ben Evers from the Bird-in-Hand in Stourport. He had five sons who all played instruments and he was therefore able to form a Stourport band. Ben failed to find a suitable site for the stand and, despite having cost £200 when it was new, he offered it to the Council for £30. The Council were not enthusiastic about its purchase and so the wealthy Reverend Gibbons of the parish church stepped in and bought it for the town.

In World War Two, the War Office wanted to take the Memorial Gates to be rendered into munitions but the Council stood against it. They were, after all, built to commemorate the fallen in The Great War.

The memorial for the First World War was originally set into the wall of the High Street. It can be seen here on the extreme left. Courtesy Gordon Ward.

A procession at Wilden celebrating the end of the First World War. Courtesy Mr Pountney.

THE SECOND WORLD WAR

Shortly after eleven o'clock on 3rd September 1939, churchgoers heard the alarming news from the pulpit that we were at war with Germany. Over the next twelve months the young men went off to fight, ration books and gas masks were issued, air-raid shelters were built and sandbags filled.

Stourport was very fortunate to be only bombed once during the next six years. It possessed a key transport system, a huge power station, four petrol depots and a number of large factories on war work. The Foundry in Gilgal was producing hand grenades while the Anglo was selected by the war office to supply the army with enamelware ranging from water bottles to grenades and bombs. Steatite and Porcelain were experimenting with the early development of radar and the whole field of telecommunications. A large community of Welsh lads were recruited to work at the Stourport branch of Smethwick Drop Forgings which was making bomb levers and other military equipment. Scottish lads were brought down to work at the Summerfield Research station north of Wilden. They were making ammunition and military hardware, and they were heavily involved in the development of solid propellants for rockets. An outside company was using the Bond Worth factory to make grenades and anti-tank bombs. Reg Hughes was working in the office and he can remember that one of the bricklayers had on his timesheet 'Working in bum shop'. Down at the far end of the factory were two large rooms with mysterious deliveries and securely locked doors. The relative of a local housewife worked in there:

"Many years after the war she told me that all the personal things from the battlefield or from civil victims were sent there. They arrived in sealed metal boxes, watches, rings, etc and everything was tagged. The workers sorted them out and sent them on to relatives."

Bill Harper was working at Parsons Chain:

"In the beginning when the war broke out I went to join up but I was told that I was in a reserved occupation as I was a toolmaker. A lot of the local men who were not of military age or unfit for national service worked at Parsons. The company itself didn't have a Home Guard as such but nearly all the people who worked there had joined the Home Guard in the

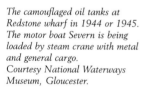

The camouflaged oil tanks at Redstone wharf in 1944 or 1945. The motor boat Severn is being loaded by steam crane with metal and general cargo.
Courtesy National Waterways Museum, Gloucester.

town, originally called the Local Defence Volunteers. There were employees from Steatite and Porcelain, Worths, Beakbanes and from Kidderminster factories, about 200 or 300 in all. They were divided into sections of twelve people and you worked with those twelve. I was a corporal. The sergeant major was Mr Richardson, a very nice gentleman.

'Most people were working seven days a week. Sometimes you had to have a Sunday morning off for a parade in the town. Every sixth night you had to go on duty up in the hills. You had to work all day, work all night then go off to work the next morning without having any sleep. One of the landmarks was Bishops Wood where you could see for miles and you had to go on watch up there. I never saw anything but my wife lived in Wilden where four big landmines were dropped. They blew up but fortunately they had been dropped in the marshes.

'There was a scare at the beginning of the war. It was our turn to go on guard one Sunday night in the summer, fairly early in the war - we hadn't even received our rifles, we only had a piece of wood each. Suddenly, all the church bells started ringing across the county (a signal that the Germans had invaded). We all went to our posts but nothing happened. Some rumour must have been put forward somewhere for that to happen.

'I have always been told that the enemy flew up the Bristol Channel then followed the Severn to the power station which was their landmark to turn off for Birmingham and Coventry. That's why it was never bombed. They usually came on moonlit nights. The night that Birmingham and Coventry were bombed they dropped flares on Hartlebury Common. My wife and I borrowed a tandem push bike and went to Birmingham then on to Coventry to look at the bombing. It was a terrible mess. You could hardly get through it. "

His wife continues:

"The war was on when we were courting. I was on nights working in a munitions factory in Kidderminster and my boyfriend was working in the toolroom at Parsons Chain. I was having trouble with the mandrels (a bar of iron fitted to a turning lathe in which articles to be turned are fixed) so I asked my boyfriend to help. I took the blueprint home and he made me one which worked very well. The managing director came round and asked how I was managing to turn out so many munitions without any problems. I told him that my boyfriend had made me a mandrel. He took me into his office and asked, 'How did he know what to do?' so I told him I had taken the blueprint home. He asked me if I knew that it was an offence. He sent for my boyfriend and told him he could get sent to prison for that. My boyfriend said, 'Well, it's all helping the war effort, isn't it?'. Everything was so hush hush then. There were posters everywhere saying 'Walls have ears' and that sort of thing."

About 500 children and vulnerable adults were evacuated to the Stourport area from Birmingham. Life on the home front was grim, especially for those with small children, as one mother explains:

"During the war you had to queue for everything. You would stand in a long queue at Marsh and Baxters for three sausages. If they had all gone by the time you reached the front that was just your hard luck. If your husband worked in the iron factory then you had extra cheese.

'I had two small children and it was very difficult standing in queues all the time. My husband was in the forces for four years and I had £2 8s (£2.40) a week to live on. There was a terrible cold winter in 1947, I had no food and no coal and the children had whooping cough. The lady next door looked after the children for me while I went to fetch some coke from the gas works. You had to queue for that. I brought it home on my bicycle, balancing it between myself and the handlebars and resting it on the frame. Everybody did the same. Then my husband came home and because he had

The Home Guard Signals outside the Larches. Bill Harper, who supplied the photograph, is fourth from the left in the middle row.

been in a foreign country we were allowed three hundredweight (approximately 152 kilograms) of coal extra. It was lovely. We lit a fire and we were able to have a nice warm house for weeks.

'The men usually worked from 3 am to 12 midday and from midday to 3 am in alternate shifts. Even after those long hours, workers had to go street watching, we had to stand there with our buckets and stirrup pump waiting for the bombs to fall. It was such a waste of time. The women went out first, then the men would take over. I came in at 10.30 pm and my husband was on duty from midnight to 2.30. The enemy wasn't supposed to drop anything between 10.30 and 12. My husband had to go to work at 5 am, whether or not he'd been street-watching. Sometimes he wouldn't bother to go to bed but just sat up for a couple of hours. He was expected to work eight hours and stand on a street corner for three hours. Some men didn't have to go to work until 8 o'clock and they could get a few hours sleep.

'Street-watching changed after a bit. Buckets were put outside houses and everybody was responsible for their own area, knocking on neighbour's doors if an incendiary bomb was dropped nearby."

One resident tells the story that her aunty was going down Mill Lane when she met this tiny, terrified man who didn't speak a word of English. He was a pilot who had come down and he was far more frightened than she was. He just wanted to be taken. She ran for help - not to the local police station or home guard but to the local publican.

Another resident describes the excitement in the town when a parachutist was seen coming down on Wilden top.

"All the men rushed out with shovels and pitchforks. Pop Millward was a big strapping man and he had got a pitchfork. He must have been a terrible sight. They found this tiny little German parachutist who was frightened to death."

Florence Wilson lived in an old cottage at Wilden:

"It had small windows which we kept open at night. About four o'clock early one morning during the war, I could hear this plane going over. There seemed to be something wrong with the engine, it was stalling. I looked out of the window and I saw this big black thing with lights on coming out of the sky and I could see that there was a cross on it. I ran into my parents bedroom and shouted 'The Germans have come!'. Mum shot out of bed but dad said, 'Get back into bed' and said to my mother, 'She's having a nightmare'. I went back to bed but I couldn't sleep. The next morning the post girl said, 'Did you hear the planes last night?' Mum said, 'I didn't but my daughter did'. The post girl told my mother that everyone said that they had dropped dummies to scare the locals.

'Food was very short but when my mother had a bit of meat extra she would make a stew with it and instead of giving it to her children she would take it over to the soldiers on duty on the line between Mill Lane and Stourport.

'Mum had this lovely aluminium jam kettle bought for her, then people came round asking for aluminium. My mum said, 'Do you think I ought to give my jam kettle?'. It was brand new. She said, 'If I don't give it I shall

During the war, everyone was issued with an identity card and an identity number. Everyone was expected to carry these at all times.

188

feel guilty and if we lose the war I won't need it anyway!'. So she gave it me to give to them."

Bob Blunt can remember rumours of parachutists landing and church bells ringing to warn of a German invasion. Did the local residents lock themselves in their houses and turn on the wireless? Not a bit of it, they flocked into Stourport, packing the main street, craning their necks to see if they could get a glimpse of the first Germans crossing the bridge.

A report of an unusual contribution to the war effort comes from Margo Addison:

"My father used to breed pigeons for the army, they would have messages tied to their legs. Sometimes one used to come home when it wasn't supposed to, then we would have to take it to the police station to have the message read. He had a large pen full of pigeons, it was raised off the floor because of the rats. He also had breeding cages."

Arthur Beard's story is told by his daughter:

"My father, Arthur Beard, was born in 1914 and died in 1991, and lived in Stourport for most of those years. He was manager of Masons, the grocers, in the High Street, when war broke out and he joined the RAF. When he was returning from a bombing raid in Germany his plane caught fire. There was just him and the pilot on the plane. While the pilot operated the controls, my father managed to put out the fire. For this he was presented with the Distinguished Flying Medal at Buckingham Palace by George VI. Almost all the other men who received the DFM were Captains and he was only a sergeant, although he later became a captain.

'He was in the 88 Squadron of Halifax Bombers, but when he was flying over the Ardennes Forest in Belgium after returning from a bombing raid in Germany he was shot down. He managed to escape and was picked up by the Marquis, an underground movement. They passed him to the Comet line, another underground movement. He went through Belgium into France and then by train and on foot to South West France He walked over the Pyranees to get to San Sebastian in neutral Spain. He managed to get a boat to Gibraltar and was flown back home. He had been missing for two months. He worked as an instructor for the rest of the war.

'In 1956 he appeared on 'This Is Your Life'. It wasn't his life but Anne Brusselman's, the French lady who helped him to get back to England. She was a member of the underground movement from 1941 to 1945 and one of the few who managed to remain undetected. She helped hundreds of men to escape and about 250 of them appeared on the show.

'When the war was over he returned to Masons. He was elected Chairman of the Urban District Council in 1973 and remained in that office to become the first Mayor of the Town Council in 1974. He was Mayor again in 1987."

The name of Beard continues in Stourport in Beard's Electrical Shop.

Life was difficult for Stourport-on-Severn High School (now Lickhill Middle). From August 25th to 3rd October, 1940, 73 air-raid warnings had sounded. On these occasions the whole school had to leave their classrooms and gather in the cloakrooms which had been converted into air-raid shelters.

The school was used as a reception and rest centre for evacuees and on one occasion the evacuees had to eat and sleep in the school overnight before they were placed with local families. The assembly hall was turned into a provisional sick bay. A further problem was that many of the evacuees were not up to educational standards, in fact 33 of them between the ages of eleven and thirteen could neither read nor write!

As if these difficulties were not enough, deep snow caused the headmaster to close the school for most of the week in January 1940, and in June 1940 24 boys were given permission to help in the gathering of sugar-beet, pea and potato crops on local farms.

One morning, the staff of Stourport High School arrived to find that the army had occupied the whole school overnight. The headmaster, Mr E J Jones, writes:

"When I arrived at school at 8.15 a.m. desks and chairs from all the classrooms were stacked on and around the quadrangle and every classroom had been converted into a dormitory. The Hall was functioning as an army canteen and soldiers where everywhere. The whole spectacle was utterly incredible! Perhaps even more incredible was the fact that in little over half an hour the situation had been completely reversed - desks and chairs were in the classrooms, beds and culinary requisites were on and around the quadrangle, and children were everywhere."

Nevertheless, Mr E J Jones was a stickler for keeping to the timetable and even on this occasion the assembly began only fifteen minutes late.

When the bombing began in 1940 the authorities of the Boys School met to decide where the children should go during an air-raid. It was agreed that if an air-raid warning was given, the children should be marched down to a shelter which had been built in the yard in Lombard Street belonging to Thomas Vale & Sons. If German bombers arrived without warning, the children were to stay indoors. Thomas Vale & Sons arrived to treat the windows with a splinter-proof solution.

A Heinkel He IIIH bomber.

Fortunately, when disaster struck, it was on a Sunday afternoon. Margo Addison heard the bombs falling:

"When the bombs fell, my fiancee (later my husband) had just come back from London. When he heard the whistle of the bomb he knew immediately what it was and he pushed me into the coalhouse (we had an indoor one at that time) and my friend, who happened to be there, was shoved under the table. We didn't understand what was going on and we thought he had gone mad. He didn't know that my little sister was sitting on the step outside and he slammed the door and shut her out. One of the bombs demolished my uncle's (Jack Sebright) toilet. He was away at the war at the time."

Several people remember seeing the bombs. Accounts vary, some say that four bombs were dropped, others six. This may be explained by the fact that there were two unexploded bombs. At least three people stood and watched them falling!:

"One Sunday afternoon in 1942 my nephew and his wife had come from Coventry for a holiday with us to give them a rest from the bombing. We heard a plane and my nephew said, 'That sounds unusual'. We went into the garden to have a look and saw this Heinkel III Day Class bomber coming over and it was dropping bombs. You could see them. They were just like the bombs you see in comics, oval shaped with the little fins. We stood there, watching it. We were absolutely barmy, beyond comprehension. It dropped six all in a line, coming towards us. If it had dropped a seventh, that would have been us."

Reg Hughes went to inspect the damage:

"I was in my early teens when the bombs fell. One summer Sunday afternoon, I was walking back home to Gibbons Crescent (off Vernon Road) after visiting a friend in Wilden Lane, when I noticed this plane circling round. It was a twin-engined plane with a short cockpit. The cockpit was circular and went all the way round the plane, perhaps to enable someone to lie on the bottom and look down. It was a nice clear day and he was banking round. The army military guns were firing up at it, you could see the tracers. One of the guns was on the railway embankment of the power station. Then I saw the bombs coming down from the aircraft and I could hear a dull thud as each one hit the ground.

'I had some way to go before I got home. I walked along the Hartlebury Road, and up Gilgal to go down Worcester Street, but then I saw that the

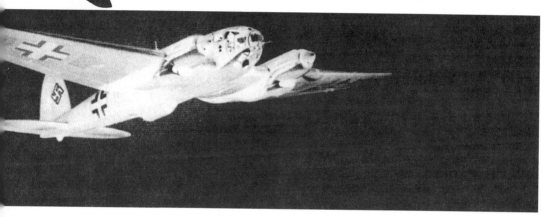

boy's school in Bewdley Road had had a direct hit. The debris had fallen right across Bewdley Road and into the playground. I went home, to make sure that my house was alright, then I went out to see where the other bombs had fallen. The second had fallen in Frank Cox's garden in Vernon Road, he was a well-known photographer. A third bomb had fallen between two houses opposite Tan Lane School, one house was at the end of Vernon Road and the other was at the end of Gibbons Crescent, and they stood at an angle to each other. The crater was touching the walls of each house. A fourth bomb had fallen higher up Vernon Road and had demolished the toilet down the garden.

'I remember there being two unexploded bombs. They were either side of Burlish Lane and I cycled out to see the large craters they had left..."

The bomb fell on the playground, part of which is now a small patch of grass on the corner of Worcester Street and Bewdley Road. The huge dome of the boys' school dropped on to the ground intact. Some of the houses round about lost all their glass, and several houses in Vernon Road took machine-gun fire to the brickwork.

Bob Blunt says that crowds turned out to see the damage:

"I remember there was a crater in Jimmy Cox's garden in Vernon Road right next to his fowl pen. The chickens were pecking their corn as if nothing had happened, and I had a nice piece of shrapnel for my collection of wartime souvenirs."

Schools were already overcrowded so that the loss of the boys' school was catastrophic. Bryan H Jarvis was a pupil at the school at the time:

"If I remember correctly, it was during the summer of 1942. I was living in Dorsett Rd., Stourport at the time and was a pupil at the "Boy's School" which was situated in Bewdley Rd. where the present Police Station is built. It was on a Sunday afternoon and I was at home in the Dining Room which faced the old railway line from Worcester to Bewdley. I noticed a German Heinkel 111 was flying quite low (we were all pretty good at aircraft recognition in those days) and all of a sudden I saw some bombs being dropped. I shouted to my father who instantly grabbed hold of me and we went straight down on the floor.

'After the raid, we all went down to see the damage. I happened to mention that my school books had been inside. A fireman, who was standing quite near heard me and said, 'Think yourself lucky that you weren't inside, young lad'.

'Afterwards, the question was where should we all go to continue our schooling? A few hundred yards up Worcester Street near St. Michaels Church was the Girl's School, and it was decided that we should share with the girls. One week the boys would use the school during the morning and the girls during the afternoon. The following week the procedure would be the other way round. Needless to say, we still had the Air Raids. If the boys were at school during the morning and the air raid warning was sounded we were sent home for the duration of the raid. If the 'All Clear' did not sound until after a certain time then we did not have to go back as there would be insufficient time to continue lessons. This, however was open to abuse, and some lads did not go back, pleading that the clock was slow. The Master would then say, 'All the more reason to return to school' (work it out).

'After a while, it was decided to use an old Chapel along the Lickhill Rd which was not very far from the town centre."

The Education Authority erected six temporary classrooms at the end of the war but even these were insufficient to meet the demand and annexes had to be used in Vale Road, Church Avenue, the Methodist Sunday School and Burlish Camp.

The American Camp

On the 18th September, 1942, 102 acres of land were requisitioned from Kidderminster Corporation at Burlish (the north-western edge of Stourport) by the War Office for the building of an American Military Hospital known as Camp Bewdley. Mary Rose Benton has collected information on the history of Burlish:

"What is now Windermere Way on Burlish Estate was, until the Second World War, a footpath. The American military broadened it out to a road, for the purpose of marching its troops to Burlish Camp, which took the area of Burlish Top, extending as far as the Birchen Coppice Estate. The area extended over what is now Elan Avenue. There were hospital quarters, concrete and timber prefab buildings, which stretched as far as what we now know as Windermere Way and Buttermere Road. The Severn Manor, recently demolished, was pressed into service as an Army hospital."

The building was completed nearly twelve months later but before it was required as a hospital it was used as an administrative command post. By May 1944 4,000 US troops were stationed there, as Reg Hughes explains:

"During the war there were two huge American Camps at Burlish. There was an upper camp on the higher ground, and a lower camp down below. From 1943 to 1944 combat troops were billeted there prior to D-Day. In 1944 General 'Blood and Guts' Patton, Commander of the Third Army, visited Burlish camp as some of the troop units billeted there were under his command."

After D-Day in 1944 both the upper camp and the lower camp were converted into a huge army hospital with a bed capacity of about 3,000. Both camps were lavishly equipped and there was even a theatre on the site to entertain the patients, it seated 500 and had dressing rooms and a projection room. The Americans brought their injured personnel straight from the battlefield by special hospital trains which were unloaded at a series of existing goods sidings on the eastern side of the Minster Road. Each train used to bring in about 300 patients and there were six or seven trains a day. Bob Blunt witnessed the arrival of the first American troops:

"We were in the middle of the war in 1943. My father was driving home from Kidderminster, we stopped at the level crossing in Stourport and a very long train pulled in. Out came hundreds and hundreds of American troops, big men, black and white, they marched in double file from the station towards Burlish. A feeling of relief, we were no longer alone!

'The following evening they were allowed out into the town. Little boys were wanting to become their guides for a shilling. The older girls were turning out to meet the Americans. Some were billeted in houses in the town, especially before D-Day 1944. As soon as they were all drafted to France the camp was turned into a military hospital.

'We quickly learned that the "Yanks" all had more pay, food and fags than our lot! It's difficult today to understand the impact that it had on the local population. People travel now and have their horizons widened by watching television. In those days there were people living in Stourport who had never seen the sea. They worked a six-day week and didn't have either the money or the opportunity to travel. I remember one old chap who walked from home to work and back again every day, and had never seen the Crown Hotel which had been rebuilt five years previously and was only fifty yards further on. That's how people were in those days."

Terry Mann was seventeen in 1944 and, while waiting to go into the army, he worked in the American Hospital:

"I was a 'go-for', that is - go for this and go for that. I was doing odd jobs round the hospital. I worked from eight until five-thirty from Monday to Friday and Saturday mornings.

'The wards were on the left hand side of Burlish Close, where the new houses are now, up the hill, with more wards on the top camp. There were large areas for those who were recovering from surgery and a lot of barrack rooms where they started their rehabilitation and therapy. When you went past the hospital on a sunny day you could see the lads lying outside in their beds enjoying the sun.

'They used to wear a denim-type maroon uniform. Our men used to wear blue serge with a red tie if they had been wounded, these men wore a combat uniform in maroon. You could often see a group of them marching down the road in Stourport, no doubt part of their rehabilitation, physical and military. There was a permanent staff of American engineers, nurses and medical people. Then there was a nucleus of us locals. We helped in the maintenance. I was repairing things, laying concrete, replacing broken windows, etc.

'The Americans had a large band with brass instruments. They used to play in the Drill Hall, the old TA centre. That used to be a regular feature every week. They also had dances in Wilden Hall by the church which was one of the local venues.

'I almost got the sack once. A group of us local lads were doing a converting job and because of the requirements of the hospital it had to be done at night. We finished in the early hours of the morning then we popped into an empty barracks for a couple of hours snooze. That was a faux pas because the military police woke us up and turned us out. We got reported and told off.

'There was one big black lad, a good six-footer, an impressive guy especially when wearing his maroon-coloured combat suit. He had badly lacerated wrists from when he had been thrown through a windscreen in France. I was walking down the High Street at about 5.30 one afternoon when I met him and we got chatting. I said to him, 'Are you off on the town?' and he said 'Yep'. I told him that he was a little bit early for that. I went on 'This is only a small town and things don't start to happen until 7.30 or 8.00. Why don't you come to my house and have a cup of tea?' and I took him home. When my dear old mother saw him she nearly dropped on the floor. It was the first black man she had seen and she was a little four feet ten inches. But he was very polite and had a cup of tea and a couple of cookies. He only stopped for an hour or so. When my father came home from work he was taken aback to see this big black guy there. Looking back, I always feel pleased in that I extended the hand of friendship."

The GIs were very generous to the locals. Every year they gave a party for all the Stourport children and provided sweets, some chocolate or cocoa, an orange and a banana. They were able to get hold of luxuries which had disappeared from British shelves during the war, like soap and stockings, and they passed them on to the local population. Local girls met the Americans in churches and dance halls, several young ladies became GI brides and went off to America. Dances were held in the Crown (in Bridge Street), in the Drill Hall and in a wooden Parish hall on the Lickhill Road, where the Christadelphian Church is now. The American camp had its own 12-piece swing band. Margo Addison was one of the many young ladies who went to all the dances. She managed to eke out her clothing coupons by making her own clothes:

"I would cut anything up. My mum would give me her old clothes. Although she hadn't got many she could always find me something."

The Americans were not always impeccably behaved. Sometimes, they would try to invade the dances when they had had too much to drink, and would cause a disturbance. In the evening, the Military Police, known as 'The Snowdrops' drove round collecting up all those who had over-imbibed. Jim Perry, who was then in his mid-teens, remembers that there was no messing about, the drunks were banged over the head with a truncheon and thrown into the back of a jeep.

Two plaques now hanging in the Stourport-on-Severn Civic Centre. They were both recognising the town's achievements in the war effort, the left one was presented by the War Office, the right one by the Air Ministry.

According to Mary Rose Benton, the more sober 'borrowed' bikes to return to camp and left them at the cottage halfway up Kingsway. Local police did not bother to collect the bikes, saying, "The owners will collect them when they want them back."

Some of the naive young GIs found themselves suffering from venereal diseases. They were asked which pub had played host to their assignations and it was put out of bounds to the entire camp.

In the same year that the camp became a hospital, a prisoner-of-war camp opened nearby, in a field alongside Torridon Close where the TV mast is now sited. Two-hundred prisoners of war arrived, chiefly Italians. They were set to work on the American camp, gardening, painting, cleaning the messes and so on.

Mary Rose Benton says that the guns on the lookout post were never fired. 'They were so large, that the American guards thought they would blow themselves up as well as any escaping prisoners'.

Ron Hughes left school in 1944 and was soon working at Jo Corbett's timber yard alongside four Italians.

"I worked at Charlton and Hartlebury, that's where I met these Italian prisoners of war. There were half a dozen of them employed stacking timber, I was working with four of them. I wasn't really in charge of them but there was only me and them. They were based at a camp at Ribbesford with the Free French Army. (I saw General de Gaulle when he visited Ribbesford House). Every day they were taken to work in a lorry and dropped off at the yard, and Corbetts was supposed to look after them. At dinner time Alf Pratley gave them each a pint of beer and a packet of fags. They weren't supposed to have the beer but Alf thought they should have it. They wore a uniform with distinctive diamond patches sewn on.

'We worked in the orchards, cutting elm for coffin boards - there was a big demand for those in the war. They were very nice, friendly people, they used to talk about their home. We had no trouble with them at all, they were glad to have some sort of employment. Some of the Italians who were working on the farms were quite happy with the situation and never went back to Italy but married local girls."

Townsfolk were mystified by two sets of lights set out at intervals on Stagboro Hill. These were dummy landing lights to fool the enemy into thinking that the uninhabited grassland was an airfield.

The War Memorial has been made into one of the chief features of the town and Armistice Day is regarded as an important event where the Mayor lays a wreath of poppies on the steps.

In front of the older memorial, dedicated to the 113 Stourport men who fell in the Great War, stands a plinth bearing the names of 34 local men who lost their lives in World War Two, and to one who gave his life in the Falklands War.

The end of the war in 1945 brought problems of a different kind, as exemplified in a comment by Betty Webb:

"When my father came back from the war my sister didn't know him. She thought her grandfather was her father. My father said he wanted a baby that would know him as dad, so that's when I was born. I was always my dad's girl."

A population explosion occurred. Soldiers came home from the war to live with their wives and they had nowhere to go.

The Americans left in July 1945 and the site was taken over as a military camp, used mostly by the British Army. When the British left, the camp was returned to the local council, to be used as temporary housing for local people. The council renovated the old hospital wards and the other buildings and converted them into temporary accommodation for families.

Terry Mann and his wife lived in one of them for a short while.

"Our accommodation was part of an old ward. Imagine a central covered alley way and running off it were the various wards turned into bungalows. It was a Council transit area for people who were waiting for new houses to be built. The size of the property you got depended on the size of your family. You had to live there for a qualifying period of approximately eighteen months to two years and from there you were moved into permanent accommodation, mainly on the Walshes. It was very basic, there was a little round cast iron stove for heating, an electric cooker, an immersion heater for the hot water and a round galvanised electric boiler for doing the washing. There was no bathroom and you had to use a tin bath on the wall in front of the fire once a week, but a lot of houses didn't have bathrooms in those days. It was very adequate. At least we had a roof over our heads and we didn't have to live with the in-laws. We had to pay a nominal rent.

'The big huts like ours were usually in the top camp. The bottom camp had more bungalow-type residences which were really up-market, this was because they had been accommodation for the American nurses. In the top camp the roads were called First Avenue, Second Avenue, Third Avenue and so on up to Seventh Avenue. A large Romney hut was converted into a shop and was kept by Mr and Mrs Thomas.

'We got married in 1947. In those days you had no coupons to spare for wedding clothes and nothing for a wedding cake or a celebration. Your rations each week were 2 oz (56g) butter, 2 oz lard, half a pound (227g) of sugar, a couple of ounces of tea and half a pound of bacon. You were lucky if you got any eggs. How could you do a reception out of that? Anyway, my sister gave me her wedding dress and at that time I was in the ATS and so they supplied the wedding cake. I had about 20 family members and they all supplied a bit. It was a very spartan buffet. My flowers were basic, just a big bunch of chrysanths.

'Even furniture was rationed. You had to give up your coupons for it. You had to be very choosey because furniture cost a lot of points. All the furniture was called Utility Furniture with two cc's stamped on it. It was very basic and solid.

'In those days they had a multibroadcast system. It was a brown box about eighteen inches square mounted on your wall and you could get several stations on it. That's how you got your music. I used to collect the money from the top camp and the bottom for Multibroadcast who were based in Kidderminster. It was about 3/6d to 5 shillings a week.

'When you moved into the Walshes, you could move into your own house more quickly if you shared a house. They were usually three-bedroomed houses, and if you shared with a family with children they would have two bedrooms and perhaps a little room at the back and you would have one bedroom. Then you each had a sitting room downstairs but you shared the kitchen and bathroom. That gave you more points to move into your own house. The people you left behind then had the whole house."

The first houses to be built on the Walsh's Farm Estate were along the side of Layamon Walk nearest to the river.

Joseph Webb was Stourport's police officer after the war and, although he was only a young man, he was well-respected. He and his wife, Betty, were both well-known in the Scout movement (see section on Scouts and Guides). Bill Hughes remarks that if you saw him, 'you ran a mile, he'd always have you for something. He was so keen that he pinched his own wife for riding a bike with no lights on. He did this to show he wasn't biased.'

Living at Burlish as a policeman's wife was not always easy. Betty says:

"When the American camp was empty, the Council housed a lot of local people there who were waiting for Council houses to be built. Various squatters also moved in, among them Ukrainians, Poles and gypsies. The Council wanted a police presence, so right in the centre they converted two Nissen huts into a police station with living accommodation.

'I had been married for three months to a policeman and we were living with my mother, so we decided to accept the offer of a Nissen Hut. One of those big black ranges had been put in for us to cook on. It did heat the room but I couldn't cook on it, I produced some terrible meals! We bought a Baby Belling and my cooking improved.

'Something happened all the time, my husband, Joe, was in the paper every week. During our first week there Joe was out on his beat when I heard this terrific banging at the door. I opened it to see this Polish man, his head had been cut open and there was blood everywhere. My brother-in-law, who was living with us, went off on his bike to telephone for an ambu-

Betty Webb and her sister standing outside their converted Nissen hut. at Burlish. Betty , who supplied the photograph, is on the right.

197

lance (we hadn't got a telephone) while I sat the Pole in the kitchen and tried to clean his head up a bit. There was blood all over the place. When I happened to look up I saw that at every window were the faces of Poles or Ukrainians looking in to see what was happening. An ambulance arrived and took him off to hospital. Evidently, he had gone to the Brinton Arms and had been hit over the head with a bottle.

'The first Christmas we were there the gypsies said to us, 'We have got a goose for you, you are a good policeman'. We had the goose, but when we were cutting it we found it was as tough as old iron. It certainly wasn't a young one.

'A friend of mine gave my nephew a bike. One day it had a puncture, he turned it upside down and came into the house to ask my husband to help him to mend it, but when he went out the bike had gone, right in front of our eyes.

'Another day, I saw a girl running up the road towards us and one of her friends had bitten the top of her finger off in an argument. She had the top of her finger in her hand. I don't know what she thought my husband could do with it.

'My husband was only beaten up once. Another time, he was arresting a gypsy and she bit his arm so fiercely that it went right through his jacket, they're very thick, those police jackets.

'We were there for two years then we heard that the police were building some new police houses in Stourport and we asked if we could have one of those. My husband still had his beat up at Burlish but it meant that we didn't have to live there.

'Joe was a policeman for 29 years, then the police force began to change. He said, 'I'm a beat man, a walker' and he didn't like going round in a police car. He was the old-fashioned type of policeman. So he left the police force and found a job as a Security Officer with the AA."

The camp was demolished in the late 1950s. Burlish Road became Windermere Way in the early 1960s and smaller roads, added over the next two years, were named after smaller lakes.

Burlish has seen many changes over the centuries but it has one great survivor, the Burlish Oak, now 280 years old. It was a mature tree when the canal was built, the railway track missed it by a few yards and the great factory of Steatite and Porcelain almost expanded to its feet. It survived the American camp and the subsequent building of housing estates. It now spreads its huge branches on a corner of Woodbury Road.

15. Parish, Council, and Parliament

On three Sundays before the 'beating of the bounds', notice would be given in the church and in the chapel. Then a crowd of dignitaries, onlookers and small boys would meet at Lower Mitton chapel. The boys would be given peeled willow sticks to smack at hedgerows and grasses on the way round. Every time the boundary deviated from a straight line the organisers 'took pains', ie pain was inflicted, on one of the boys. If it was a stream a boy was tossed in it, if it was a tree somebody's head would be bumped against it, if there was a hedge a sapling would be cut and a small boy caned, if it was a wall a bed of nettles would be found and a boy thrown in them. If it was a ditch, a boy who was too small to jump it would be chosen and then he would be offered money to try. The only departure from taking pains was if they arrived at a grassy bank. Then the boys would sit down to a treat of bread and cheese with beer. Their return to the town was met by a band and a cheering crowd.

Isaac Wedley (edited)

BOUNDARIES

There are different boundaries for different organisations. The three main boundaries are parish (for the church), parliamentary (for returning an MP) and civic (for the Council).

Upper and Lower Mitton were in separate parishes until the middle of the nineteenth century, when the Bishop of Worcester, living at Hartlebury Castle, decided that this was ridiculous and campaigned to have Upper Mitton included in the parish of Stourport. Later, West Hartlebury, Bircher Coppice and a portion of Titton were also included, adding 1000 people to the parish.

Until well into the twentieth century, parish boundaries were very important. They laid down where you were christened, married and buried.

Most people looked to the church for their social life and you were expected to attend your parish church. If you fell on hard times, they decreed who was responsible for looking after you. If you fell foul of the law, you attended at the court overseeing your parish. It was therefore essential that parish boundaries should never be forgotten.

This was the reason for walking round the boundaries.

The Parliamentary Borough of Bewdley was enlarged in about 1832 to include several hamlets including Lower Mitton and Lickhill. This gave Bewdley magistrates power to hold courts for everything except matters concerning life and limb, and to regulate fairs and markets. The Lord of the Manor at that time was Sir Edward Blount and he said that, according to his manorial rights, courts, fairs and markets were his responsibility. The matter was eventually resolved amicably.

The civic boundaries remained unchanged for many years. The villages round about were proud of their beautiful rural locations and did not want to be linked to an industrial town

Various attempts at amalgamation were bitterly opposed. It was not until 1928 that Stourport Council succeeded in combining Lower Mitton (12645 acres) and Upper Mitton (359 acres). Five years later, in 1933, necessity added Wilden and part of Areley Kings to the town. They needed new water and sewage systems which they could not afford.

In 1973, four Urban District Councils were joined together: Kidderminster Borough, Kidderminster Rural, Bewdley, and Stourport. Each of these were divided into three wards selecting three councillors, Stourport has Areley Kings, Mitton and Lickhill. For the Town Council there are six wards, Areley Kings East and West, Mitton and Central Stourport, Lickhill and Wilden. Each ward appoints three councillors for four years, the County Council election takes place in the fourth year.

ELECTIONS

Old-time elections were violent, corrupt and bloody affairs. Up until the nineteenth century, very few people were able to vote but in 1832 the Reform Bill extended the franchise to include occupants of houses or shops of £10 or more yearly value. Consequently, 158 of the inhabitants of Stourport-on-Severn had this privilege. Votes were usually placed by raising a hand at public meetings, consequently a man's political views were well known. These 158 were bribed with money, free drink and other delights. It was not unknown for voters to be kidnapped for the day and spirited away. In 1847, Pearce Baldwin paid a man £60 to take two men to London on polling day. In the same election, Bewdley paid twelve guineas for 'screaming women' to drown the political speeches and the Whigs had to employ fifty navvies at Stourport to prevent damage to Tory houses. Both parties petitioned for corruption with the result that the division of Stourport and Bewdley was found guilty of a 'most pernicious system of intimidation, kidnapping and treating', and the election was declared void.

In 1868 those who paid low rents were also allowed to vote, but feelings still ran high.

Stourport was passionately Whig while Bewdley, although in the same division, was the home of the Tories, consequently, whenever the results of an election were to be announced, Stourport men would tramp to Bewdley to hear the election results, armed with sticks and bludgeons. Members of the two opposing parties would fight for hours until they were exhausted. There were usually a couple of cracked skulls and once, two men very nearly drowned. They fought on top of a canal boat loaded with hay, fell into the canal and continued pummelling each other. Votes for all men and some women did not arrive until 1918.

COUNCILLORS

Despite the political wranglings of the nineteenth century, Stourport has been fortunate in having a number of hard working and conscientious councillors who developed the town as it is today.

The housing shortage faded away in Stourport-on-Severn, partly because of the efforts of people such as Mrs Elizabeth Mills. She was a County Councillor for twelve years and is still on the Town Council. She keeps a maternal eye on the Social Centre in William Bullock Close and was in there recently when a lady said to her, 'I have to ask you because I keep asking anybody, it's my front door, it doesn't shut properly'. Mrs Mills said, 'Alright, I'll see what I can do'. The lady continued, 'Mrs Mills, do you know how old I am? In two weeks' time I shall be 73. It's a very big age'. Mrs Mills nodded sympathetically. She is into her 80's.

"My chief interest is Housing, I like to be doing things with people. Broomy Close is a housing development with which I was involved right from the early stages. We were always keeping an eye open for somewhere suitable to build houses and we could see an appropriate space there. We discussed the type of accommodation we needed and looked at all kinds of plans. We decided on two-storey flats and bungalows, with a space for a Community Centre, as we have a lot of elderly people in Stourport-on-severn. Many of them have a caravan here and become so attached to the place that when they retire they want to live here, there are also some residential caravans not suitable for the elderly. Broomy Close is now a very popular residential development. The Council houses have recently been sold to a housing association. We have managed to provide a warden service to several housing centres.

'Another of our successes was that we got a good emergency system going for the very elderly and infirm. They wear a type of necklace, known as a helpline, which has a button on it. If they fall or need emergency help they press the button and it activates the system. We opened a centre to deal with the helplines for tenants of Council houses.

'Although I'm no longer on the District Council I still get phone calls to my house, such as 'My taps gone funny' (it probably only needs a washer). It takes too long to explain that I'm no longer a Councillor and to give them the correct telephone number so I usually say, 'Yes, alright, I'll report it and I'll see what I can do'."

Roy Crowe was Chairman of the Urban District Council in 1971, a post equivalent to that of present-day mayor.

"One venture I look back upon with pleasure is the twinning of the town, of which I was Chairman. The Stourport Urban District Council decided, in 1971, to explore the possibility of twinning. The selected town needed to be convenient for travelling, not only for officials but for the man-in-the-street. Although we could set up a municipal link, its success depended on the ordinary person.

'We contacted the French embassy and told them we were looking for a list of towns from France who were also considering twinning. We wanted a town of a similar-sized population and similar interests. The one we chose, Villneuve-le-Roi, was on the Seine and, like us, was a river town. It's near to Orly airport and not bad for coaches. Visits were then made each way and we both felt that there was sufficient similarity to go ahead. We had a ceremony at Villneuve-le-Roi where we signed the Charter and we had another ceremony here. They dedicated a garden to us and we dedicated one to them. It's been very successful and all kinds of people have come here and gone over there."

At the time of these interviews, Reginald Knott was Mayor. He was also Leader of the Town Council, Chairman of Twinning, Trustee of the Parish Rooms Committee for Areley Kings, and Chairman of the Governors of Stourport High School.

"Although I'm a Worcester person I have lived in Stourport for 23 years and I worked in the Wyre Forest for six or seven years before that. In the first ten years of our marriage my wife and I moved four times. Then we discovered Stourport, we settled here and we're happy. We have no plans whatsoever to move. It's an ideal place to live in. It's a small town, many people are surprised that we have between 19,000 and 20,000 people living here, it's so compact. Our French visitors are particularly surprised because their towns are larger and hold less people. The town is also very conveniently situated, you can easily travel to Worcester or Birmingham.

'We only wear the robes for council meetings and in Remembrance Day parades, I'm glad to say, because they get very hot. The chain of office was new when the Wyre Forest District Council was formed but the Deputy Mayor had to make do with the chain that belonged to the Chairman of the Urban District Council. If you look carefully you can see the alterations.

'I've worked at Tesco's for almost thirty years, and at the local branch for the last eight or nine years. I am now Forum representative where I have to liaise with nine stores.

'My wife and I are both on the Stourport Town Council. It's really just a large parish council. We nominate governors to schools and have various projects such as Parks and Gardens, Allotments, Town Centre and so on. Councillors are placed into various committees round the town, for example, the Town Centre Forum which is looking at how the town can be enhanced. We have allotments in Areley Kings, these are very important to people, you only have to talk to some of those who use them to realise what a major part an allotment plays in their lives. They are worried in case they get sold off for building but as it is a charitable trust there is no possibility of this.

'We carried out a joint project with the District Council on the Memorial Park and built a new community centre. It had only been up twelve months when it was burned down by vandals. It has now been rebuilt and this time it has been made vandal-proof, with shutters over the windows and that sort of thing.

'We inherited huge financial problems but these have now been solved For the first time we are going forward and are able to plan many more things that we want to do. We can spend money on the memorial park and town enhancement. At the moment we are redesigning the gardens of

202

Villneuve-le-Roi, and we are also having a look at the war memorial and the memorial park equipment, the gardens and flower beds, and the cemetery.

'This year, about 200 caravans had to be written off because of the floods. There have not been floods as severe as this since 1947 and so we are hoping that it will be another 50 years before we see the next major floods. However, the County Council have had meetings about the situation and they have come up with remedies and comments which they are forwarding to the government.

'With regard to the traffic situation in Stourport, this can never be improved until we have a second bridge. We are number one on Worcestershire's list for a by-pass, although I don't know how many years it will be before we actually get it. We will have to carry on lobbying to try and get it done. Traders worry that they will lose trade when a by-pass arrives but often, this enhances the town, making it more attractive to pedestrians so that trade improves.

'The Wyre Forest Head of Development Control is holding discussions with councillors about the empty sites at Larch Lap, Bond Worth and the Vinegar Works. The whole project needs careful thought.

'British Waterways Association has put in a planning application to upgrade the whole of the basins, laying new paths suitable for the disabled, re-opening the swing bridge, planting trees, and so on. We have had many grand schemes proposed by different companies which never come to fruition - I do hope that this one is implemented."

VILLAGE LIFE

16. Hartlebury

To the south-east of industrial Stourport, Hartlebury lies in a landscape as different from that of Wilden as it could be possible to imagine. The castle, standing on high ground above Hartlebury Common and surrounded by a reed-tinged moat, has been the Episcopal palace of the Bishops of Worcester for close on four centuries and has been in their possession since the thirteenth century.

Worcestershire by Peter J Neville Havins, 1974

HARTLEBURY COMMON

Hartlebury Common used to be known as Hartlebury Heath and its several hundred acres belonged to the church. Rare plants can still be found here, such as cotton grass, bog bean and soap wort. Bogwort used to be a popular herb for pains in the back, kidney or bladder problems. The herb was scalded or boiled in water and the liquid drunk three times a day.

The Common was enclosed by three Turnpike gates. One was near the junction of Wilden Top Road and the Hartlebury Road (then known as Jenny Holegate) at the foot of Enoch Baldwin's residence, the Mount. Another was at Crossway Green, by the Mitre Oak, where the A449 joins the A4025. A third was at the Anchor Inn, about 250 yards along the Worcester Road not far from the River Stour, and was known as Mitton Gate. This last toll gate was in three sections, the main large centre one for coaches and carts, a small gate on the right for pedestrians and a smaller gate on the left for sheep and other small animals which had to be counted one by one.

Mitton Gate was always busy and the gatekeeper in the nineteenth century, Mr Jones, was called upon any hour of the day or night. He and his wife would take half a night each. Both Mr and Mrs Jones were well-built and if there was any hint of trouble it only needed one word from either of them and the mischief-maker would pay up. They brought up eleven children in the tiny toll-house and lived to a ripe old age.

Mothers would send small boys to the Common to collect gorse which gave a fierce heat and was used for bread ovens. The boys would arrive in the early hours of the morning and try to creep past the gatekeeper while he or she was asleep to avoid payment, carefully lifting their barrows over the gate.

Sangers Circus used to camp on the Common when they paid their annual visit to Stourport. One year, Mrs Jones offered one of the elephants some cake. The following year, when they came again, to everyone's surprise the elephant refused to walk past the gate. Mrs Jones came to see what the commotion was about and, remembering her action the previous year, she fetched a cake and offered it to the elephant. Immediately the elephant moved on. This happened for six or seven years in succession.

Wedley says that one of the strangest sights in those days was that of dog carriages. Sometimes two fat men would be squeezed into a small

Bogbean

dog-carriage pulled by a team of huge dogs. They were so large they could have jumped over the toll gate except for the fact that they were tethered to the carriage.

A timber merchant, Thomas Gwillam, lived on the Common near Wiremill Farm with his team of donkeys. Wedley says:

"Seven or eight donkeys and a leader much bigger than the rest, followed by a long timber wagon, the urchins of the common dangling behind, was a sight as fit to be seen as a circus."

John Gould lived there too, a rag and bone man. His cry was 'Rags and bones, rabbit skins and hare skins, old baggin' and old ropin', broken and white glass, or any old iron'. An oatmeal man lived there who went around with a bag of oatmeal on his back, and a kipe man with a mountain of baskets for catching pike on his head. There was also a one-handed war veteran who carried tea from door to door and taught in the Methodist Sunday School.

Another resident was Billy the Saltman. Billy would travel the country with his donkey cart crying 'Salt, Salt!' He generally walked far ahead of the cart, calling to the donkey, 'Come on'. Occasionally the donkey would lag far behind, and Billy would cry out, 'Now then, come one with you, if you canna do better I'll get in the shafts myself'. His little dog went everywhere with him, Wedley says it was an ugly little thing but when Billy died, his little dog found the grave and sat there, day after day, refusing to leave.

THE GYPSIES

Also living on the Common were the gypsies. Present-day townsfolk with the surnames of Lovell, Lee, Smith, Davies, Stanley, Boswell and Loveridge may have descended from them. The gypsies made pegs and had a tremendous knowledge of natural remedies, using local herbs and shrubs.

A descendent of the Loveridges now lives in Tipton and says:

"I was always told that the gypsies originated in India and you can tell that by their colouring. A true Romany gypsy has black hair and darkish skin. They were very good at horse-breeding. I have known my uncle come back with as many as sixty horses from Kidderminster market.

'Ernie Loveridge was a champion boxer - this was bare knuckle fighting, they didn't have boxing gloves in those days. Sometimes he had to go over to Ireland to fight as bare-knuckle boxing had been made illegal in England but not in Ireland. Thousands would turn up to watch the match, they would be standing on the rooftops and everywhere. Ernie fought Richie Woodall, who later became world champion, but Richie was too good for him."

The gypsies are remembered by several older residents:

"The camp was down the back of Titton, the horses were tethered on the Common. The old lady (Mrs Loveridge) used to have a big black felt hat and a huge wicker basket almost like a clothes basket. My grandmother was the maternity lady or district nurse and sometimes I used to go with her to see the new babies. She took me into the gypsy caravan to see Loveridge's new baby. It was beautiful, so clean and tidy and respectable. They used to have fights among themselves but they never interfered with people outside. It used to be a regular thing, a fight on a Saturday after-

noon outside the Swan. The gypsies were not itinerant, you had respect for them."

Pen Lovell was born in 1778 and was famous for two reasons. The first was that, despite the fact that she smoked heavily from the age of sixteen, she lived to be 101 and died in her tent on Hartlebury Common. The second was that she was the mother of two gypsies who, in the early 1800's, were condemned for a crime they never committed. Just before they were due to be transported, two other men, who were sentenced to be hung, confessed to the crime. Wedley says that there was 'great rejoicing and free beer at the Red Lion for several days'.

Pen's funeral was attended by 500 gypsies and the chief mourners were all conventionally clad in black with black kid gloves.

Early in the twentieth century Mr Wesley Baker decided he would try to persuade the gypsies to lead a more conventional Christian life-style and pitched a mission tent on the high ridge near the Hartlebury Road. He was very successful, one outcome was that several couples who had been living together decided on a legal marriage.

John Loveridge (one of the gypsies) decided that Sunday services should be held there and they began in 1913. They were first held in a bungalow, 'the small fry of the gypsy encampment peeping out from under the table where they had been placed for safety' (Wedley). In the summer time the services were held in the open air. Then one day, John Loveridge went to see Reverend Gibbons. When he came out, without saying a word to any-one, he went straight to Kidderminster and ordered a load of wood. Some time previously he had purchased a piece of land for his family on the south side of the Common and he now offered it to the church as a site for a Mission Hall. Reverend Gibbons had accepted the offer. The parish supplied the fittings and in twelve months to a day from the beginning of the services, the wooden slatted chapel was opened and came under the direction of the Vicar of Lower Mitton. The hall was built entirely of wood, having seating accommodation for about 80 persons, a few having pews, the rest rush chairs. Outside hung the old bell from Mitton church known

A 1904 photograph of Wesley Baker's mission tent. Courtesy Brian Standish.

A recent photograph of Hartlebury village, showing the tower built by the colourful Bishop Sandys.

as the Ting Tang, a bell which always rang for five minutes before service commenced.

During the second world war the gypsies disappeared and the Mission Church remained empty. When the war was over the housing shortage was acute and people were squatting in anything remotely habitable. Mrs Helen Bower was 53 when her family moved into the Mission Church, she had attended services herself there. She told the *Kidderminster Shuttle*:

"People came from miles around to attend services. The carving in the chapel was beautiful and the hymn singing was first class. They always stuck to well-known hymns as many people couldn't read or write... There were still the old chapel lights hanging up and the pulpit in the corner of the room when we moved in. ... The stained glass windows were still there ... It was bitterly cold in winter and sometimes the roof used to bow inwards with the weight of the snow."

Mrs Helen Bower was rehoused in 1982 when she was 88. She had lived in the chapel for 35 years. By that time she had 43 grandchildren and all her children had left the little chapel for more comfortable circumstances.

In 1929 the town boundaries changed and Stourport was enlarged to include parts of Areley Kings, Hartlebury, Kidderminster foreign, Wilden and Wribbenhall which took effect from 1933. This meant that the gypsies came under the jurisdiction of the Worcestershire County Council. The gypsies were compelled to leave but some purchased nearby fields and lived there while others moved to Titton.

HARTLEBURY CASTLE

This has been the home of the Bishops of Worcester for four centuries. Many of the Bishops who lived here have been at the heart of great British events, some even helped to change them. Bishop Latimer campaigned for Henry VIII's divorce against Catherine of Aragon, Bishop Stillingfleet, who built the rectory, was Chaplain to Charles II. Bishop Fletcher was present at the execution of Mary, Queen of Scots, and made a clumsy attempt to convert her to Protestantism. Many suffered for their beliefs, Bishop Sandys supported Lady Jane Grey and went to prison for it, Latimer was burned at the stake. Some lived in great wealth, some in poverty.

There was probably an ecclesiastical building here as far back as Anglo-Saxon times when Burthred, king of Mercia, donated a piece of land. The fortifications were begun by Bishop Cantelupe, Lord Chancellor in the days of Simon De Montfort, and the moat was added by another Lord Chancellor. Successive Bishops lavished improvements and decorations upon it until it became one of the finest houses in England. John Leland, writing in the first half of the sixteenth century, described it as "well-builded" and with "fair ponds, a park for deer and a warren for conies (rabbits)".

At the time of the Reformation, Hugh Latimer was a popular Rector in Wiltshire who was very much in favour of Protestantism. Henry VIII was then looking for support in his divorce from Catherine of Aragon and consequent break from the Roman Catholic church, with the result that Latimer was appointed Bishop of Worcester. One of his tasks was to work with Archbishop Cranmer and Ridley on a Protestant version of the Homilies, to be read in a Church on "any Sunday or Holy Day when there is no sermon".

Henry VIII had underestimated Latimer's strength of character, their disagreements were many and after four years, Latimer resigned the Bishopric. Latimer lived at Hartlebury in grinding poverty. He had to sell his books and even his clothes for food. The king wanted to have him executed, but his minister, Thomas Cromwell managed to dissuade him. "Consider" he wrote to the king, "what a splendid man he is, and cast not that away in one hour which nature and art hath been so many years in breeding and perfecting". A tragic irony is that Latimer escaped execution for a more painful death later. When Henry VIII died and his Roman Catholic daughter, Mary, came to the throne, she had Bishop Latimer and Bishop Ridley, together with Archbishop Cranmer, burned at the stake in Oxford, October 16, 1555. Latimer's courage never flagged and he proclaimed that, through their sacrifice, they would 'light such a candle by God's grace in England, as I trust shall never be put out'.

Bishop Carr was an academic and a popular preacher but he arrived at the Castle with extreme financial problems. He had previously been Vicar of Brighton, and while he was there, he had become friendly with the Prince Regent, who reigned as George IV for ten years from 1820. This friendship had forced him into severe debt problems. Even the handsome stipend of Bishop of Worcester was not sufficient to clear his debts. He spent his time at Worcester shifting debts from one tradesman to another. He thought he had solved his problem when he married his daughter to a wealthy Worcester solicitor but unfortunately they soon separated. When he died the bailiffs claimed the house and the furniture. Most embarrassing was the fact that under the laws of that time, his body was considered to be a saleable item, consequently, on the day of the funeral, bailiffs at-

*An old engraving of Hartlebury
Castle.
Courtesy Brindley Arms.*

*The Winnall family in 1913 who
worked at Hartlebury Castle. Mrs
Winnall, the assistant cook, is in the
front.. On her right is her daughter
May, the housemaid, and on the left
is another daughter, Rose, the
parlourmaid. Courtesy Florence
Wilson.*

*Left: Hartlebury Castle in 1731.
Drawn and engraved by S & N
Buck.*

tempted to seize his body. So that he could have a decent burial, some of
his friends pledged their properties, which they never recovered.

Bishop Carr left debts of £100,000! At that time the Bishop of Worcester had two residences in Worcestershire, Hartlebury Castle and a house
by the cathedral, known as the Bishop's Palace. Bishop Carr's successor
was Bishop Pepys. He arrived with his wife and four children in 1841,
ready to move into the Palace only to find that creditors had locked the
gates against him, and he was not allowed to enter! A crowd gathered as he
argued with the debt-collectors. In the end, he had to leave his luggage in
the street and lodge with a local solicitor. About that time, it was decided
to slim the bishop's expenses by giving up one of his residences. Perhaps it
was because of his unpleasant experiences at the Palace, that Bishop Pepys
decided to dispense with that building and keep Hartlebury Castle. However, he reduced his expenses by getting rid of the deer in Hartlebury Park,
presenting them to the queen, a move which was not popular with the
Worcester churchmen as it deprived them of their venison dinners.

Isaac Wedley tells another story about Bishop Pepys. One fine summer
evening the Bishop decided to go for a walk along the road across the Common. He had dispensed with his Bishop's garb and was wearing an ordinary
pair of trousers and a jacket. At that time, a coach ran from Worcester to
Kidderminster across the Common and the Bishop heard the coach coming up behind him, with the driver thrashing the horses and swearing. The
Bishop stopped the coach and told the driver to have more patience, at
which the driver used more expletives and threatened to teach the med-
dlesome man to mind his own business. As the coach rolled on, the passengers said to the driver, 'Don't you know who that was?'. When the driver
learned his identity, he was horrified as the Bishop was one of his best
customers. He stopped the coach, jumped down and hurried after the
Bishop to apologise. The Bishop thought he was coming after him for a
fight and started running. The occupants of the coach were treated to the
scene of the Bishop running for dear life with the coach driver close behind. The Bishop managed to reach Hartlebury castle first and slammed
the door at which the driver began frantically ringing the bell. The footman

Edwin Sandys, Bishop of Worcester

answered the door and the coachman explained his errand, at which the Bishop came out and again told him that he should have more patience. Henry Pepys is one of the four bishops who lie in Hartlebury churchyard.

Perhaps the most colourful bishop was Edwin Sandys, a renowned scholar who lived from 1519 to 1588. He was born in Cumbria of a long-established family, his tutor held strong Protestant beliefs and was later burned at the stake for them. Edwin rose to power and helped to put Lady Jane Grey on the throne. She was overthrown after nine days' rule, the Roman Catholic Queen Mary sat on the throne, and Edwin was clapped in the Tower. After 38 weeks Queen Mary allowed him to be set free but when she told her ministers what she had done they remarked that she had just released the greatest heretic of them all. Soldiers were sent to recapture him but he had just boarded a boat for France.

Queen Mary was, of course, succeeded by the Protestant Elizabeth I in 1558. Therefore Edwin was able to return to England and was appointed bishop of Worcester. After eleven years at Worcester he became the first bishop of London and in 1575, Archbishop of York. On his travels Archbishop Sandys happened to stay at the Bull Inn, Doncaster. He had recently discharged from his service a notorious character by the name of Bernard Maude, who arrived at the inn, planning revenge. Towards evening, Maude was joined by his new employer, Sir Robert Stapleton, who also cherished designs against the Archbishop. They concealed the innkeeper's wife in a cupboard in the Archbishop's bedroom, waited until their innocent victim had retired for the night then burst into his room, accusing him of an illicit affair. Maude was carrying a dagger and at knife-point he demanded £800 for himself and the desirable Manor of Scrooby for his master. The Archbishop, however, was a noted fighter both in Church and State, and laid them both out. Queen Elizabeth, indignant at the scandalous charge laid against an exalted member of her established church, ordered her principal secretary to hold a Court of Enquiry. Sir Robert Stapleton was put in gaol for many years and a heavy sentence was passed on Maude. The court added that if Maude had not humbly confessed to his offence his ears would have been split as well.

Hugh Latimer, Bishop and martyr.
1485-1555

Hartlebury Castle today.

Archbishop Sandys was a great benefactor. He founded schools at Hawkshead (in Cumbria) and Hartlebury and in 1587, a year or so before he died, he arranged to have a tower added to Saint James Church in Hartlebury. The tower still exists, overshadowing the little village, although most of the church was rebuilt in 1836/7. The pride of the church is its bells, one is more than 600 years old, another was cast in 1678. The old and the new bishops' thrones are here and the pew-ends have the names and arms of all the bishops of Worcester dating back to 680. Thomas Garret, who was Rector here, was one of three priests burned at Smithfield for speaking out in support of the Pope. Their execution nearly caused a national uprising.

Hartlebury Castle is accustomed to royal visits. The first was of Edward I in the thirteenth century, followed by Edward III, Queen Mary Tudor when she was Princess Mary, and Elizabeth I.

Queen Elizabeth visited Worcester in the summer of 1575 and stayed at the Castle overnight. She rode side-saddle upon a white horse in her velvet riding habit, behind her streamed the ladies and gentlemen of her court. They stopped at White Ladies for a rest and refreshments, where the Queen removed her plumed riding hat and changed her habit for a richly embroidered dress. Jewels sparkled in her red hair, round her neck and on her fingers. Her face was framed by a high, gauzy ruff. The Bishop's retinue greeted her at the Mitre Oak in Crossway Green, about one-and-a-half miles south of Hartlebury.

Not all her visits were so successful. Francis Bacon (1561-1626) tells of the time that the queen was to pay a visit to the Bishop of Worcester but when she reached Hartlebury there was no-one to greet her. The Bishop had evidently forgotten or mistaken the date. The queen was furious, she stopped at the village inn, sent for the Bishop, 'rated him soundly' and departed, extremely annoyed.

Another catastrophic royal visit occurred in the late 1700's. George III arrived with his retinue but the conscientious tollkeeper closed the gate and refused to let the royal cortege through until each and everyone of them had paid the appropriate tolls.

The north wing of Hartlebury Castle is now a County Museum, many of the artefacts coming from a collection at Tickenhill House in Bewdley. The castle has the famous library of Bishop Hurd, available to the general public by appointment. Bishop Hurd was private tutor to the Prince of Wales (later George IV) and in 1807 the Prince Regent rode over to Hartlebury to see his old tutor. Visitors are given a taste of all walks of life, from the State Rooms to the collection of ornate gypsy caravans.

THE CIVIL WAR

In *The Civil War in Worcestershire, 1642-1646*, J W Willis Bund writes that although Worcestershire is one of the smaller English counties, more fighting went on during the great Civil War than in most other counties. 'In every year of the war there was more or less fighting within it'.

Upper Mitton stood between two important Royalist garrisons, the one at Bewdley guarded the bridge and another at Hartlebury Castle was so important that it was given the role of Royal Mint, making coins to finance the war.

The main route between Bewdley and Worcester ran past Upper Mitton and was well-used by the military. A small army, complete with cavalry and a thousand foot soldiers, passed through in 1644 on its way to Dudley to try and relieve the siege of Dudley Castle. At its head was Lord Wilmot. The Wilmot family owned six mills along the river Stour. An order went out to both Royalist and Parliamentarian commanders 'to forbear to plunder the cloth in the fulling mills in Kidderminster and Hartlebury, belonging to Robert Willmott, Treasurer for the Committee for the County of Stafford'.

The inhabitants of Mitton and Hartlebury must have lived in great fear. Both Royalist and Parliamentarian armies had problems getting supplies to the troops with the result that men were forced to provide for themselves by any means. This was one of the reasons why they stole anything they could lay their hands on. Thomas Brooke's house in Hartlebury Parish was plundered twice in 1646 and again later. The Rector was plundered in 1642 and in 1646 he was forced to quarter the troops at the cost of £8, a large sum in those days. In some of the households, the men were away fighting leaving only women and children to protect their property.

In 1645, any local men who were not away fighting were made to leave their daily work and help to strengthen the defences of the castle. The next year a strong Parliamentary force advanced and surrounded the castle. All the other garrisons in the region had surrendered and so Hartlebury, realising that the war was lost, followed suit.

But Mitton's troubles were not yet over. The next year it came to the ears of the new Parliamentary governor of Hartlebury Castle that a guerrilla plot was afoot, the local Royalists were planning to surprise Dawley Castle. Half a hundredweight of gunpowder was found in a field at Wolverley and one of the conspirators, Major Harcot, was brought to Hartlebury Castle and tortured by having lighted musket fuses placed on the soles of his feet. Understandably, he gave away details of the plot and revealed that a small army of 200 men were training in Boscobel Woods, near Madeley. The plotters were at once surrounded, attacked and captured.

The Parliamentarians strengthened the Castle by converting it into a garrison once again, then it was used as a prison and later demolished. Most of the present red-brick buildings have been built since the civil war and are a mixture of Stuart and Georgian styles, although parts of the original thirteenth century structure remain and some of the moat is still in existence.

During World War II, Hartlebury continued its tradition as a military base by providing a storage depot for aeroplane spares, known as 25MU, one of a series of seven depots across the country.

HARTLEBURY SCHOOL

Hartlebury school is so old that its origins have long been forgotten. Boys have been tutored here for at least six hundred years. The first building was timber-framed, fifty feet long (15.23 metres) by eighteen feet wide (5.48 metres) standing next to the church. It had one large classroom where the assistant teacher taught the younger children to read, write and count, and a smaller room where the schoolmaster taught Latin and Greek.

Bishop Edwin Sandys persuaded Queen Elizabeth in 1559 to grant the little school a Royal Charter. The original charter still survives. It was to be called 'The Free Grammar School of Queen Elizabeth' and was to have a master and an assistant 'to teach virtue and good learning, and the true knowledge of God and His Holy Word, and, at least one afternoon in every week, to teach the scholars to write and cast accounts'. About ten years later a list of statutes and ordinances had been prepared. One of them states:

"That the schoolmasters should take the profits of all cock-fights and potations commonly used in schools, and other gifts given by them by any of their friends of their scholars, besides their wages, until their salaries should be augmented."

We know that cock fighting existed by the fact that in 1616 the Order Book, kept by the Trustees, shows the cost of 'the building of a brewhouse and Chamber and Cockloft over it, for Mr Pierce our head schoolmaster'.

Twenty governors were to be appointed and as the original school only had thirty boys there was almost one for every boy. Despite the number of governors, the school was usually mismanaged. It was to be supported chiefly by renting out its farmland and property, and as the governors and their friends were tenants, rents were set at a low level. In addition, the Order Books reveal regular purchases of wine and food for meetings and other

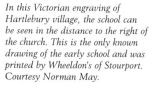

In this Victorian engraving of Hartlebury village, the school can be seen in the distance to the right of the church. This is the only known drawing of the early school and was printed by Wheeldon's of Stourport. Courtesy Norman May.

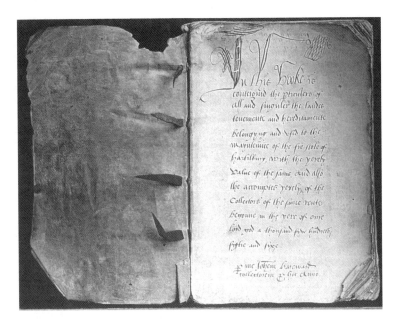

festivities (but no books). Bishop Lloyd wrote to the governors in 1705, saying that it was quite unnecessary to spend so much money on entertainment 'since you all live within the parish, where you have meat and drink at your own houses'. He added that they should not have meetings in alehouses and that the salaries they were paying were insufficient to attract good teachers.

In 1794 a new school was built up the road, this time with a playground, and in 1912, more buildings were added further up the hill. The headmaster was usually the local curate. Originally, all pupils were free, then only those who lived in the parish were free. By 1807, pupils were being charged 1/6d (approximately 7p) and the next year, fee-paying boarders were taken. No fees were paid after 1832.

In 1841 the school fell into debt and the attorney-general filed a bill in Chancery. The author of *Free Schools of Worcestershire and their Fulfilment*: states:

"From 1841 to 1852 the school was shut up, and those parishioners who could not afford to send their sons (to) a distance, had the mortification to see them growing up in ignorance, whilst the Court profoundly discussed the points at issue. Yes, a question that would have been settled in two or three days by the trustees themselves, took the Court of Chancery only eleven years to determine."

The school had the unique privilege of having a prime minister, Stanley Baldwin, as chairman. In 1938, members of the Worcestershire Association presented Earl Baldwin (their president) with a pair of exquisite wrought iron gates for Astley Hall, designed by the Bromsgrove Guild. Earl Baldwin's son presented the gates to the school in 1953 in memory of his father and they are still in use.

One morning in 1940, the boys arrived at the school to find that it no longer existed. A fire had started in the laboratory and the buildings had

School gates at Hartlebury, made by the prestigious Bromsgrove Guild. Courtesy Norman May.

burned down overnight. Even the huge school bell had melted away. However, there was no holiday for the pupils, lessons continued in Hartlebury Castle.

By the time that the sweeping educational reforms arrived in 1977, Hartlebury Grammar school was educating 120 boys. Although this was only a little country grammar school, a high percentage of pupils went on to established universities, and some of them achieved national fame, such as Julius Harrison (the composer), the queen's surgeon and the goal-keeper of the English Olympic hockey team. A private school now occupies the site.

HARTLEBURY VILLAGE

An old cross standing in the village dated 1666 was pulled down under the orders of a local farmer who claimed that it was in the way. At the same time he also demolished the stocks and the whipping post.

WARESLEY HOUSE

Originally this was the ancient manor house of South Hartlebury. For over forty years, from about 1876 to 1912, it was the home of Reverend Benjamin Gibbons, the wealthy benefactor of Saint Michael's Church in Stourport, who decided that the vicarage was not grand enough for him. Before then, it was the home of Dr John Peel, the Dean of Worcester.

17. Wilden

It was a place where I had known from childhood every man on the ground, where I was able to talk to men, not only about troubles in the works, but troubles at home, where strikes and lock-outs were unknown, and where fathers and grandfathers of the men had worked and their sons automatically went into the business.
It was also a place where nobody ever got the sack, and where we had a natural sympathy for those who were less concerned with efficiency than this generation is. There were a large number of old gentlemen who used to spend the day sitting on the handle of a wheelbarrow and smoking their pipes.
Oddly enough, it was not an inefficient community. It was the last survivor of that type of works, and ultimately was swallowed up in one of those great combinations to which the industries of the country are tending.

Stanley Baldwin, Prime Minister, referring to
Baldwin's Iron Works at Wilden

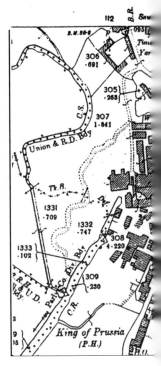

A map of Wilden in 1902. Note the course of the River Stour at the time, compared to the present day. Crown Copyright, courtesy Ordnance Survey.

Right: A very different-looking Wilden in 1890.
Courtesy Kidderminster Library.

Wilden is a most unusual village. It has one main street over a mile in length, running from Hartlebury Common to the junction of the A442 and A449 on the Kidderminster road, with most of its houses on the eastern side of the road only. On its western side, sometimes far below the road, the River Stour winds to and fro.

Florence Wilson is now in her seventies and lives at Kidderminster but she grew up in the village:

'"My uncle had a piece of land at Wilden, and on it he kept seventeen pigs, two goats, 120 fowl and various rabbits. I used to be sent off to Clarke and Cranes to buy Sharp's corn, wheat, barley and maize. My grandfather used to mix them together as a kind of porridge for the pigs. He said it would keep the purples away. He never kept the pigs in the stalls as they do today and he used to sit up all night when the pigs were farrowing. There are houses on there now.

'My uncle would also sweep chimneys. He used to sweep our chimney by tying a bunch of holly branches together with a rope and pulling it up the chimney but he also had a set of brushes. An old lady said to him, 'Will you come and sweep my chimney?' and she asked how many dust sheets she needed to put down. He told her that he wouldn't come through the house, but he would get a ladder, go up on the roof and push the brushes down the chimney. She laid dust sheets over her room but she stood in front of the fireplace waiting to see the brushes. The next time he saw her she was black from head to foot.

'Wilden wasn't modernised until after the war. There was no gas, no toilets and water came from a pump. A horse and cart used to come round and empty the toilets. Sometimes we would be biking home from the carpet factory during the dinner time and we would say, 'Whew, what's that smell?' and then we would see the horse and cart. When the driver saw us he would shout, 'I've just emptied yours!' then he'd add, 'I'll get my bread and cheese out now'. Before then, it wasn't even

218

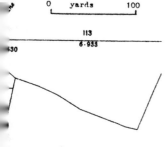

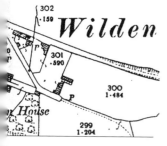

...den Works
...ron & Tinplate)

Wilden

emptied. The toilet went right down to the Stour, it was 100 yards from the house and you had to open a big garden door to get to it. The toilet was built on a slope and from time to time you had to throw a bucket of dirt on it.."

Opposite the heart of the village, and surrounded by Worcestershire countryside, is a large factory site. There was a small mill here for centuries powered by a water wheel and linked to the Stour by its own little canal. Early records suggest that by 1669 it was an iron slitting mill. By 1791 it was occupied by a Thomas Hill and owned by the Foley family, but it had to be sold because of the extravagant lifestyle of the Third Baron Foley. Wedley says that at one time it was Mr Farmer's wire works. By 1830 it had been taken over by Mr Lewty, who traded under the name of the Wilden Iron and Tin Plate Company. Mr Lewty employed about fifty people, and is remembered for his two fine black ponies.

Mr Lewty installed a beam engine and steam power. However, keeping up-to-date with these new developments was an expensive business and, like many other manufacturers of that time, in 1840 he went bankrupt. The mill was taken over by Enoch, Pearce and William Baldwin and re-named E P & W Baldwin Ltd. The company won a gold medal in Paris in 1878 for tin plate and sheet iron. Its plant included iron puddling furnaces and forges producing blackplate, tin and ternecoated plates. As the years went by puddled iron was replaced by steel, although some production of iron persisted at Wilden until as late as 1912.

By 1902 the Baldwin ventures stretched across the Midlands and into Wales. All the original owners had died out and so they came under the control of Alfred Baldwin, father of Stanley Baldwin, the Prime Minister. The company was renamed simply Baldwin Limited.

Jack Stringer was employed as an office boy before World War II:

"The Wilden works had a row of hot mills and also a cold roll mill. The cold roll mill was mainly used for polishing steel sheets.

There were a number of steam mills in a row. The Stour used to run right along the road and at one place it flowed under the works and came out in fields the other side. An old water mill was situated at this point and when the older men couldn't stand the pace they were sent to work at the water mill. You had to go down under the wheels for cleaning and repairs and for a joke, sometimes, somebody would turn the water on.

There was a pub up the road from the Wilden works which has now been demolished. When I knew it, it was called the Wilden Inn but before that it was the King of Prussia. The name had to be changed when we were fighting Germany. The men in the mills were all on piece work so it didn't matter if they left work and there was a constant stream of workmen fetching pints and bottles of beer.

'I knew Stanley Baldwin. When Parliament was in recess he would go into most of the houses in the village and talk to the elderly folk and

A general view of Wilden from an old postcard.
Courtesy Gordon Ward.

occasionally share a cup of tea with them. Sometimes, when I was walking across the fields back to work after my dinner break, I used to meet him returning home after a visit and he would stop to have a chat. He was very trustworthy and very honest. It is on record that he gave all the excess profit that he made from the first world war to the treasury.

'The Baldwin works were like a happy family. There were never any strikes or disagreements. They worked night and day, the mills never stopped, they went on from Monday morning until they closed at the weekend. If the mills stopped during the night, you woke up.

'When I went off to the war the works were known as Baldwin's Ltd but when I returned they had joined up with Richard Thomas and the company was Richard Thomas and Baldwin Ltd. Then, of course, the whole steel industry was nationalised and became British Steel."

A widow who now lives in the Walshes remembers the days when her husband worked there:

"Everything was done by hand. The steel was folded over then put in the rollers. These were like an old-fashioned mangle, and a knob could be turned to make the aperture smaller and smaller. The workers kept flipping the steel over and putting it through the rollers so that it got longer and longer and thinner and thinner. The steel started out as thick as a deep pile carpet and ended up as thin as tissue paper.

'The men would toss it like a pancake and throw it across the floor. You would think it was very dangerous but there was hardly ever an accident.

'The workers wore flannel grey shirts and leather trousers with a protective piece round the knee to stop them from getting burned. They often burned their eyebrows off and a lot of the workers had their hair burned at the front. My husband was very fair and he always had a red forehead."

Betty Webb was born in Wilden, her father, grandfather and uncles all worked at Baldwins' steel works:

"My father was a Doubler at the factory. They worked in a gang of four, there was the furnaceman who took the red hot steel out of the furnace and put it in a roller, the Catcher who caught it the other side, the Doubler who doubled the steel over, clamping it into one piece while it was still red hot, and the Stacker. The Doubler was considered to be the job which required the most expertise and so he was the highest paid. The least experienced was the Catcher.

Wilden Forge in about 1900. Alfred Baldwin (father of Stanley Baldwin, the Prime Minister) is on the extreme left.
Courtesy Kidderminster Library

'When I was about eleven years old I was allowed to walk through the Baldwin's factory at Wilden to take my dad his tea in a white enamel can with a top on and a handle. The works were very noisy, and very hot with all those furnaces. Sometimes I would take him sandwiches, which would be something like bread and dripping. The day was divided into three shifts and my dad worked different shifts each week.

'In those days nearly everybody lived in rented houses. First of all we lived by the factory, then a larger house at Wilden Top became vacant and we moved there. I think that's what killed my father. It was further to walk and when he came out of the factory he was absolutely dripping with sweat. One evening he had to walk all the way up the hill in the cold and pouring rain. He caught pneumonia and, of course, there was nothing you could do in those days. He was only 41, and he left a wife and three daughters."

The Baldwins built houses for their workers across the road, along the Wilden Lane.

In the late 1940's Richard Thomas & Baldwin Ltd was at the forefront of research into a prototype plant for the production of high grade electrical quality cold reduced strip. Their research reached such a high level that factories had to be specially built elsewhere and by 1955 Wilden was only manufacturing blackplate for the hardware trade and hot rolled silicon sheets for the electrical industry. It closed in 1956.

A field on Wilden Top belonging to Baldwins was sold to Mr West who lived in a house next to the field. He bequeathed it to the village as a sports field.

The Baldwin Centre, formerly the offices of Baldwin's factory.

THE BALDWIN FAMILY AND THE MACDONALDS

The Baldwins spent several months each year in London both on business and for pleasure. They were Methodists, and while in London they became friendly with the two sons and five daughters of a Methodist minister, George Macdonald. The daughters were petite and beautiful, like porcelain dolls in appearance but with a fierce intelligence and sharp wit. In 1856, the Macdonalds paid their first visit to Stourport.

Alfred Baldwin was the youngest of the large Baldwin family, despite this he owned a profitable share in the three Baldwin iron works. He began 'calling' on the fourth Macdonald daughter, Louisa, and in 1866 they were married. Curiously, by the time of his marriage he had become 'High Church'. They lived in Bewdley High Street where their son, Stanley, was born a year later.

1869 was a bad year for them. Louisa's father, George Macdonald, died then Louisa had a miscarriage from which she never seemed to recover. Stanley remained an only child. Alfred was the leading light of the local liberal party and became involved in a political scandal. Elections at that time were vicious, bloody affairs, he was accused of bribery and corruption and consequently withdrew from politics.

Now that his political interests were behind him Alfred was able to turn his attention to the iron works at Wilden and Stourport. The following year he bought out his brothers, George and Stanley, and began to improve the business. No doubt his workers were delighted. As a committed Christian he considered it his responsibility to make sure that his workers were well cared for. Over the years he provided medical facilities and guar-

A portrait of Alfred Baldwin.

anteed employment. He introduced eight-hour shifts instead of the standard twelve-hours. He built the church and the school, establishing a Sunday School. Both his wife and his sister-in-law taught in the Sunday School.

That same year (1870), Alfred decided to move into Wilden House, opposite the factory. During the past four years, he had been travelling the three miles to and from Bewdley and Wilden each day, sometimes walking, sometimes taking a coach. For generations it had been expected that the general manager should live at Wilden House, despite the horrendous noise and the black smuts.

Louisa's three older sisters all married penniless artists, but each of these men rose to pre-eminence in the art world. Consequently, four of the Macdonald sisters are associated with famous men. Alice, the oldest, was the mother of Rudyard Kipling; Georgiana married Sir Edward Burne Jones, one of the founders of the pre-Raphaelite movement; wheres Agnes's husband was Sir Edward Poynter who controlled the National Gallery, the Royal Academy and the Tate. Louisa's son, Stanley, became Prime Minister of England three times. The faces of the sisters stare down from many a pre-Raphaelite painting, for example, in Burne-Jones' King Cophetua and the Beggar Maid, Georgiana is the maid.

Edith, the youngest sister, never married and remained with their mother at Bewdley. In 1875 her mother died, and so it was decided that she should move in with the Baldwins at Wilden.

It must have been a busy household, despite their four servants. These were the days when food had to be prepared from basic ingredients, when the weekly wash took two days, when floors had to be scrubbed, furniture polished, water carried and coal fires lit. Various family members came to stay, often for long periods. Stanley's cousin, Harold, was left an orphan and lived with them for years. Rudyard Kipling often paid a visit. Agnes spent so much time at Wilden it was decided that her son (Ambo Poynter) and Stanley should be sent off to boarding school together. The Macdonalds suffered more than their fair share of ill-health and tragedies. Stanley's mother, Louisa, was an invalid and in a wheelchair for weeks on end.

Alfred had resumed his political life and in 1892 he became MP for West Worcestershire. He was also Director of the Metropolitan Bank and a Director of the Great Western Railway.

In 1908 he died suddenly at their London flat. He had lived at Wilden for over 40 years and at his funeral it was estimated that as many as 2,000 mourners were standing quietly outside the little church. Stanley, then 41 years of age, was asked to stand as MP for West Worcestershire in his father's place. He had been managing the steel works with his father and had been appointed 'Governing Director' in 1898. He had married Lucy Risdale, known as 'Cissie', she was healthy and robust, unlike his delicate mother. They had met at a cricket match at Rottingdean where she had impressed him by her fast bowling. At first they rented Dunley Hall, then in 1902 he moved to Astley Hall (see Astley for further information).

Stanley Baldwin in 1928 helping the ninety-year old Earl of Coventry, once a great sporting peer, to his car. Courtesy Norman May.

Many of the older residents remember Stanley Baldwin. Mrs Blunt knew him when she was a little girl. Many years later she was in the post office when he was at the counter and he dropped something on the floor. As he was getting quite elderly, she picked it up for him. He looked at her and said, 'Why, it's ...'. He had remembered not only her face but her name.

Fred Rimmel has been told by several people that:

"Stanley Baldwin from Astley Hall always went to Wilden church on Christmas morning and he carried a pocket full of half-crowns (12 1/2p). If you stood on your doorstep when Stanley emerged from church and if you were lucky enough to catch his eye to wish him, 'Good morning', you would get half-a-crown. It was a lot of money in those days and it made their Christmas."

Edith Macdonald remained at Wilden until she died in 1937. One of the post boys who delivered her daily newspaper can remember her. At Christmas time the maid would be standing on the steps in her dark uniform and white collar and cuffs, waiting for him. She would take him up the imposing staircase and into Edith's bedroom. The elderly Edith would be sitting in bed, wearing her boudoir cap and she would give him half-a-crown.

After Edith died, Wilden House was sold and the contents auctioned. The house was demolished in 1939 for a road-widening scheme.

WILDEN CHURCH

Alfred Baldwin arranged for the All Saints Church at Wilden to be built and paid for it. The cost was £3,000 in total, the site was given by the Bishop of Worcester and the church was consecrated in 1880.

From the outside it appears to be an ordinary little Victorian church, but inside, the blaze of colour from ten beautiful stained glass windows by Sir Edward Burne-Jones (1833-98) and William Morris (1834-96) is quite memorable. It is probably the only church in existence with Morris glass in all its windows.

How did such a masterpiece arrive in this tiny, out-of-the-way village? Alfred Baldwin had married one of the Macdonald sisters, therefore Lady Burne-Jones was his sister-in-law. The first Morris window was installed by Alfred and his wife in 1902, the remainder were donated by friends and relatives. Unfortunately, William Morris and Burne-Jones never saw the windows in situ for the work was not completed until after their deaths.

The church also has another treasure, here described by Flo Wilson:

"Alfred Baldwin's sister-in-law, Miss Edith MacDonald, lived at Wilden House and she helped two ladies of the local women's group to embroider this wonderful altar cloth with bunches of grapes in gold. It used to be

A recent photograph of Wilden Church, the only church in England to have a complete set of Burne Jones/Morris windows.

This is thought to be a procession to celebrate the consecration of Wilden church. The leading chorister nearest the camera may be Stanley Baldwin.
Courtesy Brian Pountney

The church choir at Wilden. Date unknown, but before 1939 and perhaps before 1914.
Courtesy Florence Wilson.

brought out every Christmas and Easter but now it's locked up in a case on the wall."

The Baldwin's were a musical family and the little Chapel of Ease outshone many larger churches in its reputation for music. Church of England people tended to live in Lower Mitton and as the little Wilden church with its high standard in music was very popular, they would walk all the way to Wilden. However, many of the workers in Wilden were Methodist and they would walk all the way to the Methodist Church at Lower Mitton. Isaac Wedley writes that every Sunday, there would be this two-way traffic between Lower Mitton and Wilden.

Wilden became a parish church in its own right in about 1895. Alfred Baldwin provided an endowment which paid for the Vicar's salary.

Florence Wilson's family were well-known in Wilden where her father and grandfather were churchwardens:

"When I was about nine I used go down to the vicarage and help mum to lay the table for all the canons and vicars who were coming. They used to take it in turns to entertain each other at different places. Mother would show me how to put the knives, forks, spoons and napkin rings.

'When I was eleven I started going to the girl guides. I used to have the key to the church, a great big thing, and I was told that at nine o'clock, when the guides had finished, I had to throw a bucket of slack on the boiler. I was told that if I was frightened, I was wicked because good girls have nothing to fear. In the church on my own I used to tremble but I wouldn't let anybody know that.

'Wilden Church was Stanley Baldwin's church (the Prime Minister). One day, he said to my father, 'You were a wounded soldier, weren't you? Can I see your wound?' and my grandfather showed him his foot which had been injured at the Dardanelles. Mr Baldwin asked him how long he had had it and my father said, 'Eight years or more'. 'And what do you get for that?'. My father told him that he didn't get anything. Mr Baldwin said, 'You ought to have a pension'. He helped him to claim for it and not long afterwards he started getting 2/6d (121/2p) a week extra.

'A channel runs down the centre of the church, covered by an iron grating. This was the heating system and a long chimney from the boiler ran along the channel. It was very efficient and the church was never cold. We could have as much coal as we liked as Baldwin's and Vale's both did a lot for the church. At the bottom end of the grating was a door to the stoke hole and we would open the grating at this point and put a bucket of water on the pipe to get it hot enough to wash the church floor. One Saturday afternoon a bucket of water had been placed on the pipe and the grating had been left open. Two ladies and a gentlemen were walking backwards in the church. One minute they were there and the next minute one of the ladies had disappeared. She had fallen twelve feet down the stoke hole. We had to fetch the doctor but she had only broken two ribs. Fortunately she was wearing this wonderful fur coat and it saved her."

WILDEN SCHOOL

When Mr Baldwin laid the foundation stone of the church, he said that he hoped to build an infants school in the very near future. He kept to his word and the little school, which is still in use, was opened in 1882. He then enlarged the churchyard and provided a house for the Vicar. After Mr

Baldwin's death the villagers paid for a memorial clock, which stands near the entrance to the churchyard.

Betty Webb attended Wilden School in the late 1920s. In those days, discipline was severe:

"The headmistress was Mrs Mills. She was very strict, she used to frighten me. There were only two classes and three teachers. I had the cane once, when the whole class had it. The headmistress had left a senior girl in charge, and it went to her head a bit. One or two started talking and wouldn't get on with their work. Afterwards she said that we had all been talking and so the whole class had the cane."

To this day, every year, on 13 July, the children of the school gather in the churchyard next door to place flowers and sing a hymn at the grave of Thomas Jones.

Thomas Jones was an agricultural labourer who lived in the Parish of Stone. He had a heavy work load and worked long hours for only twelve shillings a week.. He lived simply, with few possessions, renting one room of a house. When he knew that he was not long for this world, he sent for a retired schoolmaster, Mr Millward, to make his will. To Mr Millward's surprise, Thomas Jones began his will by leaving £50, then a large sum of money, to each of several friends. Any money which was left over he wanted to go to Alfred Baldwin. He asked that Alfred Baldwin should arrange for the children of Wilden School to go to his grave every year on his birthday and sing a hymn. Afterwards they were to receive a treat.

Wilden church, with the little school next door. Alfred Baldwin paid for both of the buildings.

Wilden schoolchildren in 1910. Courtesy Brian Pountney.

Opposite page:
One of the ten Burne Jones/Morris windows in Wilden Church.

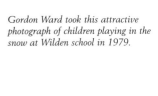

The Schoolmaster fetched Alfred Baldwin and they both said that, before drawing up the will, they needed proof that the old man had the money. After a great deal of persuasion, Thomas told the two men to lift him from his bed. When they looked under the mattress they found a small fortune comprising several hundred pounds and a bank book.

He died the next day, aged 78. This was in 1899 and ever since that day the children of Wilden School have carried out his request. At first the children received expensive presents, but now the annual income is only about £13. The custom of visiting his grave each year, placing flowers on it and singing a hymn has continued to this day.

WILDEN PARISH HALL

The people of Wilden nearly lost their parish hall in the 1950's as Jack Stringer explains:

"For many years, I was on the committee of Wilden Parish Hall, together with Stanley Baldwin's second son, Wyndham, who was the third Lord Baldwin. He was an extremely nice fellow.

'The parish hall was built in about 1930. The school at Wilden was a Church School and had plenty of land to spare and so permission was obtained to build our parish hall on land belonging to the school. All interests were vested in the Curate in Charge, Reverend Cory, later Canon Cory. Just before he died in about 1952, Canon Cory came to one of our parish meetings and told us that he was worried because the Church of England had handed the school over to the Education Authority so that the ground now belonged to them. He told us that we must get things sorted out.

'The Education Authorities wanted to kick us off! We really had to fight to keep our hall. It took us four years to get it sorted out, and in the end we bought the land for £25."

18. Lickhill

Before the canal was built, Lickhill Manor was the only place of any importance in the area. By 1429 it had authority both over its own estates and those of Lower Mitton Manor.

Isaac Wedley

A beautiful William and Mary house, Lickhill Manor, was built for a wealthy family, with a fine oak staircase and panelled rooms. By the sixteenth century the Manor was held by the Lygon family but in 1616, the year of Shakespeare's death, Sir William Lygon shocked the local gentry by conforming to egalitarian principles and selling off the land and houses to every tenant. The manor itself was sold to James Clent who passed it to John Folliott, governor of Ross Castle. Thomas, 2nd Lord Folliott, was governor of Londonderry in 1662. The walls were once hung with priceless tapestries but a later Folliott took them, together with the family portraits, to Hollybrook House, Sligo, their Irish seat.

Members of the Folliott family or their tenants lived there until 1822, when the manor was sold to Joseph Craven JP of Steeton, Yorkshire. The iron gates at Lickhill were put up when young Mr Craven got married.

The Cravens were an established aristocratic family; an ancestor, Earl Craven, was at the centre of a famous love story. He was devoted to Elizabeth Stuart, sister of Charles I, commonly known as 'the Winter Queen'. She was born in Scotland in 1596 and when she was only about seventeen she was married to the future Frederick V. In 1618 Frederick became King of Bohemia which unfortunately precipitated the Thirty Years War. King and queen were soon fleeing for their lives. The queen managed to reach the safety of Holland where, some time later, she met the Earl of Craven. He helped her and her brother, Charles I, with money and even tried to recover the Palatinate (the Royal privileges) for the queen and her husband. His loyalty only resulted in his estates in England being confiscated, although they were restored later. In 1661 she crossed to England and was given a pension by Charles II. After the death of her husband, the queen

Lickhill Manor, once the home of the Folliotts and, later, the Cravens.

lived in the Earl of Craven's house in London, and rumour has it that the two were married.

Despite the queen's upheavals she managed to produce thirteen children. Two of them fought in the civil war for Charles I (their uncle), and the twelfth child, Sophia, became the mother of George I. When the Earl died, the earldom became extinct but the barony passed to a distant relative, William Craven.

In the 1920's, a very fine maternity hospital was built at Lickhill, known as the Lucy Baldwin Maternity Hospital, named after the wife of the prime minister. Mrs Baldwin made an impassioned appeal on radio for a maternity hospital, where specialists would be on hand to treat any emergencies. Sir Julien Cahn was told about the appeal by a friend and wrote to Mrs Baldwin, offering to give her a present. She replied that she would most like to be given a maternity hospital. To her amazement, he agreed to fund the entire hospital. providing his name was not revealed until the building was completed. To hide his identity, the work was carried out through an intermediary but unfortunately, just before the building was completed, the intermediary died. Sir Julien had to come forward and reveal himself to finalise the project. It was opened on April 16th 1929. The Lucy Baldwin hospital is now used as a cottage hospital.

NEWTOWN

The old quarter at the Minster Road end of Windermere Way, including Brindley, Bishop, Lorne and Warwick Streets, was once known as Newtown. The Post Office is still known as Newtown P.O., and nearby shops are still referred to by that name.

The Lucy Baldwin Hospital, originally a maternity hospital.

19. The Christian Shores

Another member said that the people of Areley Kings may not want all the black sheep of Stourport on their side of the river, inferring that the law-abiding citizens lived on the Areley Kings side. This is how the old saying arose that the inhabitants of Areley Kings 'live on Christian shores'.

Isaac Wedley, edited, see page 65

After a life-time of sea-going adventures, Andrew Wehner has settled in Areley Kings. Surprisingly it is not the local boating facilities which have absorbed him but its early history:

"For me, history ends at 1600. It's the period before that time which interests me, the earlier the more interesting.

'Areley Kings is Stourport's southern neighbour, on the other side of the river. It was once the haunt of eagles, hence the name Ernleye, later corrupted to Areley, which means a clearing where there are eagles.

'Some time ago a water pipe was put in across the area. An archaeologist was in attendance, and I later heard some lectures he gave on local history. He told me that, in the pipe trench, he had found evidence of medieval, Saxon, Roman and even Neolithic activity in the area. This is good farmland, and so has been inhabited for thousands of years.

'He had found an indication of a Roman building on the Dunley Road, opposite the Wobbly Wheel House. This suggests that there was a big Roman estate here, then the Saxons took it over, perhaps doing away with the occupants. In time it became the Saxon Manor of Martley, and came into the hands of Edith, the wife of Edward the Confessor. It was a Royal Manor, which explains the 'Kings' part of the name, but by tradition was actually held by the Queen. When William the Conqueror arrived in 1066, he gave it to his friend William Fitzosbern, Earl of Hereford. The king gave his warlords lots of little bits instead of one big piece, so that they would not become too powerful, and Fitzosbern was also given Newent. Fitzosbern gave the income of Martley church to the Abbey of Cormeilles, in Normandy, which he had previously founded.

'Fitzosbern was killed in action in 1071, and his estates went to his son, who rebelled against the king. He was fortunate that he wasn't hung, drawn and quartered, instead, as a punishment, he lost all his estates. Consequently the Domesday Book of 1086 records that Martley belonged to the king again. It was expected to supply him with 2,625 eels a year, they were probably caught at Areley Kings, When I lived in Gloucestershire young eels, fried alive, were considered a great delicacy, and they may still be.

SAINT BARTHOLOMEW'S

'Saint Bartholomew is the patron saint of wool and cloth manufacturers. Stourport now has two parish churches. Saint Michael's was the first but when the boundaries were altered in 1937 Saint Bartholomews also found itself in the Urban District of Stourport.

'In Saxon times there was a church at Martley but no church at Areley Kings. However, it is my personal opinion that the site of Areley Kings

A stained glass window in the church commemorating its association with Layamon.

church has long been a holy site. There's a fairly prominent hill here, overlooking a river. The Saxon word 'lea' means a clearing in the forest. There is something in the soil in the churchyard which inhibits the growth of trees. Wouldn't the hill have been sacred to an animist culture of about 3,000 BC? The idea of a holy site would have lived on, through the Romans and the Saxons. In Saxon England the gospel was spread by itinerant preachers who were based at Minsters. There was a Minster at Great Witley and one at Kidderminster, so no doubt they preached on our hill."

Layamon was a priest here, ministering to his flock about the year 1200. Layamon was the first great English poet and author. He rescued from oblivion some of the greatest stories of the past. He was the first to describe the adventures of King Lear and King Arthur with his knights of the round table. His work inspired Shakespeare, Malory, Tennyson and many lesser writers. Even Harry Potter embarks on a grail-like quest. Nearly a century and a half before his time, the Norman French had conquered England and their language was used in all high places. Layamon's poem, Brut, was the first great literary work in the English language. His book, written in poetic form, tells the old legends of Great Britain since the arrival of Brut (from where Britain possibly gets its name) until 688.

'This is good farmland and so has been inhabited for thousands of years' The view looking towards the Abberley Hills from Areley Kings Church.

The base of the font is inscribed with the words: TEMPORE LA AMANNI SANTI and refers to Layamon. However Layamon died in 1200 and the lettering is of a later date. Furthermore, Layamon was never canonised.

The church was probably built straight onto the sandstone, with no foundations. All that remains of Layamon's church is one deep Norman window and some stones in the Rector's doorway in the vestry. The south tower is built of two different kinds of stones in the 14th and 15th centuries. Most of the main part of the church was rebuilt by the famous Victorian architect, F Preedy, in 1886. The pulpit is made of old oak from the roof beams. The inscribed stones at the base of the font, thought at one time to be Norman, are, in fact, fakes.

In the South West corner of the church is a tomb which has been walked over so many times it is now bare but it once read 'Our fathers have sinned, and we their children have borne their iniquities'. No-one knows the story behind it.

The Areley registers of 1633 tell of a married woman, Jane Millard, who spoke 'scandalous and diffamacious' words against Eliza Burrastone, also a married woman, and had to do penance. Wedley describes this old custom. Jane probably had to walk to church in her bare feet, enveloped in a flowing robe with a flaming torch in her hand, then she had to bend before the altar in the presence of the parson and churchwardens.

In the churchyard once stood the well-known Norchard sundial, known locally as the Wizard's Pillar. Erected by a Mr Fidkin who was thought to have magical powers, it stood originally in his cottage garden in Hartlebury. On one side it was carved with the figure of death standing on a human body, complete with a fallen hour glass, dart and spade, while on the other side was Old Father Time with hourglass and scythe. First the pointer on the dial plate was stolen, then weathering made the carving indecipherable and finally, one night in 1999, the whole sundial disappeared.

The various states of maintenance of the wall round the church is owing to the fact that each of the chief landowners was once given a piece of wall to keep in good repair. One of these landowners evidently decided to convert his piece of wall into a memorial. The letters carved into the wall on the western side of the churchyard are the remains of an inscription which once read:

Lithologema Quare
Reponitur Sir Harry

One word is Greek, two are Latin and two are English, translated it means:

A stone building - why?
Here lies Sir Harry

Sir Harry Coningsby's wall, Areley Kings churchyard.

They refer to Sir Harry Coningsby, who died in 1701. He was the son of the Lord Chief Justice of England, and as a young man Harry lived at Hampton Court in Herefordshire. The story goes that Sir Harry was playing with his little son when he let him fall from a window into the water below. The boy was drowned, and the heartbroken father shunned the world to live the life of a recluse at his small estate, the Sturt, at Areley, 'buried in his books and lost in the bitterness of his thoughts'. From there he superintended the erection of the wall. When the lumber of a house in Tewkesbury was being cleared in 1842, the burial records of Areley Kings was discovered. They confirmed that Sir Harry had been born at Hampton Court and had, indeed, died at Sturt.

Sir Harry also devised another way of ensuring that he would be remembered. He planted walnut trees in the churchyard and directed, in his will, that local schoolboys should be allowed to crack the nuts from it on his tomb on a particular day in the year. Unfortunately, the trees were cut down for gunstocks during the Napoleonic wars just over a hundred years later but they have now been replaced by young trees.

The present rector of St Bartholomews is the Reverend Andrew Vessey.

"Before I became a priest I was heavily involved in professional arts. When I arrived the chancel was in a very bad condition. We inspected the roof and found that nineteen of the original oak timbers had decayed - the whole support for the Georgian ceiling had gone. We have carefully replaced it with local oak using Georgian techniques. We had craftsmen who could use various ancient skills, for example, how to rive the oak, splitting it along the grain.

'We decided to leave open the front of the church, so that the president is not cut off from the congregation. We restored the organ and relocated it at the side of the church. The old choir stalls were turned round and set into a new rear chapel we've created. We can now have events in the round, such as poetry evenings, concerts, art exhibitions, plays and lectures. This summer we had a two-week Arts Festival. A wedding is so much better in the round when all the congregation have a good view of the proceedings.

'The chancel door desperately needed replacing so a local craftsman, Graham Taylor, made an exact copy of the original. We didn't know what to do about a lock because a modern lock would be incongruous, then I remembered that in my garage I had an old Elizabethan door which was decayed but the lock was still intact. We removed it, renovated it and now we have a genuine Elizabethan lock on the chancel door.

'What was believed to be an old washstand in my house turned out to be a Georgian altar. We put it in the rear chapel below our wonderful modern stained glass window. The old choir pews have been placed here, we had to have them stretched as the original pews were made for boys. This has created an attractive compact area for services which are usually only attended by a few people. One popular service is a ring-blessing ceremony. If a wife loses her wedding ring, she replaces it but feels she wants the second ring blessed.

'The little two-storied house in the rectory garden was built by a former rector, Richard Vernon, in 1728. Over the doorway is the Vernon shield. I have been told that he built it to escape from domestic strife and no wonder, poor man, as he had a house full of women! He had a wife, several daughters and a female housekeeper. The upstairs is lined with cupboards

A former rector, Richard Vernon, erected this building in his garden in 1728 to provide an escape from his all-female household.

built, it is said, from the sails of the old windmill. We have excavated a basement and it appears that this was the original privy, so that Richard Vernon's little house would have been quite self-contained. I have restored the top floor which is let as a studio for the artist in residence. We also have a craftsman using the other side of my house, in the old stables. This is Richard Thomas, who has a woodcraft workshop, at the moment he's working on a collapsible boat.

'In the three buildings on this site (the church, the rectory and Church House) Art and Spirituality all lock together to help create a community. People love the sublimity of music and the insight of drama. Their offerings are an arm of the church's mission. Here we have the concept of Art and Performance, we have writers, authors, poets among our church members, as well as an artist and a craftsman in residence. Our choir master is a composer, Paul Simpson, who writes music specially for us. We have had plays written for us too, such as 'Caged Lion'."

In the year 2,000, Reverend Andrew Vessey was appointed Rural Dean.

"This means that I am responsible for the care of all my colleagues between here and Tenbury Wells, including Kyre Wyard, Lindridge, Stamford, Pensax, Abberley, Witley and Wilden. We have to have an official opinion on contentious matters such as remarriage and human sexuality, and so we meet at the Deanery Synod for discussion, and I will now be in the chair. I'm an intermediary between the bishop, the archdeacon, the church wardens, and the people on the ground."

CHURCH HOUSE

The meadow, sloping down before the church, is known as Naboth's vineyard, perhaps wine was once made here by the monks or even earlier, by the Romans. Andrew Wehner explains that the vineyard was part of the parson's land and continues:

"In medieval times money for the upkeep of the nave of the Church was raised by Church Ales. The Churchwardens brewed ale, which they sold at functions which were held actually in the nave of the church, there was nowhere else suitable. In time this practice was stopped, and the drinking parties were moved out to the churchyard. Later on this too was considered unacceptable, and 'church houses' were built specially for the purpose. The lovely old half-timbered house on the edge of the churchyard may be one of them. (A restored, sixteenth century timber-framed church alehouse can be seen at Colwall, near Ledbury).

Below right:
A house in the churchyard, perhaps
built as an alehouse.

'It is within the bounds of what was once the Rector's Glebe Farm. In the eighteenth century there was an argument as to who actually owned it, a Mr Zachary or the Rector. An affidavit was sworn by a man who had been the Rector's ploughman, who said he had lived in it. So it was decided that it belonged to the Rector.

'Church House was patched up with a new floor and windows twenty years ago but it's still falling to pieces. Reverend Andrew Vessey hopes that with the help of a Landfill and Biffa Award, English Heritage and the Historic Buildings Trust, we're going to strip the whole building and convert rooms to be a gallery, lecture spaces and kitchen. We shall use it as a resource and let it out for presentations and conferences. He says that day by day it will bring businessmen into our arena and we hope that they will be touched by its holiness.

The Rectory at Areley Kings.

THE RECTORY

The large Rectory is more than two and a half centuries older than most of the church. Although it is said to be Jacobean (1603-1625), my personal opihion is that it might be even older. You can make out a medieval layout in the middle part with the great hall and the solar. During the 1700s the occupiers tried to make it fashionable by adding a balcony and a false Georgian wall. Some of the timbers in it come from the old church roof.

The rectory is a huge, rambling place, too large for the Reverend Andrew Vessey and so it's used as a parish centre for meetings and other events.

Areley Hall

ARELEY MANOR (LATER ARELEY HALL)

'In 1136 Queen Maud (wife of King Stephen) granted a fishery in the Manor of Martley to Bordesley Abbey. I have an idea she founded the abbey too. This fishery is thought to have been on the site of Areley Hall. Bordesley Abbey was dissolved in 1539. The fishery was sold off, and eventually came into the hands of Simon Mucklow in about 1594. He appears to have built himself a house on the property.

'Prince Rupert's visit was in 1644, when the royal army was moving from Worcester to Bewdley. William Mucklow is thought to have been a Major in this army, and he was certainly wounded at the second battle of Worcester in 1651. In the aftermath of the war he was fined for being a Royalist anyway, and then fined again for having commanded troops at the battle of Newark.

'They therefore sold Martley and abandoned Areley Hall but kept the right of holding Court Leet. Two hundred years and several generations later a wealthy Thomas Zachary married a Mucklow heiress and they moved back to Areley Hall. While they were having the Hall restored around 1780 they built a gorgeous Georgian home known as Areley House. Later, in the 19th century, it became the home of Joseph Rogers who owned the Tannery. The house became a private hotel after the first world war and is now a retirement home."

Areley Hall was once occupied by members of the Lloyd family who owned Lloyd's Bank. In 1841, Sarah Zachary married Sampson Lloyd and the couple lived at the Hall. The Lloyds were staunch Quakers and their ancestors had spent many years in and out of prison for their beliefs. The marriage settlement shows that Sampson was a dealer in brass, iron and tin, and owned a great deal of land and property including several iron forges along the river Stour. The Lloyd family, together with the Taylor family, had founded Lloyd's bank in 1765. When James Taylor died in the mid 1800s, the Lloyd family offered his son a quarter of the bank if he would take it over, but he declined. The Lloyd family 'were thus left to bear the responsibility of the bank alone'. Sampson became heavily involved in the running of the bank. They only lived there for a few years before Sampson took Sarah to live in Wednesbury.

During the reign of Phillip and Mary, sometime between July 1554 and November 1558, the Lord of the Manor of Martley went to dinner with the Lord of the Manor of Areley Kings. Below, in medieval English, is a price list of some of the items of their feast.

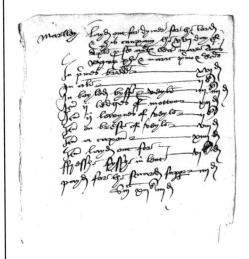

Martley   Layd on for dynner for the lord and his company and xvij of April .... Reg Phillip and Maria (not legible)

Item p(a)nes bredd	xvid	(16d)
Item ale	ijs	(2s)
Item boyyled byffe and veyle	iiijs iiijd	(4s 4d)
Item ij ledges of motton	xijd	(12d)
Item ij lownes of veyle	ijs	(2s)
Item on(e) brest of veyle	viijd	(8d)
Item a capon	xiiijd	(14d)
layd on for ffyessh in lent	vjd	(6d)
payd for the Stuard(s) supper	iiijd	(4d)
	xiijs iiijd	(13s 4d)

13s 4d is approximately 67p.

Courtesy Morton Fisher Solicitors and Worcestershire Record Office. Transcription by Elizabeth Atkins.

ARELEY COURT

Areley Court Road in the Walshes Housing Estate takes its name from a large house that once stood there. Fred Rimmel can remember the first houses being built on part of the kitchen gardens of Areley Court:

"The Court had been occupied by Mr Broome from the carpet factory and his agent used to come round for the rent. We used to chat to him and he told us that he had been Mr Broome's ostler-cum-groom and he used to have to get his carriage and pair ready in the morning for Mr Broome to go to the office. Mr Broome had needed the horses and a bottle of beer to start him off."

THE WALSHES

Part of the half-timbered sixteenth century farmhouse belonging to the Walsh family still survives. Bought by the Stourport Urban District Council in 1948 for the use of the caretaker of the local caravan site, it was sold in about 1980 and is now the Old Beams public house.

The Walsh family was of some importance, as they held estates in Shelsey and Hartlebury as well as Areley. A relative, Sir Richard Walsh lived at Shelsey Court and was High Sheriff of Worcestershire; it was Sir Richard who rounded up the gunpowder plotters in 1605. The last of the line died in Abberley in 1779. A now-illegible tombstone in the floor of Saint Bartholemew's chancel told the intriguing tale of William Walsh, who died in 1762, aged 88, "ruinated by three Quakers, three lawyers and a fanatick to help them".

Areley Kings has always been a farming community and the memoirs of Henry R Pheysey (1869-1961) give us an insight into life on the farm. Henry left school in 1884 when he was fourteen. He had already been helping on a farm two days a week after school, probably the Whitehouse farm of Mr Knowles, then went full-time until 1887. This first farm kept 150 ewes and grew fifteen acres of carrots, fifteen acres of parsnips, forty acres of potatoes, twenty acres of peas and owned several orchards of cider apples. Henry returned to the Walshes and farmed there from 1903 to 1913:

"We lived twelve miles from the Monday cattle market, so when the sheep walked, they left on the Sunday. Sometimes, if horses could be spared, sheep were taken in a wagon with hurdles all round. They then had to be off very early on Monday morning. The larger and fatter they were, the better they sold, and the sheep from this farm generally made top price in the market. Today no butcher would look at them, they would be considered too big and fat. When the sheep walked to market I was sent with a spring cart (a light cart mounted on springs) to pick up any sheep that could not travel, and also to bring the man back.

'When I left school I started farming in earnest on this farm. For about three months I got up at five o'clock and went with the carter who passed at that time. In those days there was no half day on the farm. They worked from six until six, with half an hour for breakfast and an hour for dinner. They were not paid until 6 pm on Saturdays, and after this they walked to their homes, and then some more miles to town for their shopping. Shops stayed open later then. I got to the farm in time for breakfast which was prepared by the son, and had to be finished before 6 o'clock. I can't call to mind anything except hot-buttered toast and freshly-ground coffee, both very good.

'After three months I started to live in, so I could get up a little later, but I still had to be in time to fill the men's cider bottles for them to collect at six. Every man or boy had an allowance of cider, from a pint to a gallon. At harvest time there was hardly any limit. If any man was late finishing a job, it was "Just draw so-and-so a cup of cider". I think that satisfied any overtime. Every man had his own little wooden barrel which he carried about with him - a bit of leather or hide for a handle.

'It was two miles to the other farm, and when we went drilling or horse-hoeing the field had to be finished if possible before we came home; yet no-one ever thought of riding the horses home, nor would they have been allowed to do so. I have many times come back with bleeding feet, and would have been ashamed to have been seen riding home, even in a cart. To me now it seems madness to work as we did, twelve hours every day in the week, with only one and a half hours off for meals. I have heard my employer say that when the men started to come at seven o'clock he would give up farming. I admired him, and I have worked there 'til I could drop, so that when I got to bed I could not lie easy, or sleep, for every joint ached. I remember working two full harvest days pulling a heel rake through barley stubble that had been mown badly. Often I had to stand still and pull to get the rake through. I raked the ground after the pitchers (men with pitch-forks). About mid-morning my hands were covering the rake with blood, but I felt well paid when I was told, "Well done, my lad, you beat any man".'

ARELEY COMMON SCHOOL

Three years before Queen Victoria came to the throne, in 1834, a National school for boys and girls was established at Areley Kings. It was probably both a Sunday School and a day school. No-one knows where it was held, although at that time Saint Bartholomew's had a gallery which was used for lessons and could hold 48 scholars. Perhaps the little Tudor Church House in the churchyard was used as a school, the old folk in the village call it 'The School House', although it has not been used as a school within living memory.

Eleven years later, in 1845, Francis Zachary granted a piece of land at Areley Kings to the Bishop of Worcester and other members of the clergy at the reduced price of £100 on the condition that it would be used as a school. Thus the Areley Common School began, with three rooms and a back kitchen. Only the children of labouring, manufacturing and poor classes were to be admitted. Parents paid 2d a week for the first child in each family, and a 1d per week for each subsequent child. The school lay between the Areley Common and Dunley roads; surrounded by fields, scholars had to walk along a field path to reach it. At the end of the first year the school had 25 boys and 30 girls. The school was enlarged several times and a residence for 'The Mistress' was attached.

During World War II, school buildings were understandably neglected. The government promised a new school on the Walsh's estate but by the mid 1950's, when the education authorities at last decided to fulfil their commitment, they found that they were unable to buy any land in the Walshes because it had been designated for private building. Eventually they managed to buy one-and-a-half acres next to the old school, between the old school and the Dunley Road.

A modern school, Areley Common First School, has now been built across the playground. The old school still belongs to the Education Authority and was, until the year 2000, a Music Advisory Centre. It now stands empty.

A new school, Windmill First School, was opened in 1965, followed by a Church of England Middle School three years later in adjacent buildings.

THE WINDMILL

The Windmill stood high above the road to Shrawley (the B4196) immediately after it divides from the A451. It has been converted into a Round House.

John Zachary of Areley Hall built the red-brick windmill in 1779. It was four stories high and had a boat cap to which were attached the four sails and a rudder, so that the sails could be moved in any direction to catch the wind. The miller's cottage was on the bank below with its roof level with the mill doorway so that the wind could blow straight on to the sails. The last miller was William Dawes and the ridge below the mill gets its name from his wife, known as Betty, short for Elizabeth. After the mill closed William became the village carpenter and made anything from cart wheels to coffins. He was also parish clerk, sexton, and general assistant to the Vicar and the Squire. He needed a healthy income to support his five daughters.

By 1902 it had become derelict and so about this time the Reverend Vawdrey, rector of Areley Kings, converted it into a dwelling, with circular

The inscription below the photograph reads:
"F. Mills Esq., Manager for Major J. H. Crane, Oakhampton Farm, Stourport, writes:- "We were very pleased with the results obtained from your manure, having won several prizes with the Mangolds grown with it.""
Courtesy Ray Franks.

Hop-pickers in Bridge Street in about 1900. They had probably come from the Black Country by train and were picked up by a local farmer. Stourport had a thriving trade in hops.
Courtesy Kidderminster Library.

rooms and sloping walls. By 1935 it had become a blacksmiths occupied by Thomas Hicks Fathers and his name was over the door for many years.

Isaac Wedley tells a story about William Dawes. One of the villagers paid William a visit but before he went into the mill, he tethered his donkey to the sails. While they were talking, William started the mill. The donkey sailed round and round on the sails until the rope broke. For years afterwards, a pathetic bit of rope hung from the sails of the mill.

ARELEY COMMON

There are now housing estates on each side of Areley Common Road but up until the mid 1800s, the road ran through a huge common. The only buildings were the mill, the miller's cottage and a few houses. The road itself was a rough track, used to drive flocks of sheep, herds of cows and other cattle to the Stourport market. Then, in the first few cold days of January 1846, Jeremiah Matthews arrived from Kidderminster with orders to enclose the common.

For centuries, private people had been taking over common land but in the 1700s there had been a change. Enclosures could only be done by special Acts of Parliament, each Act dealing with a certain piece of land. Between 1700 and 1845 about 4,000 of these Acts were passed and one of the last referred to Areley Common.

First, Jeremiah closed all the public footpaths. He then divided the land, giving portions to each of those who applied according to his 'respective rights and interests', so that the wealthy had the most and the poorest received the least. The majority, 26 acres, went to Daniel Zachary, Lord of the Manor. The churchwardens, as overseers, were given a large piece for the exercise and recreation of the villagers, together with five acres at a rent of £5 per year to use as allotments for the 'labouring poor'. Those who received land were told to make hedges, banks, fences or ditches round their acquisition within the next two years, and any road running across their property had to be kept clean and repaired. Some of the new pieces of land were ideal for building and rows of Victorian cottages began to appear along the road.

MURDER ON THE CHRISTIAN SHORES

The first properly organised police force came into being through various Acts in the 1830's. The first policemen wore a shiny top hat and a swallow-tailed coat, in the pocket of which he carried his staff. You can imagine him picking his way through the scene of a murder which took place on the Christian Shores in September 1836. Joseph Hawkins was seen on Thursday evening, but his shop remained closed all day Friday and the alarm was raised early on Saturday morning. The following are extracts from the *Kidderminster Shuttle*:

"The village of Areley Kings and town of Stourport were thrown into the highest state of alarm and excitement on Saturday morning last, by the discovery of a most brutal murder, committed on the body of Joseph Hawkins, who kept a huckster's shop (one selling small odds and ends) on Areley Common. The deceased was an old man and lived by himself; he was always considered a peaceable and well-disposed man, and was accustomed to attend the market at Stourport on Wednesdays and Saturdays, with bacon, cheese, &c. &c. ...

'Upon his (the constable) reaching the shop, he saw several things in confusion, and looking in a back place he beheld the body of the unfortunate man lying with the face downwards; and upon examination found that he had been shot in the belly, dragged to where he then lay, and there his skull was completely broken to pieces by a large log of wood, which was standing in the corner. Upon further inspection he found blood against the counter, and supposed that the deceased had been shot whilst in the act of

243

weighing sugar, there being some in the scale and a quantity upon the floor with the sugar scope."

An itinerant by the name of Lightband was charged with the murder. The trial was held in the Tontine Hotel and Lightband was sentenced to be hung at the gallows which stood in front of Worcester Gaol. These hangings were public entertainments, thousands would turn out to see them, pamphlets would be specially written and there would be speeches from everyone concerned. On the night before Lightband's execution, a heavy fall of snow made the roads impassable so that many of the people from Stourport who hoped to see the hanging were unable to reach Worcester.

REDSTONE

Before the bridge over the River Severn was built it was difficult and inconvenient to get from Stourport to Areley Kings or vice versa. It was necessary to go a mile downstream and cross at Redstone, either by ford or by ferry. When Lincombe Lock was built in 1844, the depth of the water between Stourport and Worcester increased by five or six feet but before then, the river here ran very shallow. The Severn was tidal at least to Bewdley, and possibly as far as Bridgnorth, so at times it was possible to ford the river at this point. It has the label 'Redston passage' in John Speed's map of Worcestershire, produced in about 1610, and the only other Severn crossings are bridges at Worcester and Upton-on-Severn.

A section from John Speed's map of Worcestershire of about 1610, showing 'Redston passage' across the River Severn.

Redstone caves on the River Severn at the end of Redstone Lane, were inhabited for over eight hundred years.

The crossing was well-used, as it lay on one of the main routes from Wales to Worcester. A traveller would go through Bewdley, along the western bank of the river Severn, round the eastern edge of Ribbesford woods, and continue southwards. Then he would turn right to go through Astley Cross to Redstone Ferry. After crossing the ferry, he would continue along the opposite side ie the eastern side of the river Severn to Worcester. The ferry was also on the main route from Ludlow to Worcester and when Henry VIIs popular young son, Prince Arthur, died at Ludlow in 1502 his long funeral cortege probably came this way. Contemporary historians say that the whole route was lined with weeping crowds.

Here, where a great cliff juts out into the Severn, is the ancient hermitage of the Redstone caves. Cut into the red rock are a long series of rock dwellings, with rooms, stairs and inter-connecting passages. Some of the ceilings are still blackened from the smoke from the fires, which were vented by chimneys cut all the way to their outlet in the hill above. One large opening, carved into a Norman arch, was a chapel. Over the altar was a large painting of an archbishop saying mass. The importance of the rock dwellings was shown by the sculptures over the entrance, now almost completely weathered away, but which included the Royal Arms, together with those of Beauchamp, Earl of Warwick, and of Mortimer, Earl of March.

Perhaps, nine hundred or so years ago, it was home to a single hermit, then it was enlarged for other monks on retreat from Worcester. Wooden projections from the rock face gave shelter to a hundred or more. The first documentary evidence is dated 1160 when Gillbertus Piscator owed the king £5. Simon of Reddestan, almost certainly a hermit, lived here in 1182 and in 1260, royal protection was granted to a religious community, described as the House of Redstone. We know that the caves were still occupied by at least one hermit, Richard Spetchley, in 1431. A century later they probably became a refuge for some of the monks who were dispossessed by Thomas Cromwell, minister of Henry VIII.

The monks would probably have been keepers of the ferry, dedicating their lives to helping the weary and hungry men who crossed by horse or boat. They would not have gone hungry. Boatmen would have made donations in return for hospitality or help in freeing grounded boats, and indulgences would have been promised to those who contributed to the support of the inhabitants.

These monks probably began as a saintly brotherhood, but as the centuries went by they seem to have become either hermits or bandits, depending upon one's point of view. There were many complaints about their greed in demanding payment. Bishop Latimer was living at Hartlebury Castle in 1553 and he described the Redstone hermitage as 'able to lodge 500 men and ready to lodge thieves as true men'. He added, 'I would not have hermits master of such dens but rather that some faithful man had it'. Ten years later it housed a population of 90. Eight bodies were found near to the hermitage in 1736 which have never been identified. They may have been monks who spent all their lives there.

In 1530, William Yarranton of 'Roodestone' purchased half a share in the ferry. This is how Redstone was then spelt and as a rood is an old name for a cross or crucifix and as the complex contained a chapel, should the caves be properly known as Roodestone and not Redstone? The other half share seems to have belonged to the Lords of the Manor of Abberley. In the early 1600s the Yarranton's acquired the caves and used them to store pig iron from the Forest of Dean for iron working mills at Wilden and Shelsey.

During the 1700s a dispute appears to have arisen over the rights of the ferry between the Yarrantons and the Glovers. However, when Stourport bridge was built in 1775, it was to the Glover family that compensation was paid for the loss of their livelihood. They probably bought the Hop Pole in Lichfield Street with the proceeds as it was kept by the Glover family for many years.

Dr Nash, the Worcestershire historian, tells us that later in the same century the caves were used for making cider, and later still it was turned into an ale-house. In the early 1800s one of the dwellings was used as a school by Mr Langford. John Noakes, the nineteenth century historian, says that five houses were occupied, the fifth by two ladies who had been evicted from the sixth house, it being unfit for human habitation, and the landlord had nailed it up. By 1868, 'poor folks' were living there, they had an alehouse, a school, a chapel, refectory and dormitories. The last people to occupy them are thought to be pea-pickers. The caves have not been inhabited within living memory except that a platoon of soldiers camped there in 1941.

On the north side of the lane was a half-timbered ferry house, with the date 1685 over the doorway. It had eighteen bedrooms, some public and some private. When the Severn was in flood, crossing by the ford was impossible and so travellers had to wait at the Ferry House until the floods went down. One day it would be empty, the next it could be crammed to capacity and the enclosure outside would be filled with carts, wagons and animals of every description. Close by stood the Angel Inn, from which a road led to the foot of the sand-dunes on Hartlebury Common, and so on to Worcester. Before it was demolished in 1890 it was known as Redstone House.

During the World War II a reserve supply of petrol was kept outside Redstone caves, well-hidden among the trees. There were three or four huge petrol vats, the tops painted with a patchy green camouflage, each holding about half a million gallons.

LINCOMB LOCK AND WEIR

Less than half a mile from Redstone is Lincomb lock and weir. The weir is entirely artifial, before the 1840's there were only green fields here. Building the lock and weir was a tremendous task which involved changing the course of the river Severn. The lock was 100 feet (30.5 metres) long and 20 feet (6 metres) wide while the weir was 300 feet (91.5 metres) long with a drop of 7 feet (2.1 metres). The Chief Engineer was Leader Williams, one of his sons became the Chief Engineer of the Manchester Ship Canal, another son became a well-known artist.

Wedley reports:

"A wild set of navvies were engaged in this work, and were the terror of the neighbourhood. William Haywood is said to have gone amongst them and to have been threatened with rough treatment if he came again. But William had no "fear of man" in such a case as this, and went at the first opportunity. opening his commission by singing at the top of his voice,"I'll

Lincomb Locks, built in the 1840s.
Courtesy Brindley Arms.

Lincomb weir in 1905.
Courtesy Ray Franks.

praise my Maker while I've breath". This created such an impression that he was left alone and not afterwards interfered with."

Great cartloads of stone were thrown into the river but when the dam was raised to half its height, the force of the water was so great that even five-ton stones were rolled away. Eventually, the builders hit on the idea of loading canal boats with stone and sinking them. The opening of the lock and weir in 1844 was celebrated by a public dinner at the Guild Hall, Worcester.

Until recent times it was possible to see salmon making their way up river at Lincomb weir. This fish was so plentiful that Bewdley tradesmen were once forbidden by statute to feed their apprentices with salmon on more than two days a week.

When George Cadbury improved the canals in the 1930's he had new boats built specially to take the Severn locks. However, Lincomb lock remained particularly difficult to manoevre.

Mr B A Lane began working for the Regent Oil Company in 1940 and in *Severn Tanking* he writes:

"The Lincomb Lock was our last lock, and it had great significance as to the amount of cargo we carried to Stourport-on-Severn depots. We had to wriggle our way into this lock here by running the engines at half speed, then turn the wheel from port to starboard and back again, repeating this until we were in the lock. To get out of the lock after lifting up, we had to move very slowly because we were actually touching the lock sill. Every morning, the lock keeper used to take the water reading off the top sill water level board. This was sent through to Gloucester to the petroleum board or the carriers, and in turn relayed to the skippers loading at Avonmouth. If there was, say, six feet two inches of water, we could get over the sill with a draft of six feet, provided we moved out steadily and

slowly and did not suck down on to the sill, which could happen if we tried to go fast. This damaged both the sill and the vessel's bottom."

Lincombe lock today.

LINCOMB HALL

Lincomb Hall was the home of the Lincomb family for generations, and was rebuilt in 1874. An iron plate was retained from the previous house and placed in the porch, showing three roses in relief and the date 1624.

There's an old story about the Lincomb family. Way back in 1253 Sir John Lincombe (or Lingayn) had a beautiful daughter, Constantia, who married Grimbaldus, the son and heir of Sir Richard Pauncefote. These were the times when every nobleman worth his salt went off to fight in the crusades, Grimbaldus did so but was captured by the Moors at Tunis. He was heard boasting of his his wife's beauty, so his captors demanded a 'joint' of his wife as ransom. Back in England, the family said that the request could not possibly be fulfilled, but their daughter was adamant and despatched a pigeon to Gloucester priory with a request that a monk should come and remove her hand. The severed limb was preserved in salt and wine and shipped abroad to secure the husband's release. Grimbaldus and Constantia were buried together in Much Cowarne Church in Herefordshire, the two effigies looking lovingly at each other and the stump of Constantia's right arm slightly elevated as if on display. In medieval times the tomb was considered to be holy and was visited by pilgrims but somehow, over the centuries, it has disappeared. Grimaldus has been dumped on the floor and the effigy of the lovely Constantia has been lost. This could have happened in 1840 when lightning struck the church and set it on fire. Richard Bradbury, Clerk to the Parochial Church Council, is anxious to hear from anyone who has any more information about the legend, the tomb or the effigy of Constantia.

20. Astley

Even apart from Astley Hall, the village is a charming example of the Worcestershire that Lord Baldwin loves, for it has a black and white mill in a perfect setting beside the Severn, and a church, high on a hill, representing many periods from the Norman times onwards, with a richness of beauty which has never been marred by injudicious restoration ... .

Companion into Worcestershire, 1939

One of the French heroes at the battle of Hastings in 1066 was Ralph de Todeni. Because of his nobility, he was eligible to be Standard Bearer to William the Conqueror, which meant that he could stand away from the battle. He declined the privilege, and, instead, chose to fight like a common soldier. As a reward William made him a Baron and gave him pieces of land throughout the country, including the ancient parish of Astley. Its origins go back to the time of Stonehenge and it has been occupied through the bronze and iron ages with Roman and Anglo-Saxon settlements.

Perhaps de Todeni regretted his bravery. He left behind the more temperate climate of Normandy to live among his enemies in a strange country with a foreign language. He made himself unpopular by draining the locality of men and natural resources in order to service and finance his projects. He had to build castles in which to live and he could not move between them without an armed guard. Evidently he was a God-fearing man, for he also built a priory close by the church and made it subject to the Abbey of St Taurin, near Rouen in Normandy, to which large sums of money was sent. This, again, did not please the locals.

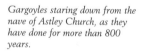

Gargoyles staring down from the nave of Astley Church, as they have done for more than 800 years.

A thriving Anglo-Saxon church already existed at Astley but in 1102, the year that he died, de Todeni arranged for it to be rebuilt on a lavish scale, with the finest of materials and workmanship.

All that remains of his priory is the brickwork of its well, known as Prior's Well. However, much of his church, Saint Peters, is still there, although the village has shifted away from it. The Norman heads still stare down from the corbels, the zig-zag ornamentation still surrounds the arch and the south chancel wall is original. Inside is a memorial to the daughter of Sir John Winford, who having died from an adder bite, is shown with an adder twined around her arm.

Over the centuries the church has been enriched by fine effigies and monuments. The earliest monument is that of Walter Blount and his wife in 1561, underneath which are their kneeling children. Next to this and from 1573 is the monument to Robert Blount and his wife. Most memorials are of the seventeenth century Winfords and the later Cookes.

Above: a memorial to Harriet Winford, daughter of Sir Thomas Winford of Glasshampton, who died in 1801 from the bite of an adder. Note the snake coiled around her arm.
Photographs of Astley Church are courtesy Rev Norkett.

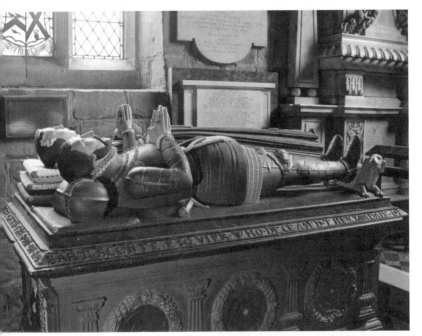

Left: recumbent effigies of Robert Blount who died in 1573 and his wife, Anne.

Below left: Walter Blount died in 1561 and his wife, Izabel, a year later.
Photos courtesy Rev. Norkett

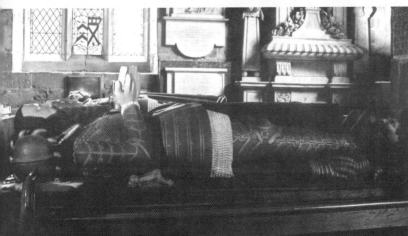

Glasshampton, the Seat of Sambrooke Freeman Esq. & Miss Winford

GLASSHAMPTON

The home of the Lords of the Manor of Astley had, until the seventeenth century, been on the banks of Dick Brook near to Priors Mill down the road from the church. They then decided to build themselves a splendid house at Glasshampton, about three-quarters of a mile from Astley in the direction of Great Witley. In the early 1800s the Reverend Denham Cookes inherited the manor, demolished the house, built an even grander one and saw it burn to the ground on its completion. He finally retired to repent what he saw as his folly.

The master carpenter, Mr Lee, lost all his tools in the fire but he considered it to be the opportunity of a lifetime. He taught himself a number of oriental languages and ended up as a professor at Cambridge University.

All that remained of the house was a walled garden and a fine stable block. At the end of the first world war, the Society of the Divine Compassion decided to found a Cistercian house within the Church of England, and began by taking over Glasshampton stables, as seen in the photograph below.

Astley Mill, also known as Priors Mill, dates back to the 17th century. Situated on Dick Brook, it was used for the grinding of corn.

251

This tiny rural village of Astley has managed to produce three great historical figures, one from each of the seventeeth, nineteenth and twentieth centuries.

ANDREW YARRANTON

Andrew Yarranton was born at Larford in 1616. The following was written by the late Gordon Lovett :

"Andrew was a very much larger than life character, who rose from being the son of a Yeoman farmer to become a figure of national repute. He made sure he got his own way, often at the expense of others, until in 1684 it was reported that "he died in London, the cause of death was a beating and thrown in a tub of water".

'His first business venture, situated in Astley, was that of iron smelting. Whilst in the wars he had noted the large quantities of iron slag at Worcester, left by the Romans, and decided to make use of it without any consent. By similar underhand means he obtained the wood for the charcoal from nearby Bayton. Sometime later his business partners sponsored him to visit Saxony to learn the German art of tin plating. Although he returned with the secrets and reported success, one of his enemies obtained a patent, that, whilst useless, nevertheless thwarted his efforts. Another of his ventures was the selling and promotion of the use of clover seed to improve the fertility of the soil.

'He was one of England's first civil engineers who improved the navigation of rivers, including the Stour, and was a proponent of canals a hundred years before Brindley. Several old tin works in the Stour valley are thought to have belonged to him.

'A strong Presbyterian, he was falsely gaoled by a local squire, Sir John Packington, in 1660 for religious plotting. Many years later it was his turn to be involved in making notorious allegations of the so-called Popish Plots that resulted in the deaths of many innocent people.

'His finest achievement was the writing of two books entitled *England's Improvement by Sea and Land*. Amongst other things they set out to show how, if a land registry was set up, money could more easily be borrowed to finance the growth of business. His idea was not put into practice until the early part of the 1900s."

Frances Ridley Havergal

FRANCES RIDLEY HAVERGAL

In the nineteenth century, Frances Ridley Havergal was born in the rectory of Astley on December 14th, 1836. Although the name may not be familiar there are few church-going people today who have not sung many of her hymns, such as 'Take my life and let it be'. They were well-known as they were written during the great Victorian religious revival, when almost everyone attended church. She died in 1879 and is buried with her father, the rector, in Astley churchyard.

STANLEY BALDWIN

In the twentieth century, Astley Hall was occupied by no lesser person than the prime minister. Stanley Baldwin was born at Bewdley, spent his childhood years at Wilden and moved to Astley Hall in 1902, ten years after his marriage. His first few years in Parliament were quiet and uneventful but when war broke out his abilities were discovered and he received promotion after promotion. He was Parliamentary Secretary, then Financial Secretary to the Treasury, then President of the Board of Trade.

Stanley Baldwin was not happy with the coalition government under Lloyd George and became a spokesman for those MPs who wanted to break away and become independent. The Independents won, Baldwin was made Chancellor of the Exchequer and when the Lloyd George died in 1923, he was chosen to lead the country. His first spell as Prime Minister only lasted a few months but he was restored to power from 1924 to 1929 and again from 1935 to 1937. He was in power during the hungry twenties and the national strike of 1926. Nine years later he was won praise for the way he handled the abdication of Edward VIII. Churchill commented, in 1935, that he had 'gathered to himself a greater volume of confidence and goodwill than any other man I recollect'.

Stanley Baldwin received criticisms as well as praise. He was made a scapegoat for the lack of armaments in Britain when war with Germany broke out in 1939. However, Britain was in no mood for another war so soon after the carnage of World War I and it was unlikely that he could have persuaded the nation to re-arm.

He loved country life and his old Elizabethan home, often treating his fellow ministers to a description of the view towards the Abberley Hills. Contemporary cartoons show him with a pipe and pigs.

He left the Commons in 1937 and enjoyed ten years retirement as 1st Earl Baldwin of Bewdley before he died. His ashes were honoured by burial in Worcester Cathedral.

A retired lady, now living near Kidderminster, began working for the Baldwins in Astley Hall in 1937:

"Lord Baldwin and the Countess, Elspeth, were very nice people and the house was lovely. I started there as a trainee maid when I was a teenager and I was under this very strict old Butler. I was determined to get to the top so I stayed on until I became the cook. We had been working very hard one day, preparing for the Ministers who were coming up from London, and the Butler said to me, 'Would you like to see into the dining room?'. I said, 'Yes please', so he took me in. It was all laid out for dinner and it was so beautiful.

'The Lady's Maid came into the kitchen and she said that Anthony Eden was the best-looking man in London. So we all got up on the landing and peered over the banisters so that we could catch sight of him. He came out of the dining room but as he did so he gave an enormous sneeze which made us all jump and frightened us to death.

'They are buried at Wilden and I still go once a year and visit their grave."

Astley Hall still exists and is now a nursing home.

Stanley Baldwin, above, lived at Astley Hall pictured below. The top picture shows the front and the lower picture the back. The photograph of Stanley Baldwin is courtesy Norman May.

21. Shrawley

The story of Shrawley in early times is the tale of a ford and a wood, a ford which was more negotiable, more easily crossed than any for some distance up and down the river Severn. Before the days of locks and weirs, and before the days of bridges, the road from Ombersley and probably Droitwich also, led down to this ford; and across it on the other side, there was gradually made a clearing in the dense forest and a little village sprang into being.

History of Shrawley by Mrs Masterman

Shrawley Wood. The woodland floor is transformed in spring by a carpet of bluebells, unsurpassed in Worcestershire, preceded in April by a display of delicate white Wood Anemones.

THE FORD

Mrs Masterman's *History of Shrawley*, written in 1928, continues:

"Possibly the indispensable salt from Droitwich was taken along this way in earliest times, to the far west. Perhaps Caractucus and his tribesmen fought with the Romans on the Shrawley river bank and kept guard from the top of the fortification on the high mound which still commands the ford. There is evidence of some early battle in the shape of bones of men and horses found buried in the river bank. Many crossings would have been made during the Pax Romana, but eventually, even the Romans departed to be replaced by invading Saxons. These Saxons burned and destroyed, driving the 'Welshmen' further and further west. They must have crossed the ford and taken possession of this little bit of the west bank of Severn to give it the present name of Shaw, or Shraw-ley (wooded pastures). The Saxons came to stay and have left their mark on all the village names round about.

'The tale goes on and tells how the Saxons, in their turn, kept guard by the ford, dreading the appearance of the long ships of the sea rovers, the hated Danes. But all in vain, Shrawley must have been deplorably harried with the rest of Doddingtree Hundred by the savage Earl Hakon. With the Norman conquest, Shrawley came under the overlordship of Ralph de Toni, the Conqueror's standard bearer. "

SHRAWLEY WOOD

Centuries ago many woods across Britain were made up of small-leaved lime trees but most of them have died out and Shrawley Wood is one of the few left in Britain. The sylvan woods were not always quiet and peaceful. During the civil war of 1646/49, they were inhabited by deserters from the various armies. It is said that there was a gang of fifty men from one village alone.

The Forestry Commission took over half of the woods in the 1950s and, in its wisdom, decided to poison some of the limes to plant conifers.

Oaks from Shrawley Wood were selected to repair the Houses of Parliament after the bomb damage of the second world war

THE CASTLE

Through Ralph de Toni, Shrawley fell by marriage to the Beauchamps of Holt Castle. Earthworks down by the pool mark the site of a Norman castle. In the fifteenth century it came into the hands of Richard Neville, Earl of Warwick, known as 'Warwick the Kingmaker'. However, it is unlikely that he lived there.

During the civil war, according to tradition, it was held by William Chylde, an ardent Royalist. Fierce fighting took place, with hand-to-hand fighting in the woods and Cromwell's army bombarding the castle from a field on the other side of the river, still known as Battle meadow. A quantity of human bones were found near here in the early 1800s but it is uncertain which battle they came from. After Cromwell's triumph, William Chylde was fined heavily by the Parliamentary party.

Shrawley passed through various hands until, in 1700, Shrawley came into the possession of the Vernon family of Hanbury. They were Lords of the Manor for three centuries and provided several Rectors. During the 1930's Sir George Vernon fell out with the church and arranged that after his death he should be buried in the grounds of a favourite cottage in the wood, overlooking the Middle Pool, rather than in unconsecrated ground 'by prating priests'. The cottage is now a ruin but his grave is still there.

THE HERMITAGE

The wood rises to a steep escarpment with the remains of an old cave known locally as Rock Seat. This is thought to be one of a series of caves where hermits lived, earning a living by helping travellers across the ford. According to the Reverend J L Molliott of Abberley, the hermits had another important role. He writes:

"In the parish of Shrawley, on the banks of the Severn, there are some curious caverns, called the Red Rocks, anciently the abode of hermits, and it is reported that they occupied their leisure time in fishing out of the river certain baskets, pitched on the outside, containing children supposed to have been launched on the surface of the stream from Bewdley bridge. These children in Christian charity they baptised and nurtured, giving them the name of the river, and if they seemed in good condition, educated them and settled them for life."

There is no record of the fate of those not in good condition. They were all given the surname of Severne, which first appears in Shrawley in the sixteenth century. The Severne family certainly seems to have been a large one, as the memorials inside Shrawley church testify. Reverend Molliott added that there were many more Severnes buried in old Abberley churchyard, beneath the north wall. Perhaps further proof is provided by an entry in the Abberley church register of 1741 when a baby was given the name of Delarivere Severne (of the river Severn).

The Severnes lived high up, overlooking the river, at a place with the quaint old name of "Cockbaylis". It was rebuilt and renamed Severn Bank House some hundred years ago by one of the Vernon family .

256

St Mary's Church at Shrawley, dating back to the 12th century.

A very early gravestone of 1696 with a crudely incised face at the top.

THE CHURCH

This little church has guarded the morals of the village below for almost 900 years. Here, the Severne babies were baptised and eventually buried. The twelfth century font still has staples used originally to hold a padlock to secure the consecrated water from witches.

Shrawley is well-known for its epitaphs. A sad inscription to Mrs Vernon reads:

> Two babes were laid in earth before she died;
> A third now slumbers at the mother's side.
> Its sister twin survives, whose smiles impart
> A trembling solace to her father's heart.

Another in the churchyard is to a blacksmith:

> My sledge and hammer lie reclined
> My bellows, too, have lost their wind;
> My fire is spent, my forge decayed
> And in the dust my vice is laid:
> My coal is spent, my iron gone,
> My nails are drove, my work is done.
> My fire dried corpse here lies at rest.
> My soul, smoke-like, soars to be blest.

THE WELL OF SAINT KEYNE

In this peaceful setting is the well of St Keyne. Many churches and wells throughout England are named after her, together with Keynsham in Somerset which is where she went with the intention of founding a nunnery. The Lord of the Manor gave her a piece of land, but it was so infested with huge venomous snakes that no-one would come forward to join her. Saint Keyne is supposed to have turned the snakes into stone and tradition claims that the fossilised ammonites which are common in that area are the remains of these reptiles. After a holy life she returned to Wales to die. It is said that anyone contemplating marriage should first drink the water from the well.

FETES

Special cakes were made for the wake, held every year on 6th November at the Wyre Inn, once situated by the ford. Unfortunately, the inn was demolished by the authorities who suspected that poachers from the surrounding woods were using it as a hide-out. The Wake has been replaced by a Fete held each Saturday of the August bank holiday. The proceeds go to support the church and village hall, the latter is the old school, bought by the villagers when it closed in 1977.

The well of Saint Keyne, close to the church, with the old lifting mechanism still in place.

Shrawley has seen a declining population. While the population of Upper Mitton soared from 147 in 1801 to 1,418 in 1901, that of Shrawley decreased from 504 to 414 during the same period.

WITHIN LIVING MEMORY

A more recent history of Shrawley is provided by Bill Walker:

"In earlier centuries the village was virtually self-sufficient in basic food supplies and rural crafts. My own great grandfather was the village tailor and was obviously a fairly well-educated man since he wrote and read letters and documents for the villagers. He also wrote out the parson's sermons.

'My father used to tell me that in the days before bus services, if he and his four brothers wished to go to Stourport they would do so in a group, as it was certain that if the young men of Astley found out they were on their way, it would be a case of having to fight their way through.

'During my own school days while at the village school, the various terms had their own activities - swapping cigarette cards, bowling a hoop, whipping a top from home to school, (no traffic problems in those days). "Top dog" was the boy who had managed to acquire a motor tyre. The girls had skipping, hop-scotch, Jack of five stones and forming moving circles while chanting weird incantations.

Part of Shrawley village and Shrawley woods.

'As a boy and a young man I sang in the church choir, one generous sponsor being a Mrs Allen from the "Big House". Each Christmas every member received a book. I still have several of mine from the 1930's. During the summer we were treated to a day trip by the seaside, usually Weston or Rhyl. I remember one year we went to Bournemouth and were rather looked down on by the genteel old ladies and retired colonels of the town. After a 2/6d (12.1/2p) lunch in a posh restaurant the parson visited each table to ask how we enjoyed our meal. The village undertaker, a bass in the choir, replied, "It was very nice but was two bob's (10p) worth of waiter and a tanner's (just over 2p) worth of grub".

'The young men of the village served in two world wars, sixteen were lost in the First World War and one in the Second. In the second a search-light battery was mounted on the Church Farm ground and a decoy airfield was constructed on outlying fields by the RAF whose men were billeted through the village.

'At that time there was a thriving farming community, now sadly depleted. The villagers could earn extra seasonal money fruit picking, pea picking, sprout picking, and sugar beet hoeing and pulling but now all of these have virtually disappeared, together with old village families, most of whom have moved from the district. As houses have become vacant they have been snapped up by people from the urban areas and the old community ways and customs have gone for ever."

Shrawley looks to the future. In a prominent position overlooking a bend in the road passing the church, an obelisk has been recently erected with the following inscription:

THIS OBELISK WAS PLACED
ON MIDSUIMMER DAY 2000 TO
COMMEMORATE THE THIRD
MILLENNIUM - BENEATH LIES
A TIME CAPSULE FROM THE
20TH CENTURY

THE CAPSULE SHOULD BE ADDED TO AT
THE END OF EVERY CENTURY HEREAFTER
XXIV VI MM

Until I was eight years old, I lived in the Black Country. I was a sickly child, with pneumonia every winter. As soon as I came here, my health improved. I simply blossomed. Coming to Stourport from the dark, satanic mills was marvelous. We had no money, mother had to go out and work in the fields just to keep body and soul together, but I didn't care. I'm 80 in December, I'm still living here, and I love it to this day.

Fred Rimmel

A quiet evening at the Clock House basin, Stourport-on-Severn.

BIBLIOGRAPHY

Arkell V T J, *Britain Transformed*, Penguin Education, 1973
Baylis T J S, (President of the Worcestershire Federation of Head Teachers Associations) *Stourport 1770-1970*, Published by Stourport Committee
Baylis T J S, *Stourport-on-Severn in old picture postcards*, European Library, 1983.
Boucher Cyril T G, *James Brindley Engineer 1716-1772*, Goose & Son Ltd, Norwich, 1968
Boughey Joseph, *Hadfield's British Canals* David & Charles, 1950
Bund Willis J W, *The Civil War In Worcestershire 1642-1646 and The Scotch Invasion of 1651*, Alan Sutton, 1979
Crowe Nigel, *Canals*, B T Batsford, London, 1994
Dallow Margaret, *A Brief Guided Walk along the towpath of the Staffordshire and Worcestershire Canal*, Stourport-on-Severn, 1993
Darlingtons Handbook - The Severn Valley, J Bartholemew, 1897
Federation of Women's Institutes, *The Worcestershire Village Book* ,Countryside Books, Newbury, 1988
Fraser Maxwell, *Companion into Worcestershire*, Methuen & Co Ltd, 1939
Grazebrook Sydney, *The Heraldry of Worcestershire* , T Russell Smith, London, 1873
Gwilliam Bill, *Worcestershire's Hidden Past*, Halfshire Books, 1991
Hadfield Charles, *The Canals of the West Midlands*, David & Charles (Publishers) Ltd, Devon, 1966
Havins Neville Peter J,*Portrait of Worcestershire*, Robert Hale, London, 1974
Hopcraft W H, *A History of the Baptist Church*, published by Stourport Baptist Church in 1973
Hoskins W G, *The Making of the English Landscape*, Pelican, 1955
Lane B A, *Severn Tanking* , Douglas McLean, 1991
Lloyd Humphrey, *The Quaker Lloyds in the Industrial Revolution*, Hutchinson, 1975
Lovett Gordon, *Astley*, self-published 1998
Masterman Mrs S, *The History of Shrawley*, printed in 1928 and given to Mr S Comley by Mrs Averill when he recently visited Falmouth.
Mee Arthur, *The Kings England - Worcestershire*, Ebenezer Baylis & Son Ltd, Worcester, undated
Pevsner Nikolaus, *The Buildings of England - Worcestershire*, published Penguin, 1968
Pheysey Memoirs (1869-1961) *Around the Land in Eighty Years*, currently looking for a publisher.
Redgrave Sam, *Worcestershire, A Portrait of the County*, photographs by John Bradford, Halfshire Books, 1996
Skipp Victor, *The Centre of England* , Eyre Methuen, London, 1979
Stafford Carole Ann and Crowe Alan, *Us Kids*, QuercuS, 1998
Standish Brian, *Worcestershire Once upon a Postcard*, Amber Graphics, 1987
Stanton E W FRGS, *Stourport-on-Severn. A Dissertation for London University Geography Diploma*, 1962
Taylor Joe and Cook Jas, *Walks in Shakespeare Country* Thornhill Press, 1989
Thomas Memoirs, by Norah, Kath and Janes thomas, chiefly on the originas of the Roman Catholic Church, refers to early 1900s
Turley Adrian and Neil, *The US Army at Camp Bewdley*, published by the authors, 2000
Victoria County History, A History of the County of Worcestershire, University of London Institute of Historical Research, 1913

Voice David and Thompson Melvyn, *The Illustrated History of Kidderminster and Stourport Electric Tramway Co Ltd*, David Voice Associates, 1998

Wedley Isaac L, *Old Stourport*, Kidderminster Shuttle Press, 1912

Wedley Isaac L, *The Passing of Mitton*, Kidderminster Shuttle Press, 1920

Wedley Isaac L, *Twixt Severn and Teme*, Kidderminster Shuttle Press, ?1928

Wedley Isaac L, *Stourport - Its Rise, Decline and Final Triumph*, a series of articles in *The Kidderminster Shuttle* during 1933

White FO, *Lives of Elizabethan Bishops*, Skeffington & Son, 1898

Free Schools of Worcestershire and their Fulfilment. Unfortunately, only a fraction of the book has been preserved but librarians suggest that this could have been written by George Griffith and published by Charles Gilpin, Longdon, 1852. However, there are dates in this book after 1852.

Other guides, brochures, pamphlets, leaflets, trade directoris etc have been used, too numerous to list.

INDEX

Abbott, Holt   15, 16-18

Addison, Margo   189, 190, 194

Ale/Beer   96

Allen, Mrs (Shrawley)   258

Allotments   202

Alveley   136

American Chain & Cable Co   55

American Camp at Burlish   192-198

Amo   9, 12, 30, 98, 98, 160

Anchor Inn   91, 96

Anderson, Mr (Beau Nash)   86

Anderson, Lawson & Co   39

Angel   9

Angel, later Redstone House   246

Anglican National Society
(see National Schools)

Anglo-American Tin Stamping Co/   35, 53.
Anglo Enamel Company   185

Anglo Corner   35, 54,89

Anglo House   89

Apollo Glee Union   149

Areley Castle   62

Areley Common   243

Areley Common School   241

Areley Court   239

Areley House   238

Areley Kings   65, 200 231-246

Areley Kings' Church   231-236

Areley Kings' First School rules   130

Areley Kings' Rectory   236

Areley Manor (Areley Hall)   237, 238

Arthur, Prince   245

Astley   82-253, 258

Astley Cross   245

Astley Hall   216, 253

Aston (horse boat)   9

Athlete (Tug)   8

Atkins, Bernard   59-60

Avonvale   16

Babcock Inernational   55

Bailey, Thomas   9, 95

Baines, Mr E   155

Baker, Richard   85

Baker, Wesley   208

Baldwin, Alfred   220, 221-228

Baldwin Enoch   37, 178ff

Baldwin, E P & W   219

Baldwin family   106,113,151, 222,226

Baldwin Iron Works   35-37 94, 95, 185

Baldwin, Joseph Thomas   113, 125

Baldwin, Pearce   200

Baldwin Road   55,36, 116,174 91

Baldwin's Best Butts   35

Baldwin, Stanley (Prime Minister)   35,47,51,80,114, 117,216,218,220, 223,224,253

Baldwin, Thomas   35

Baldwin, Wyndham   228

Banbury Buiildings   59

Band Stand   178, 184

Banks of Buggery   92

Baptists   116-117

Barber, George & Kath   103

Barber, Rev   109

Barclays Bank   116

Barges   8

Barnett, Miss   121

Bartholomew, Saint   231

Baylis, Ted   129

Baylis, Mr   151

Beakbane, Henry (Tannery)   34-35

Beard, Arthur   189

Beard, Howard   99

Beating of the Bounds   199

Beatrice   9, 12, 30, 160

Beauchamps   256

Beaver   13

Beech, John   150

Belle View   120

Belsom, Ralph   146

Belsom, Joan   146

Bennet, Graham   58

Benton, Mary Rose   133,192,195

Berkeley Castle (horse boat)   9

Berrows Worcs Journal   7

Bewdley Road   47,50,115,116, 124,128,191,192

Bewick, Thomas   70

Bibb, Thomas and Urbane   88

Bickerton, Betty   42-43

Bickerton family and business   80-81, 115, 140

Birch, Betty   34

Birchen Coppice Estate   192, 199

Bird-in-Hand   184

Bird, Ivor   151

Bird, William   33, 88

Birmingham Vinegar Brewery Co Inc   43

Bishops at Hartlebury   209

Bishops Wood   186

Black Star   27

Blackstone Ford   119

Blount, Sir Edward	199	Brusselman, Anne	189
Blount family	250	Brussels carpets	38
Blundells Mill	31	Brut	232
Blunt, Bob	44,62,83-84,	Bullock Close, William	71, 147,
	160,189,191,193		201
Blunt family and business	83, 84	Burlish Camp	
Blunt, Mrs	224	(see American Camp)	
Board of Education	128	Burlish Close	193
Board of Guardians	174	Burlish Crossing	133, 136
Boat-building	32	Burlish Halt	133
Boat Club	150	Burlish House	115
Boats for hire	163	Burlish Lane	191
Boat, The, Public house	90	Burlish Oak	198
Bonavista	9	Burlish Road	198
Bond, Thomas	40	Burlish Reservoir	46
Bond-Worth	39, 42, 48, 49,	Burne Jones, Sir Edward	223-226
	154, 100, 106,	Burrastone, Eliza	233
	185, 202	Buttermere Road	192
Boots	79	Cadbury, George	14, 247
Boswell (gypsy family)	207	Cadbury's	22
Bower, Helen	209	Cahn, Sir Julian	230
Bow-Hauliers	20	Calder, Philip	54
Bowling	99, 156	Camp Bewdley	
Boys' school	190	(See American Camp)	
(see also National Schools)		Canal Company	4, 87
Bradburn, Mrs	65	Canal building	4
Bradley, Lawrence	46	Canal Control C,tee	
Bridge in flood	167	of Board of Trade	14
Bridge Inn	68	Canal Pleasurecraft Ltd	17, 33, 85
	103-105	Caractucus	254
Bridges, first, second and present	63-68	Carbolate	12
Bridge Street	19,63-69,70, 71,	Carnival	142-143, 163
	113,117,	Carpets of Worth	38, 43
	121,124,139,	Carr, Bishop	210-211
	165, 167	Carradine, V	155
Bridge: over Stour	91	Carrington, Mr	53, 54
Brindley	1-6, 12,	Cattell, Miss	170
	18, 39, 120	Chamberlain W	155
Brindley Arms (Station Hotel)	96, 103, 135,	Charity Sundays	77, 124, 142
	141, 155	Charles, T P	78
Brindley's Bridge	63	Charlton	195
Brindley Street	136	Cheapside	14, 38,
Brinton Arms	198		52, 87,88
Brinton, John	36, 39,	Chess Club	145
	72, 116	Chesshire, Rev Cecil	110
British Electric Authority	52	Childe, David	58
British Medical Journal	69	Childhood	120
British Steel	220	Cholera	176
British Vinegars	44	Christian shores	65
British Waterways	17, 60, 202	Church Ales	235
British WireProducts	53-55	Church Avenue	121, 124,
Bromley, Mr	70		126, 192
Brooke, Thomas	214	Chylde, William	256
Broome, Samuel	36, 39, 239	Cinemas:	
Broomy Close	201	Electric	25, 157
Brown, Joel	121	Woodbury	157
Brown, Spencer	45	Circus	86, 206

Civic Centre 70
Civil War (1642-48) 178, 213ff
Clarke and Cranes 218
Clarke, Frank 92
Clarke, Joby and family 19
20-25,
Clarke Tim 20, 22
Clent, James 229
Clock Warehouse 11, 59, 151
Coaches (horse drawn) 132
Cobhams, Alan, Flying Circus 141
Cock-fighting 215
Coffee Tavern 74-75, 149
Coleman, John 170
Collyer, Thomas 75
Congregational Church 89, 115-6
118, 168
Coningsby, Sir Harry 234
Cook, Henry 85
Cooke's Building Yard 169
Cookes family 250
Cookes, Rev Denham 251
Co-operative Society 35, 46, 92
Corbett Jo 14, 23, 56, 195
Corbett, Phyllis 55
Cork, Mr 74
Cory, Canon 228
Cotton's Lock 16, 27
Court, Henry 178
Cox, Jimmy 191
Crane, Major J H 241
Craven family 229
Crewe, Terry 30, 50
Cricket 154
Crowe, Roy
109,128,129,145,
146,164,165,201
Crown (See Old Crown)
Dadford, Thomas 4
Danby, Samuel 33
Danks, Mr 65, 66
Danks, Venn & Co 32, 179
Darbyshire, J 36
Davenport, Rev Ellis 115
Davies, David Rev 106-107
120, 177
Davies family (gypsies) 207
Davis, Mr 174
Dawes, Betty and William 85, 241-242
Day Centre 71-72
Dick Brook 115, 251
Diglis 13, 16, 133
Dock Compay Ltd 14, 33
Doctors 176
Dog carrriages 206
Domesday Book 1, 31
Drew, Mr 157

Drew R 155
Drew, Sam 69
Drill Hall 45, 179
182, 194
Druids 97
Duke of Bridgwater 2, 4, 6
Dunley 115
Easthope, Martin 148
Eaton, William 121, 130
Edwards, Ted 15
Eels 231
Elan Avenue 192
Elections 99, 200
Electric Theatre (see Cinema)
Electric Tramway Company 139
Elf Manufacturing 31
Elgar, Edward 147-148
Elizabeth I 212, 213, 214
Empire Day 179
Empress 9
Enclosures Act 4
Enterprise (tug) 150, 179
Evans, Richard Rev 106, 116, 175
Evans, Bob 109
Evers, Ben 184
Everton, Charles 107
Fairs 86, 143
Farm Bed 36, 39
Farmer's Wire Works 219
Fathers, Thomas Hicks 242
Fawcett & Watson 39
Feathers Inn 89
Ferry House 246
Fidkin, Mr 233
Fire Brigade 101, 163, 172
First World War 182-184
Fitzgerald, Mr 142
Fitzosbern, William 231
Fletcher, Cyril 148
Floods 163,202,165ff
Fly Boats 19, 20
Fogs 82
Foley family 219
Folliott family 229
Football (See Swifts)
Forbes, Bob 109
Forest Fencing 59
Foundry Street (previously 36, 37, 62, 94
    Holborn Street, then New Street) 132,139
Franks, Ray 167ff
Freeze-ups 170
Funerals 176-177
Galahad Way 73
Ganderton, Mary Maria 114
Ganderton, PC 86
Ganderton, Thomas Henry 86, 114
Gardening & Pet Shop 147

Garret, Thomas	213	Hastings, Charles (of the BMA)	69
Gas Works	52	Hatton, Harry	9
George III	213	Havergal, Frances Ridley	252
Gheluvelt Court	73	Haw Bridge	50
Ghosts	81, 101	Hawker, John	57-58
Gibbon's Crescent	191, 103-105	Hawkins, Joseph	243
Gibbons Lock (See Cotton's Lock)		Hay, Stan	53
Gibbons, Rev Benjamin	107,110,125,128,	Haywood, William	118-119,
	144, 184, 208		246-247
Gilgal	22, 36, 90, 132	Head, George	12
Girl's Schools (in High Street)	80	Head, John	40
Girl's School (near Church)	192	Hearts of Oak	23, 56
(see also National Schools)		Heath House	91, 92, 147
Glasshampton	251	Heath Nurseries	71, 147
Glee Club	145, 148	Heath Rev	112
Glover family	151, 246	Heath Richard	121
Goodman, Jack	74	Heinkel III	190, 192
Goodman, Mr	116	Henshall Hugh	3, 6
Gould, John	206	Heywood, William	106
Grace W G	83	Hickin Bold	43
Great Western Way	135-136	Hickman, John	85
Gregory, George	128, 155	High School	128-131
Gregory, Roland	109	High Street	39,70,74--84,75,
Griffin, Mr ((Tallow chandler)	85		77,106,115,120,
Griffiths, George	133		139,181,182,189,
Grinnall family and business	81		194
Grinnall, Frank	79, 160ff, 181	Hill, Alan	145
Groves, Peter and Mary	106	Hill of Zion	90
Guides	157	Hill, Mr	112
Guild of Help	72, 114, 143	Hill, Thomas	219
Gwillam, Thomas	207	Hoare, Richard	32
Gypsies	207-209	Hobley, John	43
Hadfield, Charles	118	Hodges, Captain	8
Hafren Way	73	Hodges, C D F	176
Hakon, Earl	254	Holbrooks Ltd	
Hall, H G	133	(See Vinegar Works)	
Hall, Jock	56	Holder, Len	9
Halmshaw, Mr	141, 147	Holly Bush	144, 105
Harcot, Major	214	Holt (horse boat)	9
Harding, Tom	85	Home Guard	185-187
Hardwick family	103	Hopcraft, John	54
Harker. John	50	Hope and Anchor	70
Harper, Bill	53, 152, 155,	Hope-Jones organ	109, 111
	185-187	Hop Pole	246
Harper, Mrs	187	Hop Trade	97
Harris, George	39, 74, 106,	Hornblower, Ann	78
	91,178	Horticultural Society	145
Harrison ,Charles	39, 144, 179	Horton, William	121
Harrison, Julius	148, 217	Howells, Rev Ivor	111
Harrisons Screw Works	36	Hughes, Bill	14-16, 20-25,
Hartlebury	136,138,168,178,		56-60,96,171
	195,199,206	Hughes, Bert	20-25
Hartlebury Castle		Hughes, Jessie	21
209,213,214,217		Hughes, Reg	45-47,141,143,
Hartlebury Church (St James)	213		151, 157, 185,
Hartlebury Common	72,169,179,206		191,193
Hartlebury Grammar School	148	Hughes, Ron	195

Humphreys, Mr (Deputy Head) 129ff, 167
Hunt, Isaac 134
Hurd, Bishop 213
Hutton, Clive 154
Hutton, R 155
Hyde, Tony 46
Idris 20, 21
Income Tax 88
Infants School (see also Tan Lane) 124
Ingram, Lily 93
Inland Waterways Association 16, 18
Instrumental Society 145, 149
Ireland, Samuel 63, 64
Island Mills 39
Jacks, Ruth 147
James, Stan 24
Jarvis, Bryan H 192
Jason, Miss 12
Johnson, Neil 179
Jones, E J (Headmaster) 128,129, 190
Jones, George 164
Jones, Jean 78
Jones, John 79
Jones, Mr 115
Jones, Mr & Mrs (Tollkeepers) 206
Jones, Thomas 227-228
Jukes, Richard 69
Keenan, Sam 52,96,135-138
Kenricks 36
Ketley, Thomas 103
Keyne, Saint 258
Kidderminster Shuttle 144, 147, 209, 243
King, Mrs (Headteacher) 130
King of Prussia 220
Kingstonian 12, 30
Kingsway 195
Kipling, Rudyard 223
Knight F 155
Knight family 31
Knott, Reginald 202
Knott, William 43
Knowles, Mr 239
Lady Foley, Honor and May 9
Lady Hatherton 96
Landon, Edwin (Tailor) 86
Landon, Sarah Ann 114
Lane B A 28-30 247-248
Lane, Jane 68
Lane, Joe 46
Larches 187
Larch Lap 55-61, 202

Latimer, Bishop 210, 245
Layamon 73, 233
Layamon Walk 197

Leap Gate 136
Lee family 207
Lee, John 175
Lee, Mr 251
Leland, John 89, 209
Lewty's at Wilden 35, 219
Lewty's at Post Office 78
Lichfield House 40
Lichfield Street 4,15,55,58,87, 112,168,246
Lickhill 1, 7, 199, 200, 229-230
Lickhill Manor 72, 167, 229
Lickhill Middle School 45, 129-131
Lickhill Road 45,46,72,115,118 122,157,162,192
Lightband, Mr 244
Lincomb 8,13,30,152
Lincomb Hall 248
Lincomb Lock and weir 244, 246-248
Lion Hill 34,86-87, 141,143
Lion Hotel (See White Lion)
Literary Institute (See Stourport Literary Institute)
Lively, Jack (Cheap Jack) 86
Lloyd, Bishop 217
Lloyd, Sampson 238
Local Education Authority 128
Lock-keeper's cottage 85
Lock Shop 17, 84, 85
Lodge Road 118
Lombard Street 33,46,62, 92,93, 94,101,139,145, 157,172 ,177,190
London, Midland & Scottish Railway 20
Longboat Lane 136
Long Lane 72
Long Warehouse 33
Lovell, gypsy family 207-208
Lovelock, Mr 104
Loveridge 207-208
Lovett, Gordon 252
Lower Mitton Church (See Saint Michael's)
Loyalty 27
Lucy Baldwin Maternity Hospital 230
Lydney 8
Lygon 229
Lyttleton, Lord 144
Macdonald, Edith 224,226
Macdonald family 222-223
Macdonald, Louisa 222-223
Mann, Mrs 55, 196ff
Mann, Terry 193, 196

Mansion, The	74	Monkey boats	32
Mantle, Rev John	112	Monk, Thomas	32
Map of town	66,67	Moor Hall	72-73,85,178
Marina	166	Moor Hall Lane	72-73
Markets	143	Morgan Matroc	
Marsh & Baxters	186	(See Steatite & Porcelain)	
Mart Lane	14, 16, 17, 23,	Morris, Mrs	118
	54, 87, 165	Morris, William	224-226
Mart Lane Abattoir	93	Moulden, Ashley	17
Martley	231, 237	Moulder's Arms	95
	238	'Mousey'	151
Mason, Miss	127	Mucklow, Simon	237-238
Masons, Grocers	189	Mulberry Tree	92
Massey, Sid	58	Murder	243
Masterman		Murphy, Louisa	129
(Medical Officer of Health)	62	Murray, Dr (Bond Worth)	100
Masterman, Mrs	254	Murray, John	106, 178
Matthews, Jeremiah	243	Musical Evenings	149
Matthews, Ron	134	Music Society	147
Matthews, Thomas	152	Nabarro, Gerald MP	18
Maude, Bernard	212	Naboth's Vinyard	235
Maud, Queen	237	Narrow boats	4
Mayo, Tom	25-26	Nash, Dr	246
Mayor	143	National Schools	121-126
McKay	176	National Standard	53-55
Memorial Park	154, 178	Nelson Wharf	14,22
	184, 202	Nestle	44
Methodists	112, 122, 125,	Neville, Richard	256
	222, 226	Newbury, William	43
Methodist burial ground	106	Newnham, Keith	47,50, 94,
Methodist Church	34, 38, 77, 118,		145-147
	121, 192	Newman, Margo	8
Midland Bank	182	New Street	70,75,81,120,143
Midland Industrial Plastics	50	Newtown	230
Midland Red	9	Nicholdson, George	70, 106
Millard, Jane	233	Noakes, John	246
Mill Lane and Mill Road	31, 91, 188	Norchard Sundial	233
Mills, Elizabeth	157, 201	Nunney, Sgt Isaac	179
Mills, F	241	Oakhampton Farm	241
Mills, Mrs	227	O'Dowd (Father)	118
Millward, Mr	227	Oil Depot	166
Milner, Bill	147	Old Beams	146, 161, 239
Minster Road	126, 134,	Oldest House (41 Mitton St)	89
	139, 193	Old Crown	68, 167, 195
Mission Hall	208	Old Rising Sun	95, 103
Mitchley, Victor Stout	99ff, 172	Osborne, Bill	157
Mitre Oak	213	Outback Pub	145
Mitton Cemetary	38	Packet Boats	32
Mitton Gardens	89, 113	Packington, Sir John	252
Mitton Mill	31, 119	Pall Mall	102
Mitton Street (Drury Lane)	81,89, 92,93,118	Palmer, Samuel	9
Mitton, Upper, Lower and Over	1, 7, 89, 199	Pannier Tank Engine	136
Mitton Wake	101, 142	Pansington	169
Mitton Walk & Close	89	Paradise Court	89
Mitton Works	40	Park Avenue	73
Moffat, Mrs	72	Parker, Thomas	145
Molliott, J L	256	Parkes Passage	74, 84, 112,

	120, 121
Parochial Church Council	110
Parsons Chain	53-56
Partridge, Mr	175
Passenger Steamers	9, 140, 185ff
Patton, General	193
Pauncefote, Sir Richard	248
Pawn Shop	175
Pennington, Jessie	100
Penny Readings	144
Pepys, Bishop	211
Perry family and business	92-94
Perry James	3
Perry Jim	71-72, 151
	194
Perry (young lad in Poor House)	175
Perseverence	9
Pheysey, Herbert Richard	132, 239
Philip, Father	106
Phillips, Florence	16-18
	171
Philpot, Bishop	106
Piccadilly	90
Pierce, Headmaster	215
Piscator, Gillbertus	245
Playland	164, 169
Police Station	72, 86, 192
Police	142, 175
Poor House	91,174-175
Population	62, 96, 182
	202, 258
Porcelain & Steatite	15
Post Office	78-79
Potter, Mr	115
Power Ptroleum Company	50
Power Station	23,5153,136,191
Power Station Road	53
Poynter, Sir Edward	223
Pratley, Alf	14, 56, 195
Preece, Jimmy	47
Preedy, F	233
PRHA (Refreshment Association)	100
Priarie Tank Engine	138
Price, Mr	116
Price, R	155
Primitive Methodism	115
Prince Albert	33
Priors Mill, Astley	251
Private Eye	111
Purser, Betty	120
Putting Green	152, 158,
	164, 167
Quack Doctors	177
Quarterman, Alfred	147
Quinby	36
Railways	13, 46, 82,
	133-138,158
Randall J	18
Randle (Miss) Tea Rooms	117
Ratcliff, F D	44
Raven Public House	117
Raven Street	70,109,115,117,
	120,121,175
Raybould, F W M	118
Ready family	69, 164
Ready, Margaret	158, 164
Ready, Mr, Senior	143, 162
	166, 167
Red Lion (see also Steps House)	90
Redstone	244-246
Redstone Caravan Park	167
Redstone Hermitage	245-246
Redstone Wharf	185
Regent King, Regent Queen,)	28, 50
Regent Jack and Regent Jill)	51
Regent Oil Company	28
Regent Petrol Depot	172, 185
Ribbesford	33
Rimmel, Fred	35,44,47,
	50,88,114,
	158,166ff,172,
	178,224,239
Ring o' Bells	102
Risdale, Lucy	224
Rising Sun (see Old Rising Sun)	
River King	12
Robson, Chris & Steve	161
Rock	119
Rock Seat	256
Rogers family (The Tannery)	34, 92, 119
Rolt, Tom	16
Roman Catholics	116-118, 146
Rose, James (Church builder)	106
Rothesay	16
Round House	242
Round o' Beef	102
Rowley, Mr	112
Rugby Club	154
Rupert, Prince	237
Russian Oil Products	27
Saint Bartholomew's Church See Areley King's Church	
Saint Michael's Church	90, 106-111,
	121, 209
Saint Michael's Lodge	108
Saltman, Billy the	207
Samantha's Flowers	81
Sanders, George, Circus	141
Sandys, Bishop	212, 215
Sarsons	44
Saturn (fly boat)	24
Saunders, Rev John	113
Sav ings Bank	87
Scarth, Richard	52-3

Scouts	156	Spry, Constance	42
Scott, Sir Gilbert	108-111	Squirrel, Public House	156
Sebright, Jack	190	Stafford, Carole Ann	158
Second World War	185-197	Staffordshire & Worcestershire	3, 7, 12,
Self Service Supermarket (first)	93	Canal	13, 27
Sequah (Quack doctor)	176	Staffs & Worcs Canal Co	11-13,21,96
Severn & Canal Carrying Co	9, 25, 27	Staffordshire Building Society	79
Severn Bank House	256	Staffordshire, Worcestershire &	
Severn Commission	13-14	Shropshire Electric Company	52
Severn Merchant	29	Stagboro Hill	195
Severne family	256	Stanley gypsy family	207
Severn Manor	192	Stanton, Lionel	120
Severn Merchant	61	Stanton, William (Blacksmith)	88
Severn Navigation Company	13	Stapleton, Sir Robert	212
Severn (passenger steamer)	9	Station (see also Railways)	134
Severn Road/Lane	55,87	Station Hotel (see Brindley Arms)	
Severnside	51	Steatite and Porcelain	47-50, 72
Severn Steamboat Company	12		154, 185
Severn Steam Yacht Company	9	Steps House (Red Lion)	90, 102, 142
Severn Submarines	50	Stocks	90
Severnvale	16	Stour, artificial branch	91
Severn Valley Mills	40, 88, 89	Stourbank House	44, 87
Shaw, Thomas & William	121	Stour Lane (Hell Lane)	89, 102
Shell Mex Seven	50	Stourmouth	1
Shepherd, J	155	Stourport Bridge (see Bridge)	
Shirley, Robert	39	Stourport Gas, Coal & Coke Co	38
Shrawley	254-259	Stourport-on-Severn First	
Shrawley Church (Saint Mary's)	257	School - see Tan Lane School	
Shrawley Fete	258	Stourport-on-Severn High School	189, 190
Shrawley Ford	254	Stourport-on-Severn High School	
Shrawley Hermitage	256	and Language College	129-131, 147
Shrawley Wood	254		147
Simcock, Samuel	3, 4,5	Stourport Junior Girls	124
Simon of Reddestan	245	Stourport Literary Institute	114, 143ff
Simpson, Paul	235		144
Sincerity	27	Stourport Reading Society	143-144
Sion Gardens	120	Stourport Rifles	178
Smethwick Drop Forgings	185	Stourport Urban District Council	92
Smith family	169	Stringer, Jack	154, 220, 228
Smith family (gypsies)	207	Stringer, Margaret	72
Smith, Jack	53	Summerfield, Rocket Research	47, 185
Smith, Mr (Church builder)	108	Sunday Schools	121, 143
Smith, Richard & Sons	39	Swan Hotel	98-101, 145,
Smith-Rutter, Eliza	120		182, 208, 170
Smythe, Thomas	150	Swann, Charles	43, 87, 98
Snell & Thompson	110	Swan Passage	117
Snider, Peter (Tollkeeper)	68	Swifts Fottball Club	154, 155
Society of Divine Compassion	251	Swimming Pool	152, 170
Society of Females	101	T & S Element	23
Southall H	155	Tan Lane	34, 94, 116
Sovereign	9		147, 191
Speed, John	245	Tan Lane Infants School	94,109,126-127
Spence, John	54	Tannery	33-35, 85, 92,
Spetchley,. Richard	245		114,116,157,172
Spragg Ernie	15, 58	Taylor, Graham	234
Spragg family	148	Temperance Hall	115, 116
Springfield House	92	Tettenhall	5

Thomas, D   155
Thomas family   117-118
  149, 158
Thomas, Mr & Mrs (Burlish)   196
Thomas, Richard   235
Thomas, Richard and Baldwin Ltd   220, 222
Thomas Vale Construction Ltd
  (see Vales)
Thompson, Melvyn   38-43
Thorp, Sam   11
Timmis, Paul   15,56-58
Tinker Watson & Biddy   95
Titton   168, 169, 199,
  207, 209
Todeni, Ralph de (or Toni)   249-250
  254, 256
Tolley, Philip   89
Tolls and toll-keepers   19, 22
  133
Toll gates (Hartlebury)   206
Toll Office   85
Tontine (formerly Areley Inn,   9, 27, 96-98,
  then Stourport Inn)   153, 244
Tontine system   97
Torridon Close   195
Town Hall   70
Trader   28
Traffic   202
Trains (see railway)
Trams   79, 139-140
Travelling Theatre   141
Trent & Mersey Canal   3, 5
Trows   8
Tugs   8
Turks Head   24
Turner, Jimmy   86
Twinning   201
Twins (The)   9
Tyler & Humphries   39
Tyler, Harold   45
Tyler John   9
Union Inn   87
United Reform Church   110, 111
Vale, Ernest   44
Vale family   44
Vale House   183
Vale Road   44,92, 115, 118,
  143,192
Vale, Thomas & Co   35,44-47,64,69
  70,92,93,117,45
  157,179,190,226
Vaughan, Samuel   101
Vawdrey, Rev   241-2
Venables, Mr   90
Vernon family   256
Vernon Hall   115
Vernon, Richard   234-235

Vernon Road   191
Vernon, Sir George   256
Vessey, Rev Andrew (Rural Dean)   106, 234-235
Villneuve-le-Roi   146, 201
  (See also Twinning)   202
Vinegar Works   43-44,52
  170, 202
Voice, David, Associates   139-140
Wainwright, Tereh   102
Wakeman, Joe & family   107
Walker, Bill   258
Waller, Rev   108
Wallfield Bridge   106
Walsh family   239
Walshes Caravan Park   161
Walshes Estate   196,
  239-240
Walshes Farm (now Old Beams)   85
Ward bequest   113
Ward, Joseph   79, 113
Ward, Thomas   34
Waresley House   107, 217
War Memorial   182, 184, 195ff
Warner, Fred   46
Water Witch   33
Watkins, Mr (Tailor)   86
Watson, Kenrick   69
Weaver, Mr   8
Weaver's Committee   39
Weaver, John   91
Webb, Betty   156, 195, 197ff,
  221, 227
Webb, Jo   197
Wedgwood, Josiah   5
Wedley, Isaac   13,47,65,74,79,
  85,86,88,95,97,
  98,102ff,107,113,
  118,125,139,142,
  148,170,176,182,
  199,206,208,211,
  219,226,233,242
Wehner, Andrew   231-246
Wesley, John   84-85, 112
West, Mr   222
Westminster Bank   79
Westwood J   155
Wharton, Rev   107, 121
  124, 128
Wheeldon, F   154
Wheeldon, Joseph   74
Wheeldon, Thomas   78, 215
White Gates   85
Whitehouse Farm   239
White Lion   86, 99, 101-102
White, Phil   151
Whittall, Matthew   103

Wilden   35,141,186, 188,
                                          200, 218-228,
                                          253
Wilden Church (All Saints)   224, 227
Wilden Girl Guides   156
Wilden Home Guard   186
Wilden House   223, 224ff
Wilden Inn   220
Wilden Iron Works   136, 184,
                                          219-222, 246
Wilden Lane   222
Wilden School   226-228
Wilden Top   222
Wilden Village Hall   194, 228
Wilkes, Roy   56
Willetts, Ivan   102
Williams, Leader   246
Williams, Mr   132
William the Conqueror   231, 249
Wilmot family   89, 91, 106
                                          214
Wilson, Florence   188, 218ff
                                          226
Windermere Way   192, 198
Windmill   241
Windmill Bank   242
Windmill Schools   241
Windsor Castle   9
Winford, Sir John and family   250
Winnall family   211
Winter Queen   229
Wobbly Wheel House   231
Wombwell's Menagerie   141
Woodbury Road   157
Woods, Rt Rev Robin   111
Woolworth's   74, 79
Worcester & B'ham canal   19
Worcester Evening News   179
Worcester Road (Buggy Lane)   91, 169, 179
Worcestershire Methodist Circuit   112
Worcester Street   33,36,126,191
Workmen's Club   114, 144, 145
World War I   181-184
World War II   185-196
                                          246, 259
Worth Carpets (see Bond Worth)
Worth family   40
Worthington, Jonathon   72, 85
Worth, Roland B   117, 179
Wulstan & Thomas Canterbury
    RC Church (See Roman Catholic)
Wyre Inn, Shrawley   258
Yaranton, Andrew   252
Yarranton, William   245, 246
York, Aaron   72, 84, 106, 112
York House   84, 176

York Street   4, 17, 23,
                                          72,84,120,
                                          143,168,175
Young Men's Reading Institution   144
Young, Sylvia   114
Zachary, Daniel   243
Zachary, Francis   241
Zachary, John   241
Zachary, Mr   236
Zachary, Sarah   238